...AUGHNESSY MEB FABER **DAVID MERKEL** NORBERT KEIMLING **STAN ALTSHULLER** TOM MCCLEL...

...D DILLIAN RAOUL PAL **BARRY RITHOLTZ** KEN FISHER **CHRIS MEREDITH** ASWATH DAMODARAN

...RLSON DAVE NADIG **JOSH BROWN** COREY HOFFSTEIN **JASON HSU** WES GRAY **JOHN REESE** LA...

...EDROE **CULLEN ROCHE** JONATHAN CLEMENTS **MICHAEL KITCES** CHARLIE BILELLO **JOHN MAULD...**

...DAM BUTLER JASON ZWEIG **GARY ANTONACCI** MORGAN HOUSEL **BEN HUNT** TODD TRESIDDE...

...TRICK O'SHAUGHNESSY MEB FABER **DAVID MERKEL** NORBERT KEIMLING **STAN ALTSHULLER** TO...

...CLELLAN **JARED DILLIAN** RAOUL PAL **BARRY RITHOLTZ** KEN FISHER **CHRIS MEREDITH** ASWAT...

...MODARAN **BEN CARLSON** DAVE NADIG **JOSH BROWN** COREY HOFFSTEIN **JASON HSU** WES GR...

...REESE LARRY SWEDROE **CULLEN ROCHE** JONATHAN CLEMENTS **MICHAEL KITCES** CHARLIE BIL...

HAUGHNESSY **MEB FABER** DAVID MERKEL **NORBERT KEIMLING** STAN ALTSHULLER **TOM MCLE**

D DILLIAN **RAOUL PAL** BARRY RITHOLTZ **KEN FISHER** CHRIS MEREDITH **ASWATH DAMODARAN**

RLSON **DAVE NADIG** JOSH BROWN **COREY HOFFSTEIN** JASON HSU **WES GRAY** JOHN REESE **LA**

EDROE CULLEN ROCHE **JONATHAN CLEMENTS** MICHAEL KITCES **CHARLIE BILELLO** JOHN MAUL

1 BUTLER **JASON ZWEIG** GARY ANTONACCI **MORGAN HOUSEL** BEN HUNT **TODD TRESIDDER** P

HAUGHNESSY **MEB FABER** DAVID MERKEL **NORBERT KEIMLING** STAN ALTSHULLER **TOM MCCLEL**

RLSON **DAVE NADIG** JOSH BROWN **COREY HOFFSTEIN** JASON HSU **WES GRAY** JOHN REESE

D DILLIAN **RAOUL PAL** BARRY RITHOLTZ **KEN FISHER** CHRIS MEREDITH **ASWATH DAMODARAN**

EDROE **JONATHAN CLEMENTS** MICHAEL KITCES **CHARLIE BILELLO** JOHN MAUl

THE BEST
INVESTMENT WRITING

Also by Meb Faber

*The Ivy Portfolio: How to Invest Like the Top
Endowments and Avoid Bear Markets*

Shareholder Yield: A Better Approach to Dividend Investing

*Global Value: How to Spot Bubbles, Avoid Market Crashes,
and Earn Big Returns in the Stock Market*

*Global Asset Allocation: A Survey of the World's
Top Asset Allocation Strategies*

Invest with the House: Hacking the Top Hedge Funds

THE BEST INVESTMENT WRITING

Selected Writing From Leading
Investors and Authors

VOLUME 1

Edited by
Meb Faber

Hh

Hh Harriman House

HARRIMAN HOUSE LTD
18 College Street
Petersfield
Hampshire
GU31 4AD
GREAT BRITAIN
Tel: +44 (0)1730 233870
Email: enquiries@harriman-house.com
Website: www.harriman-house.com

First published in Great Britain in 2017
Copyright © Meb Faber

The right of Meb Faber to be identified as the author has been asserted in accordance with the Copyright, Design and Patents Act 1988.

Hardback ISBN: 978-0-85719-619-4
eBook ISBN: 978-0-85719-620-0

British Library Cataloguing in Publication Data
A CIP catalogue record for this book can be obtained from the British Library.

All rights reserved; no part of this publication may be reproduced, stored in a retrieval system, or transmitted in any form or by any means, electronic, mechanical, photocopying, recording, or otherwise without the prior written permission of the Publisher. This book may not be lent, resold, hired out or otherwise disposed of by way of trade in any form of binding or cover other than that in which it is published without the prior written consent of the Publisher.

Whilst every effort has been made to ensure that information in this book is accurate, no liability can be accepted for any loss incurred in any way whatsoever by any person relying solely on the information contained herein.

No responsibility for loss occasioned to any person or corporate body acting or refraining to act as a result of reading material in this book can be accepted by the Publisher, by the Author, by the Contributors, or by the employers of the Author or Contributors.

Contents

Introduction — 1
By Meb Faber

INVESTMENT STRATEGIES & EDGES

A Portrait of the Investing Columnist as a (Very) Young Man — 7
By Jason Zweig

What You Should Remember About the Markets — 20
By Gary Antonacci

Sustainable Sources of Competitive Advantage — 26
By Morgan Housel

Who's Being Naïve, Kay? — 30
By Ben Hunt

Five "Must Ask" Due Diligence Questions Before Making Any
Investment — 41
By Todd Tresidder

Alpha or Assets — 56
By Patrick O'Shaughnessy

50% Returns Coming for Commodities and Emerging Markets?
— 75
By Meb Faber

MARKET CONDITIONS, RISKS & RETURNS

Estimating Future Stock Returns — 83
By David Merkel

Predicting Stock Market Returns Using Shiller-CAPE and PB —
88
By Norbert Keimling

Risk Parity and the Four Faces of Risk — 102
By Adam Butler

The Biggest Challenge for Hedge Funds in 2017 — 117
By Stan Altshuller

Bond Market Knows What Fed Should Do — 122
By Tom McClellan

The Interest Rate Issue — 126
By Jared Dillian

India — 132
By Raoul Pal

The Frightening Global Rise of Agnotology — 145
By Barry Ritholtz

Bull Market Charges on Regardless of a Growing Revolt — 149
By Ken Fisher

PRICING & VALUATION: FROM MICRO TO MACRO

Price-to-Book's Growing Blind Spot — 155
By Chris Meredith

Superman and Stocks: It's not the Cape (CAPE), it's the Kryptonite (Cash flow)! — 167
By Aswath Damodaran

The Greatest Bubble of All-Time? — 180
By Ben Carlson

How Illiquid are Bond ETFs, Really? — 185
By Dave Nadig

Everyone is a Closet Technician — 194
By Josh Brown

THE BEHAVIORAL SIDE OF INVESTING

Even God Would Get Fired as an Active Investor — 201
By Wesley R. Gray

Outperforming by Underperforming — 209

By Corey Hoffstein & Justin Sibears

The Confounding Bias for Investment Complexity — 219

By Jason Hsu & John West

Would You Bail on Warren Buffett? Investors Make that Mistake all the Time — 227

By John Reese

Thinking Can Hurt Your Investments — 230

By Larry Swedroe

How to Avoid the Problem of Short-Termism — 236

By Cullen Roche

PERSONAL FINANCE & WEALTH-BUILDING

Reflect, Pause and Focus — 243

By Jonathan Clements

The Four Phases of Saving and Investing for Retirement — 247

By Michael Kitces

The Passive Investor Test — 256

By Charlie Bilello

20 Rules of Personal Finance — 264

By Ben Carlson

Life on the Edge — 268

By John Mauldin

FREE EBOOK EDITION

Every owner of a physical copy of this edition of

The Best Investment Writing – Volume 1

can download the eBook for free direct from us at Harriman House, in a format that can be read on any eReader, tablet or smartphone.

Simply head to:

ebooks.harriman-house.com/bestinvestwriting

to get your free eBook now.

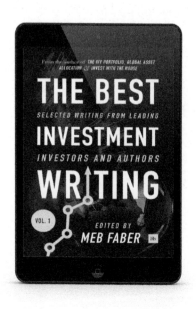

Introduction

BY MEB FABER

It wasn't always this way...

Investing in, say, 1975, was a relatively arduous process. Back then, if you wanted to buy a stock, your best bet was to trek to the local library to read newspapers and financial periodicals on the company of interest. Of course, there wasn't always plentiful information.

The other option was to contact a company directly (or ask your broker to). You would request the latest financial reports. It would take days or weeks – if the company even responded – before you'd have the information.

But let's say you went to all this effort. And let's assume your research paid off – you found a great company and you're ready to invest...

Actually, you're not ready.

Before you break out your checkbook, how much are you going to offer for the shares? You'd typically get your pricing information from the newspaper. But it would show you yesterday's price. If the stock had risen 3% that morning, the price you might have prepared to pay would be insufficient.

And then there was the cost of broker commissions. Remember how expensive they could be? According to a report in the *Journal of Economic Perspectives*, an average broker commission for a stock trade as recently as 2001 was $210. At this price, you really had to be committed to that purchase.

The reality is, investing decades ago could be a pain... but that pain protected you from a huge problem: the overload of market data available to us now, combined with technologies that make trading easier and faster than ever, which together, often results in impulsive, rash investment decisions that lose us money.

Today, our world is all about *now*, *more*, and *faster*. Instead of the library, we have our smartphones. Financial reports that used to take weeks to obtain now download in seconds. Online commissions have fallen to below $5, and at some brokerages, are completely free.

Now, to be sure, the technological advances that have streamlined investing and lowered trading costs are wonderful – if only our investment choices themselves were as wonderful…

But therein lies the dark underbelly of all these *improvements*: too many *market experts* shouting too many conflicting opinions at us. The result? Bad investment decisions, while at the meantime investing has never been easier or more accessible.

It's a bit like handing your child the matches…

There are the headlines, the pundits, the investment professionals, the newsletter writers, the friends, the friend of a friend who has the *inside scoop*…

Who do we believe? Which expert knows best? If he was right yesterday, does that mean he'll be right tomorrow?

Consider a visit to the popular investment site, Seeking Alpha. Here, market experts post articles evaluating stocks, funds, strategies – you name it.

I picked a stock at random – Intel – and looked under the 'Latest' section.

Here are just a few of the headlines at the time of this writing…

- Intel Should Fear AMD
- AMD's Assault on Intel is Barely Noticeable
- Intel Threats Compound
- Intel: Adding Growth To A Solid Dividend Play
- Intel Set For An EPYC Meltdown
- Intel: Expansion Time

So according to these headlines, Intel should be fearing a barely noticeable assault by a competitor. Its threats are compounding and it's set for an EPYC meltdown, yet it's simultaneously a solid dividend play that's expanding…

Super helpful, thanks.

We're not wired for this much information – and this much *contradictory* information. After all, Seeking Alpha boasts that they have over 13,000 contributors that have authored over 700,000 articles!

Virginie Maisonneuve, head of global and international equities at Schroders, recently warned about this in a research paper…

> "Overloaded investors have been shown to make worse decision, but have more confidence because information gives the illusion of control. This results in short-termism, overly aggressive trading and higher market volatility."

So what do we do?

Enter *The Best Investment Writing – Volume 1*.

The pages that follow are written by some of the brightest, most insightful minds in investing. They are real experts, speaking to you from years of research and experience. And the wisdom contained in this compilation is the kind that can make a real, tangible difference in your portfolio.

The first piece you'll read is Jason Zweig's excellent article, titled 'A Portrait of the Investing Columnist as a (Very) Young Man'. In it, Jason describes his experiences as an antiques collector (at the age of about 14, interestingly enough).

One of the things I found most fascinating in the article was the immense time and energy Jason invested in his research. He describes going through encyclopedias in order to write down, and then memorize, the dates of when America's greatest authors published their first works (so that at estate sales, he could quickly bypass anything except first editions). He did the same thing with paintings, memorizing dates, styles, and compositions.

Jason was a true expert. This gave him an advantage over the would-be collectors wandering about the same estate sales, overlooking the treasures directly in front of them.

As investors, wouldn't we all be better off taking counsel from someone equally an expert? Someone who could help us identify the real treasures while bypassing the junk?

These market experts do exist, but they can be difficult to find amidst the hoard of imposters shouting at us. Like great investments, they are rare.

We've done the hard work of identifying not only the writers, but also curating some of their best writings, and compiled them for you in this book.

You could think of it as a masters in investing.

And so, rather than wax on any longer, our experts will take it from here. My hope is you'll find the following pages as valuable, entertaining, and insightful as I have.

Good investing,

Meb Faber

Meb Faber is donating to charity his author royalties from the sales of this book.

INVESTMENT STRATEGIES

STRATEGIES

—— & ——

EDGES

A Portrait of the Investing Columnist as a (Very) Young Man

BY JASON ZWEIG

When an inmate in federal prison reminisces about what you were like as a child, you pay attention.

For the past couple years, I've been mulling over an article in which the art collector and convicted felon Ralph Esmerian describes me when I was a boy. In 2011, Mr. Esmerian, a dealer in luxury jewelry, a prominent collector of American antiques, and a former chairman of the Museum of American Folk Art, was sentenced to six years in federal prison for embezzlement and bankruptcy fraud. In 2014, from the minimum-security Canaan prison camp in Waymart, Pa., Mr. Esmerian emailed a reminiscence of his collecting career to Scudder Smith, editor-publisher of *Antiques and the Arts Weekly*. Someone called my attention to the following passage, which is so well-written that it's worth quoting in full:

> In 1973, just one year after the Durands, I had another fortuitous first-time visit to a dealer in Salem, N.Y. Martin Zweig had a strong reputation as an excellent picker for several of the antique dealers in New York City and New England. I was greeted at the door by him and his wife, and we immediately began a walk through their home to view the inventory set up in various rooms. Martin appeared shy and self-conscious, ill at ease with perfunctory small talk, but he came alive and sparkled when pointing to objects and discussing their relevance as antiques. Upon completing the house tour, the Zweigs suggested we sit down in the living room – adding the caveat that none of the pieces in the parlor were for sale.
>
> As I entered this dimly lit room, I was mesmerized by the sight of a great white rabbit carousel figure. Short-tailed, glass eyes and long-

eared with an original paint surface showing slight wear and tear, the rabbit dominated the room and all the inventory I had seen – giving a reason for my visit as it appeared to bound over its surroundings of formal furniture and folk art.

Not for sale was the very quick retort to my question. As we talked some more, I exclaimed over certain pieces but always returned to the fabulous rabbit. Perhaps 15 minutes later, the husband asked his wife to call Jason from his room, explaining that Jason was their son whom I had not met on my tour. Martin admitted that he was never comfortable discussing not-for-sale objects for fear of risking a client's hostility at the apparent conflict of interest between being a dealer and a collector as well. Thus he wanted his son included in our conversations. I nodded sympathetically, feeling for the man's innate awkwardness.

Enter Jason – my expectation of the adult son evaporated on the sight of a boy, small of stature but serious of demeanor. We shake hands, exchanging names, as his father explains my interest in folk art and the rabbit. Jason immediately picks up when Martin has finished and proceeds to elaborate on the Zweigs' love of pieces and that they are not meant to be teasers but simply the furnishings they want to live with. I am impressed by the kid's delivery and merely repeat my request to have the rabbit, adding that I own a rooster and horse carousel figures that I feel are of similar workmanship quality as the rabbit.

Jason never takes his eyes off me, listening intently, then turns to his father and declares that the family should sell the figure to me, that the rabbit would have a good home. Martin asks if he is sure of his decision. Although shocked by the turnaround, I never get the sense that I am being set up, listening to a duet sung by good cop, bad cop. Jason never breaks stride and affirms he would sell it. Martin then instructs him to put a price on the figure since that is his decision.

Jason has yet to smile since entering the room. He continues to look at me and without glancing away out of embarrassment or hesitancy, proceeds to price the rabbit at a value three times the individual costs of my horse and rooster. As politely as I can, I ask Jason his age. "I'm 10," he says. I stare back, slumping slightly in my chair as I feel the room spinning. Have I followed Alice down the hole in Wonderland? Maybe Dorothy's tornado has tossed me into this scenario, starring a live American Gothic dealer and wife, a 10-year-old son precocious beyond the experience of most lifetimes, and the four of us absorbed by the great white rabbit.

Still smiling and noticing that even Martin was aghast at his son's temerity, I asked Jason how he had determined the price so quickly, so definitely, all on his own. Without hesitation he elaborated, and I got up to shake a congratulatory hand and to thank the Zweig family.

And so the white rabbit came home, a superb painted carved figure from the Dentzel works in Philadelphia at the beginning of the Twentieth Century when carousels twirled their spin throughout the country. Every time I looked at him I remembered a very first visit with a dealer in Salem, a memory filled with a youngster's fluency and audacity that matched the magic of a white rabbit. I paid two more visits to the Zweigs over the years, but never saw the filial prodigy. I have heard that a Jason Zweig is considered one of the more respected financial writers in this country. No surprise for one who remembers his 10-year-old presence and reasoning.

It is a strange feeling to find yourself written about without, at first, remembering what the writer describes about you. But, yes, that was me. My parents – literate, cultured, ambitious people – raised me to be peculiarly knowledgeable about the past at a very young age. I was, effectively, junior partner in their antiques business before I was a teenager, although I hadn't thought about those days in many years until I read that reminiscence.

I remember Ralph Esmerian well, although I confess I don't recall the specific conversation he describes. And a few of his details are incorrect – understandable, of course, with the passage of four decades. My father's name was Irving; my family isn't related to Martin Zweig, the mutual-fund manager who died in 2013. My parents weren't itinerant pickers who scavenged antiques from yard sales and the like, but respected dealers who exhibited at prestigious antique shows and frequently sold to fine museums.

Nor was my dad quite as shy as Ralph described; he was contemplative, but not diffident. My dad had taught political science at Ohio State and seemed to have committed every significant moment of American history to memory – no trivial advantages for him once he became an antique dealer.

He also had been the proprietor, editor and publisher of newspapers in small towns for more than a decade, so he could turn any great antique into a great story. Finally, I would have been 14, not 10, at the time of the event Ralph is recounting – although I probably looked as if I was 7.

But everything else Ralph says sounds right to me. He had extraordinary taste and elegant manners, even as he insisted that I call him "Ralph."

My parents did trust me in the way he described. I accompanied them on most of their buying trips to auctions and shows, and I regularly crawled around under tables, peered behind desks, turned furniture upside-down, rummaged through boxes of old books, went into attics and basements and barns with a flashlight, and so forth. Every once in a while I would spot something wonderful that everyone else, including my parents, had missed. That was partly because my parents had taught me extremely well – and partly because I was patient.

I think my youthful enthusiasm for the hunt and chase, the intellectual puzzle of connoisseurship, must have appealed to Ralph, a kindred spirit. I had no qualms about going down on my hands and knees in dust or dirt to distinguish fake from real, or about going through enormous piles of old papers in search of one document of historical importance, or about turning the bottom of a drawer back and forth in the sunlight for ten minutes until I could finally read a feather-faint pencil inscription that my intuition had told me could be the cabinetmaker's signature.

I have no recollection of what price Ralph paid us, but I know my only motivation would have been to match the rabbit with its rightful owner at a price warranted by its quality. I would simply have said what I thought it was worth; if he was worthy of owning it, then he would accept the price – as he did. And he is right that my dad wasn't using me as a kind of stooge; we often would set prices in this kind of informal discussion, right in front of the customers. Warren Buffett does something similar when he buys businesses: He asks the seller to name a price. If it's acceptable, Mr. Buffett buys; if not, he politely declines to negotiate and walks away. While my father did like to haggle when he bought, he refused to haggle when he sold. It was as if, once he owned something rare and beautiful, it was beneath the object's dignity for him to negotiate over it.[*]

---

[*] I interviewed Ralph Esmerian briefly over the phone this week (December, 2016); he was released in March after serving four-and-a-half years in federal prison.

We were all fond of that rabbit, partly because of its spectacular vigor as a sculpture but also because of its radiant condition, still in all its original pigments and with most of its patina intact. You hardly needed to imagine it on a carousel to picture it leaping up and down; you could see the wooden muscles coiled to spring under the wooden fur, and the joy on its face as it prepared its wooden leap. I still remember sitting on it and imagining what it would be like to be a boy in the 1890s escaping to the carousel for a quick spin on this magnificent sculpture – which did evoke the rabbit in *Alice in Wonderland*, just as Ralph says.

Our adventure with the rabbit wasn't unusual. In the 1970s – before the duopoly of Sotheby's and Christie's had grown to dominate the art world, before *Antiques Roadshow* became a public-television hit, and before Google put a universe of knowledge at everyone's fingertips – the market for art and antiques was extraordinarily inefficient. Prices could be, and often were, out of whack by several orders of magnitude.

In financial markets, information asymmetry often favors the sellers; those who have held an investment have access to inside knowledge and may be far better informed than those who are interested in buying it. In the art and antiques business of the 1970s, however, that information asymmetry was inverted: Buyers could often know far more than the sellers.

He told me the price I gave him for the rabbit was $3,500 (or approximately $20,000 today, adjusted for inflation). "That came right out of your mouth," he said. "You were staring at me. You didn't look to either of your parents for approval. I had never seen anything like it, this little kid acting that way."

The rabbit was one of four carousel figures my parents had bought for a total of $750, so we earned a good return, although that wasn't the point. We had bought these magnificent sculptures – the others were two snorting, rearing horses and a cat with a fish in his mouth and his tail in the air – from the manager of the town dump in Salem, N.Y., who ran a junkyard down the road from the dump. They were propped against an exterior wall of his shed, exposed to the sun and rain and snow. We felt as if we had salvaged them from the brink of oblivion. When part of Ralph's collection of American folk art was sold at Sotheby's in 2014 to satisfy creditors in his bankruptcy, David Schorsch, a leading dealer in Woodbury, Conn., paid $106,250 for our carousel rabbit. David was kind enough to send an email letting me know that he had bought it on behalf of a private collector and that it would have "a wonderful home in a great collection of folk art."

I thus learned a lesson, as a child, that has never left me and that has stood me well when, as an adult, I sought to understand the financial markets:

> Things are not what they seem: Much of what most people think is treasure is, in fact, trash. And much of what they think is trash is, in fact, treasure.

To tell the difference, art dealers and value investors alike must develop what the great investor Michael Steinhardt has called variant perception. You have to know much more than most of the other people in the market, and that knowledge becomes most valuable when it is at odds with the common perception of the other participants.

When I was a kid, that variant perception was based on vast amounts of study and preparation, along with stubborn – almost ornery – patience.

Realizing that rare books were chronically undervalued and easily overlooked, I spent a few days one summer, probably around the age of 13, going through our encyclopedia and writing down the dates when America's greatest writers first published their works. Author by author, one to an index card, I listed all their major books by date (some, like Mark Twain, required more than one card). Then I memorized all the dates, flash-card style.

That way, I knew, I would be able to spot first editions almost instantaneously. In the 19th century, book publishers typically didn't designate that a book was a first edition on the title or copyright page; but if you knew which year great books were published in, you could work your way through a crate full of dusty old volumes at remarkable speed. Knowing which ones didn't matter enabled you to focus your attention on those that did.

I did the same thing with paintings in art-reference books and at museums, memorizing dates and styles and compositions until I could see a landscape or portrait from the other side of the room and instantly identify the artist and, within five or ten years, when it was painted.

Speed, in an inefficient market, is important. An enormous value can exist, because the market is inefficient; but it might not persist, because its very enormity may call the value to someone else's attention. Whoever is first to appraise it correctly wins.

So my parents taught me to move through a display booth, a room, a house – even a lawn strewn with items for sale – at high intensity. You rake your eyes everywhere: from floor to ceiling, from one end of the area to the other. But you don't look at one object at a time; that would take forever, and devil take the hindmost.

Instead, you train your eye to take in whole groups of objects at once: everything on this table, all the objects on that wall, that cluster of furniture, the entire contents of this cabinet. You are searching for the incongruous, the oddball, the thing that doesn't belong there – the mahogany chair at the oak table, the silver porringer amid the modern dishware, the oil painting or watercolor tucked in among the photographs or prints or posters, the hand-woven rug alongside the rolls of synthetic carpeting. My parents also gave me prompt and unambiguous feedback – one of the keys to developing expert intuitions.

Only much later in life did I learn that similar training is the basis for many forms of pattern recognition by experts in a variety of fields.

As Herbert Simon, the great polymath and Nobel Laureate in economics, wrote:

> The situation has provided a cue; this cue has given the expert access to information stored in memory, and the information provides the answer. Intuition is nothing more and nothing less than recognition.

At an estate sale in the early 1970s, I walked up to a table covered in old books, swept my eyes across it looking for the gold-stamped leather bindings that typified early editions, and instantly took in that all the volumes were 20th-century – except one, which I immediately picked up. It was *The Song of Hiawatha*, by Henry Wadsworth Longfellow; I opened it, and the publication date, 1855, matched the entry in my mental database. I bought it for 10 cents.

At another auction, I went through what must have been two dozen boxes of old books until my hands were so dusty it looked as if I were wearing tan leather gloves. At the bottom of the last box was one book bound in magnificent red Moroccan leather. I opened it without even looking for the title. The inner covers were lined with superb Florentine marbled end papers, and the pages were edged with gold leaf. It wasn't just a first edition of *A Connecticut Yankee in King Arthur's Court* by Mark Twain (1889); it was one of 250 presentation copies the publisher had printed, and tucked inside the back cover was an original Christmas card drawn by Dan Beard, Twain's illustrator. This copy had evidently been given to Beard by Twain, although the book wasn't autographed. I stuffed it back under the rest of the books it came with; we bought the entire box for $40 and gave all the other books away.

But vast preparation and expert pattern recognition were only half the battle; patience and stubbornness mattered at least as much.

We never assumed, on any buying expedition, that we wouldn't find anything good enough to be worth owning. My dad often said, "If you don't see anything good, you haven't looked hard enough yet."

He often took that principle to extremes. My dad was one of the most intelligent people I've ever known, but he did commit one cognitive error: the sunk-cost fallacy. He hated to come home from any expedition empty-handed and would often devote absurd amounts of effort to find something – anything – worth buying in order to "justify" the trip.

On one such wild goose chase, we had driven to a house in Schoharie, N.Y. for the preview of an estate auction. Everything in the house turned out to be junk at a glance: the pieces of Chippendale and Hepplewhite furniture that had looked enticing in the ad were reproductions, the pottery and porcelain was chipped and cracked, the rugs were tattered, the paintings were poor quality, and so on. My parents kept trudging from one room to another and up and down the staircase in endless loops of frustration, trying to find something worthwhile.

After all too many of these laps, I refused to waste any more energy and flopped down on a sofa in the dim and dingy living room; I was a teenage boy, after all. The upholstery expelled a musty puff of dust. I coughed and squinted my eyes shut. When I opened them, I found myself looking at the same hideous painting, propped up against the fireplace, that we and a couple hundred other treasure-seekers had already walked past almost a dozen times.

The auctioneers had retrieved it from the attic; the surface of the painting was so dirty it looked as if it had been varnished with a mix of caramel and coal dust. Some of the paint was peeling off the canvas in an upper corner. The picture had almost certainly been moldering in the attic for decades: Its giant gilded frame was chipped and cracked and almost black with dust. Mud wasps had built nests between the elaborate curlicues of the frame.

I was just bored enough to look at the painting just long enough to realize that something about it was bothering me.

Why would anybody put such an ugly painting into such an ornate picture frame?

The instant the idea came into my head, I stopped wondering when my parents would give up and started wondering about the painting. It was some kind of landscape. A few trees, some clouds, maybe a river – nothing else was discernible through the murk.

But the frame was huge and heavy and had once been beautiful.

No one, in a thrifty community of Dutch and Scotch-Irish farmers, would have let an empty picture frame sit around; it would have been sold for whatever it would fetch. And no one would ever have bothered putting any frame at all onto this ratty old painting once it had gotten so dirty in the attic.

Which meant that the painting must already have been in this beautiful frame when it went into the attic long ago. Which meant that long before that, before landscapes in ornate frames became unfashionable, somebody must have thought this one was valuable.

Behind the sofa, the curtains were partly drawn. I stood up and pulled them all the way open. A shaft of sunlight hit the painting and cut through the grime. It was as if I had set off a miniature nuclear explosion: Brilliant pink and orange clouds boiled above a line of trees and a waterfall. I walked around the sofa and over to the fireplace, then crouched in front of the canvas and stared at it from a few inches away. Under the accumulated dirt of five or six decades, water cascaded over rocks, wind whipped through a line of trees, and those clouds erupted into towers of fire.

I knew instantly that I was looking at a long-lost masterpiece of the Hudson River School of 19th-century American landscape painters. My thumb had an intuition of its own: I licked it and pulled it lightly across a rock in the bottom left corner. "F CHURCH 1848," I read through the little window I had just opened in the dirt. *My mind raced: Frederic Church, born in 1826, one of his earliest major paintings.*

Here it is, after subsequently being cleaned and restored to its original glory. I can assure you it looked nothing like this on that day in 1975:

I shot up the stairs like a rocket. I found my parents, grabbed each of them by the arm and hissed, "There's a Church downstairs." My parents, understandably, hesitated – there could be no place of worship in this house of junk. Then they looked in my eyes, and they knew what I meant. I led them downstairs. We lugged the painting outside into the sunlight to look at it – then wordlessly, breathlessly carried it back into the living room.

The sale was the next day, held in the back yard, as so many auctions were in those days. We waited patiently for the painting to come up. The auctioneer, not knowing what it was, called it "an old landscape" and told the crowd that the frame might be worth salvaging if you could find someone to repair it. The audience was astonished when we paid about $2,000 for what one woman sitting in front of us called "a dirty old rag." The underbidder was a dealer who often followed us around and bid on whatever we did, assuming that anything my parents wanted must be good; my dad called him "the pilotfish." If not for him, we would have been the only bidder; there were no other takers at any price.

When we got the Church painting home, we worried about its condition. Working with cotton balls dabbed in art-restorers' cleaning solution, we got most of the grime off it. But parts of the paint were loose and flaking away.

It needed urgent care. Before we could even get it to a restorer, Donald Webster, an attorney and art dealer who ran the best auction house in Washington, D.C., C.G. Sloan & Co., visited. He bought the painting on the spot, for what I remember as about $16,000 (or a bit more than $70,000 in today's money). We hated to part with such a tour de force, but Mr. Webster agreed that the first thing he would do was to take it to the same restorer we would have used.

As always, we didn't think of what we had done as profiting from the ignorance of others; we thought of it as rescuing an artistically and historically important work of art from oblivion. What would have happened to these treasures if we hadn't found them? In many cases we were all that stood between them and another century in somebody's attic or pantry or toolshed – or, eventually, the town dump. I have no doubt, even today, that had we not identified the Church painting for what it was, it would have gone unsold that day and ended up in a landfill.

Shortly after Mr. Webster bought it from us, the painting found its way into the collection of the White House, where (at least as recently as 1990), it hung in the Oval Office.

President-elect Trump and his family have what we might describe, diplomatically, as different taste in interior decorating.

But I hope there will still be a place in their White House for the magnificent Frederic Church landscape that my parents and I rescued from oblivion so many years ago.

As I think back on my childhood and adolescent career, two things stand out for me:

First, how fortunate I was to be raised by such a brilliant mother and father who imparted so much knowledge and intellectual excitement to me at so early an age. And with their zest for the hunt as my inspiration, it's no wonder value investing had such attraction for me when, later in life, I studied the financial markets.

Second, how important it is to be in the right place at the right time. The art and antiques business in the 1970s was a remarkable confluence of inefficiencies and opportunities to exploit them. Back then, we could drive a few hours in any direction on any weekend and come home with a stationwagon full of beautiful old objects whose intrinsic value almost no one else had recognized. Nowadays, you could comb much of New England for weeks on end and find nothing except art and antiques priced at *more* than they are worth. The bargains that once abounded have been replaced by immense quantities of overpriced, undesirable mediocrities being passed off as rare and valuable. In a world in which it takes a few seconds to Google what an object sold for on eBay, undervalued art and antiques have all but disappeared.

I'm not nostalgic for my childhood, nor do I regret that I no longer practice much connoisseurship, because I know full well that those days are gone. The market for art and antiques today bears almost no resemblance to the world of my childhood, and the return to those skills, if I tried to earn my living by exercising them again, would be close to nil.*

The analogy to investing seems, to me at least, so obvious that I hesitate even to point it out. Decades ago, stock-picking was a handicraft in which information moved slowly and unevenly, so the person who knew the most could perform the best – by a wide margin. Think of Warren Buffett buying such tiny flecks of corporate plankton as Sanborn Map and Dempster Mill Manufacturing. Today, with more than 120,000 chartered financial analysts and 325,000 Bloomberg terminals worldwide and with Regulation FD requiring companies to disclose material information simultaneously to all investors, the playing field is close to perfectly level.

If you're applying the tools that worked so well in the inefficient markets of the past to the efficient markets of today, you are wasting your time and energy. An investor who devotes weeks or months of research to analyzing a single widely-traded stock is like an antique dealer driving across the back roads of New England searching for bargains that, for the most part, disappeared decades ago. It isn't impossible that you will find a bargain, but the odds that the rewards will justify the pursuit are low.

Today, being able to identify mispriced investments isn't nearly enough; you also must be able to identify where mispriced investments are still likely to be found.

---

* Once a decade or so, on average, I do find a great antique or work of art at a bargain price. And when I do, I buy it. But if I spent every intervening moment looking for more such opportunities, I would be foolishly wasting my time.

If investors are to prosper from inefficient markets, they have to evaluate which markets still *are* inefficient. Areas like microcap stocks or high-yield bonds, where index funds can't easily maneuver, offer some promise. Areas increasingly dominated by index funds offer little.

An individual investor can still benefit from time arbitrage: You can buy into a stock when bad news poisons the price with negative emotion and then hold for years until euphoria finally returns. That's a luxury most institutional investors no longer have.

But the skills that worked in inefficient markets rarely yield sufficient returns in efficient markets to make them worth bothering with.

Take it from one who has been there.

ABOUT JASON ZWEIG

Jason Zweig became a personal finance columnist for *The Wall Street Journal* in 2008. Zweig is also the editor of the revised edition of Benjamin Graham's *The Intelligent Investor* (HarperCollins, 2003). He is the author of *Your Money and Your Brain* (Simon & Schuster, 2007), one of the first books to explore the neuroscience of investing, and *The Devil's Financial Dictionary* (PublicAffairs, 2015), a satirical glossary of Wall Street.

Before joining *The Wall Street Journal*, Zweig was a senior writer for *Money* magazine and a guest columnist for *Time* magazine and cnn.com. From 1987 to 1995, Zweig was the mutual funds editor at *Forbes*. Earlier, he had been a reporter-researcher for the Economy & Business section of *Time* and an editorial assistant at *Africa Report*, a bimonthly journal. Zweig has a B.A. from Columbia College, where he was awarded a John Jay National Scholarship.

A frequent commentator on television and radio, Zweig is also a popular public speaker who has addressed the American Association of Individual Investors, the Aspen Institute, the CFA Institute, the Morningstar Investment Conference, and university audiences at Harvard, Stanford, and Oxford.

Zweig was for many years a trustee of the Museum of American Finance, an affiliate of the Smithsonian Institution. He serves on the editorial boards of *Financial History* magazine and *The Journal of Behavioral Finance*.

What You Should Remember About the Markets

BY GARY ANTONACCI

Because I have been an investment professional for more than 40 years, I sometimes get asked my opinion about the markets. These questions usually come from those without a systematic approach toward investing. Here are some typical questions and answers:

Question: How much do you think the stock market can drop?

Response: 89%.

Question: What?!!

Response: Well, that is the most it has dropped in the past. But past performance is no assurance of future success, so I guess it could go down more than that.

Question: I just looked at my account, and it is down. What should I do?

Response: Stop looking at your account.

Question: What are you doing now?

Response: What I always do… following my models.

After these responses, I am usually not asked any more questions.

Simple But Not Easy

Some say investing is simple, but not easy. This is due to myopic loss aversion. This combines loss aversion, where we regret losses almost twice as much as we appreciate gains, with the tendency to look at our investments too frequently.

We should remember that we cannot control the returns that the markets give us, but we can control what risks we are willing to accept. If we do not have systematic investment rules, it is easy to succumb to emotions that cause us to buy and sell at inappropriate times. The Dalbar and other studies show that investors generally make terrible timing decisions. The most common mistake investors make is to pull the plug on their investments, often at the worst possible time.

But investing does not have to be difficult if we have firm rules in place to keep us in tune with market forces. A sailor cannot control the wind, but she can determine how to take advantage of it to get her where she wants to go.

Trend Following

I have found the most important principle to keep in mind is the old adage "the trend is your friend." As some say, "the easiest way to ride a horse is in the direction it is headed." To remind me of how important it is to stay in tune with the long-term trend of the markets, I have this on my office wall:

Source: Quotatium.com

Many are familiar with that saying, but few have the ability to always adhere to it. Much of Warren Buffett's success is because he had the vision to stick with his approach over the long run. Buffett said, "You don't have to be smarter than the rest. You have to be more disciplined than the rest." This discipline applies not only to staying with your positions. It also means re-entering the markets when your approach calls for it, even though uncertainties may still exist.

What gives me the ability to stay with the long-term trend of the markets? First is knowing how well trend following has performed in the past.

Absolute Momentum

There are different approaches to trend following, such as moving averages, charting patterns, or other technical indicators. The trend following method I prefer is absolute (time-series) momentum. It has some advantages over other forms of trend following. First, it is easy to understand and to back test. It looks at whether or not the market has gone up or down over your look back period.

In my research going back to 1927, absolute momentum had 30% fewer trades than comparable moving average signals. From 1971 through 2015, our Global Equities Momentum (GEM) dual momentum model had ten absolute momentum trades that exited the stock market and had to reenter within a three-month period. A ten-month moving average had 20 such exits and reentries. The popular 200-day moving average had even more signals. Fewer trades mean lower frictional costs and fewer whipsaw losses.

You do not need to enter and exit right at market tops and bottoms to do well. In fact, if your investment approach is overly sensitive to price change and tries to enter and exit too close to tops and bottoms, you will often get whipsawed.

Because of whipsaw losses and lagging entry signals, trend following often underperforms buy-and-hold during bull markets. This is the price you pay for the protection you get from severe bear market risk exposure.

But since absolute momentum has a low number of whipsaw losses, the relative momentum part of dual momentum can put us ahead in bull markets over the long run. Absolute momentum can then do its job by keeping us largely out of harm's way during bear markets. The tables below show how absolute momentum, relative momentum, and dual momentum (GEM) have performed during bull and bear markets since 1971.

Bull and Bear Market Performance January 1971–December 2015

Bull Markets	S&P 500	Absolute Momentum	GEM
Jan 71–Dec 72	36.0	32.6	65.6
Oct 74–Nov 80	198.3	91.6	103.3
Aug 82–Aug 87	279.7	246.3	569.2
Dec 87–Aug 00	816.6	728.4	730.5
Oct 02–Oct 07	108.3	72.4	181.6
Mar 09–Jul 15	227.7	136.8	106.4
Average	277.7	218.1	292.7

Bear Markets	S&P 500	Relative Momentum	GEM
Jan 73–Sep 74	−42.6	−35.6	15.1
Dec 80–Jul 82	−16.5	−16.9	16.0
Sep 87–Nov 87	−29.6	−15.1	−15.1
Sep 00–Sep 02	−44.7	−43.4	14.9
Nov 07–Feb 09	−50.9	−54.6	−13.1
Average	−36.9	−33.1	3.6

Results are hypothetical, are NOT an indicator of future results, and do NOT represent returns that any investor actually attained.

Robustness

My research paper, 'Absolute Momentum: A Simple Rule-Based Strategy and Trend Following Overlay' showed the effectiveness of absolute momentum across eight different markets from 1974 through 2012. Moskowitz et al (2011) demonstrated the efficacy of absolute momentum from 1965 through 2011 when applied to equity index, currency, commodity, and bond futures. In '215 Years of Global Asset Momentum: 1800–2014', Geczy & Samonov (2015) showed that both relative and absolute momentum outperformed buy-and-hold from 1801 up to the present time when applied to stocks, stock indices, sectors, bonds, currencies, and commodities.

Greyserman & Kaminski (2014) performed the longest ever study of trend-following. Using trend following momentum from 1695 through 2013, they found that stock indices had higher returns and higher Sharpe ratios than a buy-and-hold approach. The chance of large drawdowns was also small compared to buy-and-hold. The authors found similar results in 84 bond, currency, and commodity markets all the way back to the year 1223! Talk about confidence building. These kinds of results are what give me the ability to stay with absolute momentum under all market conditions.

Market Overreaction

I have some clients though who are less familiar with and sanguine about trend following. They still get nervous during times of market stress, such as August of 2015. They need to also understand that stocks do not trend all the time. The stock market can overextend itself and mean revert over the short run. During such times it is important for investors to stay the course and not overreact to short-term volatility.

To remind me to remind others about short-term mean reversion, I have this coffee mug in my office:

Source: Quotatium.com

This tells me to ignore market noise and calmly accept occasional market overreactions that are often followed by mean reversion.

There is no way to get rid of short-term volatility and still earn high returns from our investments. We should, in fact, embrace short-term volatility since it is what leads to superior returns over the long run.

What to Remember

Rigorous academic research confirms the existence of trend persistence and short-term mean reversion. Whatever your investment approach, if you respect these two forces you should be able to invest with comfort and conviction. Being aware of these principles gives us the two qualities required for long-run investment success. First is the discipline we need to follow one's proven methods unwaveringly. The second is patience.

Warren Buffett said the stock market is a mechanism for transferring wealth from the impatient to the patient. Like Buffett, we also need to patiently accept inevitable periods of short-term volatility and underperformance with respect to our benchmarks.

If you have trouble always remembering the concepts of trend persistence and mean reversion, then do what I do. Get yourself a poster and coffee mug.

ABOUT GARY ANTONACCI

Gary Antonacci is author of the award-winning book, *Dual Momentum Investing: An Innovative Strategy for Higher Returns with Lower Risk*. His research introduced the investment world to dual momentum, which combines relative strength price momentum with trend following absolute momentum.

His research on momentum investing was the first place winner in 2012 and the second place winner in 2011 of the Wagner Awards for Advances in Active Investment Management given annually by the National Association of Active Investment Managers (NAAIM).

He received his MBA degree from the Harvard Business School in 1978. Since then, he has concentrated on researching, developing, and applying innovative investment strategies that have their basis in academic research.

Sustainable Sources of Competitive Advantage

BY MORGAN HOUSEL

David Paul Gregg invented the CD, which is amazing and changed history. But you've probably never heard of him because CDs aren't difficult to make, and lost relevance over time.

Most things work this way. As soon as a smart product or business idea becomes popular, the urge to copy it and commoditize it is the strongest force economics can unleash. Jeff Bezos summed this up when he said "Your margin is my opportunity."

The key to business and investing success isn't finding an advantage. It's having a sustainable advantage. Something that others either can't or aren't willing to copy once your idea is exposed and patents expire.

Finding something others can't do is nearly impossible. Intelligence is not a sustainable source of competitive advantage because the world is full of smart people, and a lot of what used to count as intelligence is now automated.

That leaves doing something others aren't willing to do as the top source of sustainable competitive advantage.

Here are five big ones.

The ability to learn faster than your competition

Someone with a 110 IQ but the ability to recognize when the world changes will always beat the person with a 140 IQ and rigid beliefs. The world is filled with smart people who get nowhere because their intelligence was acquired 20 or 30 years ago in a vastly different world than we live in today. And since intelligence has a lot of sunk costs – college is expensive and hard, for example – people tend to cling to what they learn, even while the world around them constantly changes. So the ability to realize when you're wrong and when things changed can be more effective than an ability to solve problems that are no longer relevant. This seems obvious until you watch, say, Kodak or Sears trying to solve 1980s problems in the 2000s.

Marc Andreessen promotes the idea of "strong beliefs, weakly held," which I love. Few things are more powerful than strongly believing in an idea (focus) but being willing to let go of it when it's proven wrong or outdated (humility).

The ability to empathize with customers more than your competition

Forty-seven percent of mutual fund mangers do not personally own any of their own fund, according to Morningstar. That's shocking. But I suspect something similar happens across most businesses.

What percentage of McDonald's executives frequent their own restaurant as a legitimate customer interested in the chain's food, rather than a fact-finding mission? Few, I imagine. How many times has the CEO of Delta Airlines been bumped from a flight, or had his bags lost by the airline? Never, I assume.

The inability to understand how your customers experience your product almost guarantees an eventual drift between the problems a business tries to solve and the problems customers need solved. Here again, a person with a lower IQ who can empathize with customers will almost always beat someone with a higher IQ who can't put themselves in customers' shoes. This was apparent in the 2016 US presidential election, when understanding the electorate's mood far exceeded the power of traditional campaign strategies.

It's also why the best writers are voracious readers. They know exactly what readers want and don't want because they themselves are customers of content.

The ability to communicate more effectively than your competition

Business success doesn't necessarily go to those with the best product. It goes to whoever is the most persuasive. George Soros may be one of the brightest minds in finance, but he would fail miserably as a financial advisor. Not one person in ten who reads his books understands what the hell he's talking about.

Most business edges are found at the intersection of trust and simplicity. Both rely on the ability to tell customers what and why you're doing something before losing their attention.

This is one of the crazy things that gets harder to do the smarter you are. There's a bias called "the curse of knowledge," which is the inability to realize that other people with less experience than you have don't see the world through the same lens you do. I saw this firsthand when a financial advisor told an utter novice grandmother that a higher bond allocation (which she wanted) didn't make sense "because of the slope of the yield curve." She had no idea what this meant, and told me experiences like this eroded trust since she couldn't distinguish her confusion from his obfuscation.

The willingness to fail more than your competition

Having no appetite for being wrong means you'll only attempt things with high odds of working. And those things tend to be only slight variations on what you're already doing, which themselves are things that, in a changing world, may soon be obsolete.

Here's Bezos again: "If you double the number of experiments you do per year, you're going to double your inventiveness."

The key is creating a culture that allows you to fail often without ruin. This means not docking employees for trying things that don't work, and not betting so much on a single idea that its failure could cripple the company.

Amazon and Google, I'm convinced, are successful because they're better and more willing to fail than any other company. Accepting lots of small failures is the only way they're able to eventually find a few things that take off.

The willingness to wait longer than your competition

Rewards sit on a spectrum: Small, unpredictable ones in the short run, big, higher-odd ones if you wait longer.

It's amazing how much of a competitive advantage can be found by simply having the disposition to wait longer than your competitors.

Waiting longer gives you time to learn from, and correct, early mistakes. It reduces randomness and pushes you closer to measurable outcomes. It lets you focus on the parts of a problem that matter, rather than the chaos and nonsense that comes in the short run from people's unpredictable emotions.

If you can wait five years when your competitors are only willing to wait two, you have an advantage that is both powerful and uncorrelated to intelligence or skill.

Which is about as close to a free lunch as it gets in business.

ABOUT MORGAN HOUSEL

Morgan Housel is a partner at The Collaborative Fund.

He is a two-time winner of the Best in Business award from the Society of American Business Editors and Writers and a two-time finalist for the Gerald Loeb Award for Distinguished Business and Financial Journalism. He was selected by the *Columbia Journalism Review* for the *Best Business Writing 2012* anthology. In 2013 he was a finalist for the Scripps Howard Award.

Who's Being Naïve, Kay?

BY BEN HUNT

All great literature is one of two stories: a man goes on a journey or a stranger comes to town.

> — Leo Tolstoy (1826–1910)

Satan: Dream other dreams, and better!

> — Mark Twain, *The Mysterious Stranger* (c. 1900)

Twain spent 11 years writing his final novel, *The Mysterious Stranger*, but never finished it. The book exists in three large fragments and is Twain's darkest and least funny work. It's also my personal favorite.

Harold Hill: Ladies and gentlemen, either you are closing your eyes to a situation you do not wish to acknowledge, or you are not aware of the caliber of disaster indicated by the presence of a pool table in your community!

> — *The Music Man* (1962)

The Pied Piper legend, originally a horrific tale of murder, finds its source in the earliest written records of the German town of Hamelin (1384), reading simply "it is 100 years since our children left."

Stanley Moon:	I thought you were called Lucifer.
George Spiggott:	I know. "The Bringer of the Light" it used to be. Sounded a bit poofy to me.
George Spiggott:	Everything I've ever told you has been a lie. Including that.
Stanley Moon:	Including what?

George Spiggott:	That everything I've ever told has been a lie. That's not true.
Stanley Moon:	I don't know WHAT to believe.
George Spiggott:	Not me, Stanley, believe me!

— *Bedazzled* (1967)

A must-see movie, and I don't mean the 2000 abomination with Brendan Fraser, but the genius 1967 version by Peter Cook and Dudley Moore. Plus Raquel Welch as Lust. Yes, please.

Wade Wilson: I had another Liam Neeson nightmare. I kidnapped his daughter and he just wasn't having it. They made three of those movies. At some point you have to wonder if he's just a bad parent.

— *Deadpool* (2016)

Shape clay into a vessel;
It is the space within that makes it useful.
Cut doors and windows for a room;
It is the holes which make it useful.
Therefore benefit comes from what is there;
Usefulness from what is not there.

— **Lao Tzu (c. 530 BC)**

It's like trying to find gold in a silver mine
It's like trying to drink whiskey from a bottle of wine

– **Elton John and Bernie Taupin, 'Honky Cat' (1972)**

Michael:	My father is no different than any powerful man, any man with power, like a president or senator.
Kay Adams:	Do you know how naïve you sound, Michael? Presidents and senators don't have men killed.
Michael:	Oh. Who's being naïve, Kay?

— *The Godfather* (1972)

As Tolstoy famously said, there are only two stories in all of literature: either a man goes on a journey, or a stranger comes to town. Of the two, we are far more familiar and comfortable with the first in the world of markets and investing, because it's the subjectively perceived narrative of our individual lives. We learn. We experience. We overcome adversity. We get better. Or so we tell ourselves.

But when the story of our investment age is told many years from now, it won't be remembered as a Hero's Journey, but as a classic tale of a Mysterious Stranger. It's a story as old as humanity itself, and it always ends with the same realization by the Stranger's foil: what was I thinking when I signed that contract or fell for that line? Why was I so naïve?

The Mysterious Stranger today, of course, is not a single person but is the central banking Mafia apparatus in the US, Europe, Japan, and China. The leaders of these central banks may not be as charismatic as Robert Preston in *The Music Man*, but they hold us investors in equal rapture. The Music Man uses communication policy and forward guidance to get the good folks of River City to buy bond instruments. Central bankers use communication policy and forward guidance to get investors large and small to buy financial assets. It's a difference in degree and scale, not in kind.

The Mysterious Stranger is NOT a simple or single-dimensional fraud. No, the Mysterious Stranger is a liar, to be sure, but he's a proper villain, as the Brits would say, and typically he's quite upfront about his goals and his use of clever words to accomplish those goals. I mean, it's not like Kay doesn't know what she's getting herself into when she marries into the Corleone family. Michael is crystal clear with her, right from the start. But she wants to believe so badly in what Michael is telling her when he suddenly reappears in her life, that she suspends her disbelief in his words and embraces the Narrative of legitimacy he presents. I think Michael actually believed his own words, too, that he would in fact be able to move the Family out of organized crime entirely, just as I'm sure that Yellen believed her own words of tightening and light-at-the-end-of-the-tunnel in the summer of 2014. Ah, well. Events doth make liars of us all.

Draw your own comparisons to this story arc of *The Godfather*, with investors playing the role of Kay and the Fed playing the role of Michael Corleone. I think it's a pretty neat fit. It ends poorly for Kay, of course (and not so great for Michael). Let's see if we can avoid her fate.

But like Kay, for now we are married to the Mob … err, I mean, the Fed and competitive monetary policies, as reflected in the relative value of the dollar and other currencies. The cold hard fact is that since the summer of 2014 there has been a powerful negative correlation between the trade-weighted dollar and oil, between the trade-weighted dollar and emerging markets, and between the trade-weighted dollar and industrial, manufacturing, and energy stocks. Here's an example near and dear to the hearts of any energy investor, the trade-weighted dollar versus the inverted Alerian MLP index (ticker AMZ), a set of 43 midstream energy companies, principally pipelines and infrastructure.

US Trade Weighted Dollar & Alerian MLP Index

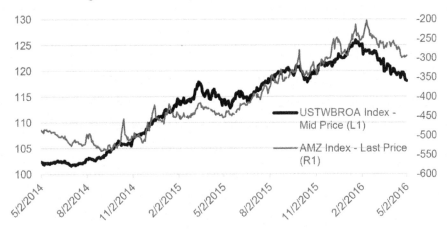

© Bloomberg Finance L.P. as of 05/02/2016. For illustrative purposes only. Past performance does not guarantee future results.

This is a -94% correlation, remarkably strong for any two securities, much less two – pipelines and the dollar – that are not obviously connected in any fundamental or real economy sort of way. But this is always what happens when the Mysterious Stranger comes to town: our traditional behavioral rules (i.e., correlations) go out the window and are replaced with new behavioral rules and correlations as we give ourselves over to his smooth words and promises. Because that's what a Mysterious Stranger DOES – tell compelling stories, stories that stick fast to whatever it is in our collective brains that craves Narrative and Belief.

There's nothing particularly new about this phenomenon in markets, as there have always been "story stocks", especially in the technology, media, and telecom (TMT) sector where you have more than your fair share of charismatic management storytellers and valuation multiples that depend on their efforts.

My favorite example of a "story stock" is Salesforce.com (ticker CRM), a $55 billion market cap technology company with 19,000 employees and about $6.5 billion in revenues. I'm pretty sure that Salesforce.com has never had a single penny of GAAP earnings in its existence (in FY 2016 the company lost $0.07 per share on a GAAP basis). Instead, the company is valued on the basis of non-GAAP earnings, but even there it trades at about an 80x multiple (!) of FY 2017 company guidance of $1.00 per share. Salesforce.com is blessed with a master story-teller in its CEO, Marc Benioff, who – if you've ever heard him speak – puts forth a pretty compelling case for why his company should be valued on the basis of bookings growth and other such metrics. Of course, the skeptic in me might note that it is perhaps no great feat to sell more and more of a software service at a loss, particularly when your salespeople are compensated on bookings growth, and the cynic in me might also note that for the past 10+ years Benioff has sold between 12,500 and 20,000 shares of CRM stock every day through a series of 10b5-1 programs. But hey, that's why he's the multi-billionaire (and a liquid multi-billionaire, to boot) and I'm not. The next chart shows the five-year chart for CRM.

Not bad. **Up 138% over the past five years.** A few ups and downs, particularly at the start of 2016, although the stock has certainly come roaring back. But when you dig a little deeper...

Five-year chart for Salesforce.com (CRM)

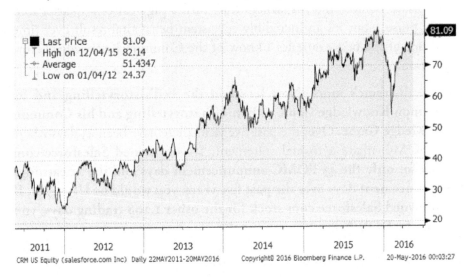

© Bloomberg Finance L.P. as of 05/20/2016. For illustrative purposes only.
Past performance does not guarantee future results.

There are 1,272 trading days that comprise this five-year chart. 21 of those trading days, less than 2% of the total, represent the Thursday after Salesforce.com reports quarterly earnings (always on a Wednesday after the market close). **If you take out those 21 trading days, Salesforce.com stock is up only 35% over the past five years.** How does this work? What's the causal process? Every Wednesday night after the earnings release, for the past umpteen years, Benioff appears on *Mad Money*, where Cramer's verdict is always an enthusiastic "Buy, buy, buy!" Every Thursday morning after the earnings release, the two or three sell-side analyst "axes" on the stock publish their glowing assessment of the quarterly results before trading begins. It's not that every investor on Thursday believes what Cramer or the sell-side analysts are saying, particularly anyone who's short the stock (CRM always has a high short interest). But in a perfect example of the Common Knowledge Game, if you ARE short the stock, you know that everyone else has heard what Cramer and the sell-side analysts (the Missionaries, in game theory lingo) have said, and you have to assume that everyone else will act on this Common Knowledge (what everyone knows that everyone knows). The only logical thing for you to do is cover your short before everyone else covers their short, resulting in a classic short squeeze and a big up day. Now to be sure, this isn't the story of every earnings announcement... sometimes even Marc Benioff and his lackeys can't turn a pig's ear of a quarter into a silk purse... but it's an incredibly consistent behavioral result over time and one of the best examples I know of the Common Knowledge Game in action.

But wait, there's more. **Now let's add the Fed's storytelling and its Common Knowledge Game to Benioff's storytelling and his Common Knowledge Game.** Over the past five years there have been 43 days where the FOMC made a formal statement. **If you owned Salesforce.com stock for only the 43 FOMC announcement days and the 21 earnings announcement days over the past five years, you would be UP 167%. If you owned Salesforce.com stock for the other 1,208 trading days, you would be DOWN 8%.**

Salesforce.com stock price appreciation

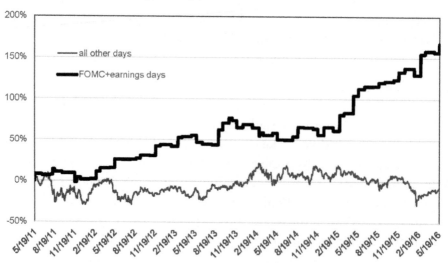

© Bloomberg Finance L.P. as of 05/19/2016. For illustrative purposes only. Past performance does not guarantee future results.

Okay, Ben, how about other stocks? How about entire indices? Well, let's look again at that Alerian MLP index. **Over the past five years, if you had owned the AMZ for only the 43 FOMC announcement days over that span, you would be UP 28%. If you owned it for the other 1,229 trading days you would be DOWN 39%. Over the past two years, if you had**

owned the AMZ for only the 16 FOMC announcement days over that span, you would be UP 18%. If you owned it for the other 487 trading days you would be DOWN 48%. Addition by subtraction to a degree that would make Lao Tzu proud.

Alerian MLP Index Price Appreciation

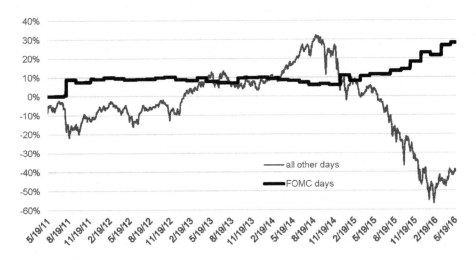

© Bloomberg Finance L.P. as of 05/19/2016. For illustrative purposes only. Past performance does not guarantee future results.

I'll repeat what I wrote in 'Optical Illusion / Optical Reality'… it's hard to believe that MLP investors should be paying a lot more attention to G-7 meetings and reading the Fed governor tea leaves than to gas field depletion schedules and rig counts, but I gotta call 'em like I see 'em. In fact, if there's a core sub-text to *Epsilon Theory* it's this: **call things by their proper names**. That's a profoundly subversive act. Maybe the only subversive act that really changes things. So here goes. **Today there are vast swaths of the market, like emerging markets and commodity markets and industrial/ energy stocks, that we should call by their proper name:** *a derivative expression of FOMC policy*. Used to be that only tech stocks were "story stocks". Today, almost all stocks are "story stocks", and the Common Knowledge Game is more applicable to helping us understand market behaviors and price action than ever before.

You see this phenomenon clearly in the entire S&P 500, as well, although not as starkly with a complete plus/minus reversal in performance between

FOMC announcement days and all other days. **Over the past five years, if you had owned the SPX for only the 43 FOMC announcement days over that span, you would be UP 17%. If you owned it for the other 1,229 trading days you would be UP 28%. Over the past two years, if you had owned the SPX for only the 16 FOMC announcement days over that span, you would be UP 5%. If you owned it for the other 487 trading days you would be UP 2%.**

S&P 500 Index Price Appreciation

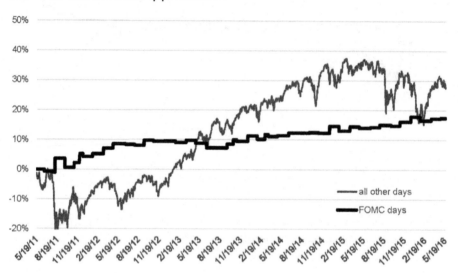

© Bloomberg Finance L.P. as of 05/19/2016. For illustrative purposes only. Past performance does not guarantee future results.

What do I take from eyeballing these charts? The Narrative effect and the impact of the Common Knowledge Game have accelerated over the past two years (ever since Draghi and Yellen launched the Great Monetary Policy Schism of June 2014); they're particularly impactful during periods when stock prices are otherwise declining, and they're spreading to broader equity indices. That's what it looks like to me, at least.

So what does an investor do with these observations? Two things, I think, one a practical course of action and one a shift in perspective. The former being more fun but the latter more important.

First, there really is a viable research program here, and what I've tried to show in this brief note is that there really are practical implementations of the Common Knowledge Game that can support investment strategies dealing with story stocks. I want to encourage anyone who's intrigued by this research program to take the data baton and try this on your favorite stock or mutual fund or index. You can get the FOMC announcement dates straight from the Federal Reserve website. This doesn't require an advanced degree in econometrics to explore.

I don't know where this research program ends up, but it's my commitment to do this in plain sight through *Epsilon Theory*. Think of it as the equivalent of open source software development, just in the investment world. I suspect it's hard to turn the Common Knowledge Game into a standalone investment strategy because you're promising that you'll do absolutely nothing for 98 out of 100 trading days. Good luck raising money on that. **But it's a great perspective to *add* to our current standalone strategies, especially actively managed funds.** Stock-pickers today are being dealt one dull, low-conviction hand after another here in the Grand Central Bank Casino, and the hardest thing in the world for any smart investor, regardless of strategy, is to sit on his hands and do *nothing*, even though that's almost always the right thing to do. Incorporating an awareness of the Common Knowledge Game and its highly punctuated impact makes it easier to do the right thing – usually nothing – in our current investment strategies.

And that gets us to the second take-away from this note. The most important thing to know about any Mysterious Stranger story is that the Stranger is the protagonist. **There is no Hero! When you meet a Mysterious Stranger, your goal should be simple: survive the encounter.**

This is an insanely difficult perspective to adopt, that we (either individually or collectively) are not the protagonist of the investing age in which we live. It's difficult because we are creatures of ego. We all star in our own personal movie and we all hear the anthems of our own personal soundtrack. But the Mysterious Stranger is not an obstacle to be heroically overcome, as if we were Liam Neeson setting off (again! and again!) to rescue a kidnapped daughter in yet another *Taken* sequel. At some point this sort of heroism is just a reflection of bad parenting in the case of Liam Neeson, and a reflection of bad investing in the case of stock pickers and other clingers to the correlations and investment meanings of yesterday.

The correlations and investment meanings of *today* are inextricably entwined with central bankers and their storytelling. **To be *investment survivors* in the low-return and policy-controlled world of the Silver Age of the Central Banker, we need to recognize the impact of their words and incorporate that into our existing investment strategies, while *never* accepting those words naïvely in our hearts.**

ABOUT BEN HUNT

Dr. Ben Hunt is the chief investment strategist at Salient Partners and the author of Epsilon Theory, a newsletter and website that examines markets through the lenses of game theory and history. Over 100,000 professional investors and allocators across 180 countries read Epsilon Theory for its fresh perspective and novel insights into market dynamics. As chief investment strategist, Dr. Hunt helps develop investment strategy for the firm, works with portfolio managers and key clients to incorporate his investment views into their decision-making process, and manages certain portfolios directly. Dr. Hunt is a featured contributor to a wide range of investment publications and media programming.

Dr. Hunt received his Ph.D. in Government from Harvard University in 1991. He taught political science for 10 years at New York University and (with tenure) at Southern Methodist University. Dr. Hunt wrote two academic books: *Getting to War* (Univ. of Michigan Press, 1997) and *Policy and Party Competition* (Routledge, 1992), which he co-authored with Michael Laver. Dr. Hunt is the founder of two technology companies and the co-founder of SmartEquip, Inc., a software company for the construction equipment industry that provides intelligent schematics and parts diagrams to facilitate e-commerce in spare parts.

Dr. Hunt began his investment career in 2003, first in venture capital and subsequently as a portfolio manager of two long/short equity hedge funds. He worked at Iridian Asset Management from 2006 until 2011 and TIG Advisors from 2012 until 2013. Dr. Hunt joined Salient in 2013.

Five "Must Ask" Due Diligence Questions
Before Making Any Investment

———————————

BY TODD TRESIDDER

How To Avoid Losing Investments Before They Cost You Money

Key ideas:

1. Learn how to profit from the "business common-sense test."

2. Discover the most important question you should always ask first... before anything else.

3. Get five extra bonus due diligence questions to protect your money.

Ignorance about investing isn't bliss… it's expensive.

What you don't know about investing will cost you money.

But the cure is simple – due diligence.

Due diligence is the critical skill that separates professional investors from amateurs.

Amateur investors act irresponsibly by risking their hard-earned dollars on hunches, articles they read, brokerage investment advice, or hot tips without first performing due diligence. This invites unnecessary and avoidable risk resulting in catastrophic losses.

Professional investors do the opposite by investigating all investments first before ever putting a dime of capital at risk.

Sure, it's a pain and sometimes takes hard work, but getting answers to the tough questions up front can save you from expensive losses down the road.

There's simply no substitute for investment due diligence because it's what you don't know about investing that will cost you.

Below are the five due diligence questions you must ask yourself before making any investment.

Due Diligence Question #1: How Can I Lose Money With This Investment?

This question is so important I'm tempted to throw away the remaining four questions and just repeat it over and over again until you get it in your bones.

You don't know an investment until you understand all the ways you can lose money with it.

> *"Rule No. 1: Never lose money. Rule No. 2: Never forget rule No. 1."*
>
> — **Warren Buffett**

I can't overemphasize the importance of this question. You must first focus on the return of your capital, and only second concern yourself with the return on your capital.

The first question in my mind when analyzing any investment is to find all the ways I can lose money by identifying in advance all the major risks that can lead to losses.

Once these risks are fully identified, the second step is to proactively manage away whatever risks are manageable. I explain this two-step due diligence process in greater detail below:

The First Step in Risk Management is to Identify the Risk Profile

Your first job is to identify all the ways you can lose money with a particular investment. You do this by identifying and grouping the risks associated with that investment.

You may be surprised just how much risk is manageable.

With proper portfolio design and investment strategy, you can usually manage away every significant risk (except one or two) to acceptable proportions.

These one or two remaining risks define the specific, uncontrolled risk profile for that investment. It's the leftover risk you must live with.

In order to manage away the risks of loss, you must first know what risks are inherent to the investment you're considering.

Using the stock market as an example, there are almost a limitless number of risks, but for practical purposes, they can be profiled down to a few major categories:

1. "Company specific" risks include things like accounting scandals, lawsuits, and mismanagement – anything unique to the company that's not part of the industry. These risks are managed away by diversifying among multiple companies. Mutual funds and exchange traded funds (ETF) are great examples of simple, cost effective tools to diversify away company specific risk.

2. "Industry specific" risks include a downturn in demand for widgets, changes in consumer tastes, disruptive technology changes, and industry law changes. This risk is controlled by not concentrating your portfolio in a single industry.

3. A closely related risk is "investment style" risk such as value vs. growth, or large cap vs. micro cap. The market will vary how it rewards or punishes different investment styles over time. For this reason, you should manage this risk by not concentrating too heavily in any one specific investment style like micro cap, value, or growth.

4. "Market" risk is associated with a general downturn in investor's appetite for stocks, causing an overall reduction in the valuation level of equities. This risk is manageable through a sell discipline, hedging, or by diversifying into non-correlated markets such as real estate, commodities, cash, or international equities rather than solely domestic equities.

Again, the above risk profiles are designed to illustrate stock investing. However, the same principles can (and should be) applied to every asset class in your portfolio.

"All of life is the exercise of risk."

— **William Sloane Coffin, Jr.**

For example, if you invest in real estate, you wouldn't want to over-concentrate in one property, or one city, or one type of property. It's wiser to diversify away those risks that can be managed, rather than concentrate them.

The Second Step in Risk Management is to Create a Controlled Risk Profile

Once the risk profile for an investment is fully understood, your job as risk manager is two-fold:

- First, you must design ways to manage away whatever risks can be eliminated.

- Second, you must accept only investments where the remaining uncontrolled risk profile doesn't overlap with other investments in your portfolio.

The end result is a minimization of the total risk for the entire portfolio, because it's composed of mostly uncorrelated, managed-risk investments.

Why bother with all this? Because lower risk means losing less money when you're wrong. That's important because losing less when you're wrong results in making more when you're right.

> *"Often the difference between a successful person and a failure is not one has better abilities or ideas, but the courage that one has to bet on one's ideas, to take a calculated risk – and to act."*

> — Andre Malraux

Your ability to manage risk is limited only by your knowledge and creativity.

The critical point to understand is that each investment has unique risk management tools available that are directly related to the unique characteristics of the investment and the market it trades in.

For example, one of the largest risks to income-producing real estate is a change in interest rates, since mortgage interest is one of your biggest expenses. This risk can be managed by locking down long-term, fixed-rate, fully-amortizing financing.

You can also limit your loss in real estate to the amount of your down payment through the use of non-recourse financing, thus controlling the risk of widespread capital losses impacting your entire portfolio should one property turn into a loser.

Notice that these two financing tools for managing risk are unique to real estate and aren't available to investors in business or paper assets (the other two primary paths to wealth).

Each market has its own unique characteristics for managing risk, and the paper asset markets are no different.

For example, most securities markets offer high liquidity and low transaction costs, making them a natural candidate for cost effectively managing many risks through a sell discipline.

In fact, many mutual funds have zero transaction costs and daily liquidity through their commission free exchange privilege.

However, using a sell strategy in real estate to control downside capital risk doesn't make sense compared to paper assets because of the prohibitively high transactions costs, and possible low liquidity during tough market conditions when you would want to sell.

In short, each market has unique characteristics that can be exploited to effectively manage the risk inherent in that market. What works in one market to lower risk may not apply in another market.

In summary, your first due diligence question is to uncover all the ways you can lose money with an investment.

The first step in this process is to profile what the risks are inherent in that investment.

The second step is to develop strategies to control losses that match the unique character of that asset should the worst come to pass.

This is the essence of active risk management.

> *"And the day came when the risk to remain tight in the bud was more painful than the risk it took to blossom."*
>
> — **Anais Nin**

After you have managed away all risks that can be eliminated, you're left with a specific, uncontrolled risk profile for that investment. This leads to your final risk management step, which is to make sure the remaining risk profile doesn't correlate with other investments in your portfolio.

For example, when I purchase apartment buildings, they are financed with long-term, non-recourse debt to control both interest rate risk and to minimize total risk of loss should Murphy's Law prevail.

In addition, each building is located in a different geographic market to assure the uncontrollable risk profile associated with location doesn't correlate to other assets in my portfolio.

The risk of loss on each apartment building similarly has no correlation to the risk inherent in my paper asset portfolio or my business. Each risk profile is unique to the asset.

This excessive focus on risk might seem pessimistic to many, but my experience is quite the opposite. All it really does is bring balance because investing is by definition a game of greed.

The objective is to make money so the game is naturally played offensively by looking for the profit. By disciplining yourself to look for the loss, you'll balance offense with an equally strong defense to create a winning team.

Stated another way, the hallmark of great investors isn't just strong positive returns, but consistent returns through all market conditions.

This can only be achieved by focusing on controlling losses through disciplined risk management.

Due Diligence Question #2: How Will This Investment Help Me Achieve My Personal and Portfolio Objectives?

The portfolio objective for most investors is to maximize profit with minimum risk.

You achieve this goal by building a diversified portfolio of non-correlated, risk managed, high mathematical expectation investment strategies that capitalize on a competitive advantage in business, real estate, and/or paper asset investing. (Sorry, I know it's a mouthful. Read it twice. There is a lot of meat in that sentence.)

But it's not enough to just have a portfolio objective – you must also have a personal objective.

Your personal objective for investing is to achieve your portfolio objective in a way that honors your personal values, skills, and interests.

You're a unique human being who must travel his own path to success. After all, there's no point in climbing the ladder to success if it's leaning against the wrong wall.

> *"Success with money, family, relationships, health, and careers is the ability to reach your personal objectives in the shortest time, with the least effort and with the fewest mistakes. The goals you set for yourself and the strategies you choose become your blueprint or plan. Strategies are like recipes: choose the right ingredients, mix them in the correct proportions, and you'll always produce the same predictable results: in this case financial success."*
>
> — Charles J. Givens

Investment success is a lifelong process, and humans aren't robots. The only way you'll stay the course long enough to succeed is when your investment strategy fits your interests, skills, goals and resources, thus providing emotional satisfaction.

Stated another way, one of the biggest obstacles to success is getting distracted by the endless opportunities that will cross your path.

There are many ways to make money investing, but I recommend you find the one or two that are going to work for you, and not get diverted by all the rest. You must stay the course long-term until you succeed.

For example, I've worked with successful real estate investors in single family homes, commercial real estate, mini-storage, office parks, mobile home parks, notes, apartments, and more. Yet, seldom do I meet successful investors who are actively working more than one of these investment niches at any one time.

The smorgasbord approach to investing doesn't work because each investment specialty has its own twists and turns that require specialized expertise.

Each niche has its own network that you must plug into for success. Each niche requires its own specialized skills and competitive advantage.

Nobody can (or should) be a master of all investment strategies because any one offers more than enough opportunity to reach financial freedom.

For that reason, you must determine which niche has the inherent characteristics that best fits your interests, investment goals, and risk tolerance because that's where you'll discover wealth, happiness and fulfillment.

Not every investment alternative is suitable for every investor. Your job is to find the one uniquely suitable for you.

For example, every investment has an "active" and "passive" component to it. If you don't want to be a "hands on" real estate investor, then professionally managed apartment complexes make more sense than single family homes.

Even greater passivity can be obtained through paper asset investing if that fits your objective.

> *"Success is the progressive realization of worthwhile, predetermined, personal goals."*
>
> — **Paul J. Meyer**

However, if you're age 55 and just starting to build for retirement, then beware of investment advice pushing you toward passive investments like paper assets. Your situation may require the leverage only available in business and real estate to allow you to make up for the late start and still achieve your financial goals.

In summary, if you want to succeed with investing, you must make sure Step 2 of your due diligence process analyzes each investment for congruence with your personal and portfolio objectives.

Below is a summary of the key points in the second due diligence question:

1. Each paper asset investment strategy must have a positive mathematical expectation, and each business or real estate investment strategy must have a competitive advantage or exploitable market edge to place the odds for profit in your favor. This is the source of your investment return.

2. The source of investment return must persist long enough into the future to be reliably exploited (adequate sample size).

3. The investment strategy must be consistent with your personal skills, interests, values and abilities.

4. The investment strategy must be consistent with your portfolio objectives.

5. You must follow the investment strategy long enough to benefit from the competitive advantage without being distracted by other investment alternatives.

When your investment passes these tests, then it's worth putting your hard-earned capital at risk to try and reach your personal and portfolio objectives.

Your financial coach can be particularly valuable in clarifying these principles and how to apply them because he has no conflict of interest biasing his investment advice since he sells no investment products.

Due Diligence Question #3: What's My Exit Strategy?

You should always have your exit planned before acquiring any investment.

Why? No investment is appropriate forever.

Times change, market conditions change, and your objectives change.

You have a reason for acquiring an investment, and when those reasons are violated, it's time to exit without delay. By knowing your reasons in advance, there's no confusion or hesitation with the sell decision.

The reason it's important to sell is because your portfolio is a living entity. Selling is to your portfolio what pruning deadwood is to a tree – it makes room for new growth to occur. It's healthy.

You should never marry your investments.

Polaroid was once a darling blue chip stock that got decimated by technology changes. The rust belt was a real estate boom at one point, and the railroads were the king of transportation … but not anymore.

Everything changes, and you must change your portfolio to be congruent with the times.

There's no such thing as a "permanent investment". I've never met an investment I wouldn't sell given the right circumstances. My job as the manager of my portfolio is to understand what those circumstances are, so that I'm ready to take action when conditions warrant it.

> *"Affairs are easier of entrance than of exit; and it is but common prudence to see our way out before we venture in."*
>
> — **Aesop**

I must know the assumptions and premises under which I enter an investment so that I can exit as soon as they are violated. Wherever possible, I must pre-define exit points in terms of price to control losses when things go wrong.

For example, I was a partner in a company that invested in real estate tax liens. We developed an entire business model to acquire valuable real estate for little more than back taxes. Yes, we actually purchased valuable real estate free and clear for pennies on the dollar of what it was really worth.

However, despite it being profitable, we exited the business because we learned how a legal assumption critical to the success of our model was simply wrong.

Once we uncovered the false premise of our model, we exited with our profit and moved on to greener pastures. We knew the reasons behind our model, and we knew when that model was invalidated.

Some would question our logic because the model had previously been profitable, but we knew it was just a question of time until the invalid assumption would bite us in the rear.

Similarly, when I enter equity positions, I predefine the point at which I'll exit based on price behavior that would prove my decision was incorrect.

In summary, you must always predefine your exit strategy because the first loss is usually the best loss.

You must conserve capital when the inevitable mistake arises so that you're prepared to invest in the next opportunity. By consistently pruning your portfolio of troubled investments, you're making room for new growth to occur.

"A prudent question is one half of wisdom."

— Francis Bacon, Sr.

Due Diligence Question #4: How Does This Investment Make Business Sense?

Investing is ultimately about business, so every investment must make business sense.

What that means is the earnings, valuation, and return on investment must be congruent with the competitive advantage and barriers to entry possessed by the underlying business.

Let me clarify this idea with a little bit of Economics 101.

The world of business and finance is competitive. Above market returns and excessive valuations can only be supported if a significant competitive advantage coupled with barriers to entry for future competitors exists.

Otherwise, the high valuations and returns will attract competition until returns and valuations are forced down to market level. In plain language, that means your investment loses money – which is a bad thing.

For example, when the NASDAQ indexes were selling at over 200 times earnings in 2000, it didn't take a genius to figure out this made no sense. How could a broad equity index representing a claim on the earning power of many companies in competition with each other be worth 200 years of earnings?

The truth is it wasn't, and prices declined accordingly.

Similarly, when looking at various Southern California apartment deals in 2005, it didn't take a genius to figure out they made no business sense when they were selling at prices so high you couldn't service the debt with zero vacancy, no operating costs, zero taxes or insurance, and the lowest interest rates in the last 40 years.

There isn't a valuation model in existence that can make business sense out of such inflated prices except the greater fool theory.

In summary, you can use the business common sense test to help you avoid dangerous investment manias and speculative bubbles that can lead to losses.

Investment Advice: How To Avoid Fraud With The Business Common Sense Test

But the business common sense test isn't just limited to avoiding investment manias and speculative bubbles, because you can also use this same test to sniff out potential frauds.

For example, a common fraud I see is the classic Ponzi scheme where someone is offering you outrageous interest rates on your money and "guaranteeing" your principle to invest.

The business idea supporting the investment usually sounds plausible on the surface, but is often laced with techno-babble terminology to intimidate the novice from asking the following necessary and obvious questions:

1. How does it make business sense for the promoter to go through all the headaches of soliciting many small investors, when a legitimate business could attract all the capital needed from professionals with one phone call and at lower interest rates? (Answer: It probably isn't legitimate, and a professional would figure that out with due diligence – amateurs don't do their due diligence.)

2. How are the exorbitant returns being promised adequately earned by the underlying business, and what are the barriers to entry that will keep those returns from being competed away (assuming the business is legitimate)?

3. What's really behind the "guarantee" and what's really being guaranteed anyway? (Investment advice: the more somebody "guarantees", the closer you should look at the guarantee and what you're being guaranteed from.)

Knowledge is the nemesis of the con man, and an informed investor who's willing to ask questions is his worst enemy.

The way you learn is by asking questions and listening – that's what due diligence is all about.

Amateurs want to hope and believe they found an easy road to wealth so they don't ask questions and don't want to know the truth. The result is usually expensive.

I see investment fraud cross my desk with remarkable regularity. They're out there, and if you invest, you must apply business common sense and do your due diligence to flush this stuff out.

I've saved many clients hundreds of thousands of dollars just by coaching them on how to ask the right questions ... and I can help you, too.

> *"Just wanted to thank you for your advice about the (name withheld for legal reasons) investment. I recently cashed $220K out of his deals making over 20%. The money was over a month late but it arrived. A real estate lawyer thought it was the worst contract he had ever seen; from the first sentence he knew it was bogus. Working with you really helped. I got an education and learned to do my due diligence and let the numbers be the basis for my decision."*
>
> — **Name Withheld For Legal Reasons**

(This scam was later uncovered by the S.E.C. – investors who didn't get out early lost everything.)

Always remember that your investment represents a claim on either the assets or earning power of the underlying business. Whether it's debt, equity, or real estate, you must ultimately be able to make business sense of the return you're being promised.

If it doesn't make business sense, then it probably isn't real.

Remember, if it sounds too good to be true, then it probably is. That's just common sense investment advice for a competitive business world.

Due Diligence Question #5: How Does This Investment Affect The Risk Profile And Mathematical Expectancy Of My Portfolio?

For the statistically or financially trained, what we are talking about here is efficient frontiers and modern portfolio theory. For the rest of us, I'll try to translate into plain English.

You should never add an investment to your portfolio unless it either lowers your portfolio's risk, or raises its return. Preferably, you should get both.

How do you do this?

Let's say you have an investment strategy in stocks that returns 8% compounded over multiple cycles in the market, but loses money during bear markets. If you add an inversely correlated asset (something that zigs when the other asset zags) with a return expectancy of 12%, you'll lower the risk of the whole portfolio while increasing the return.

Examples of assets with low or negative correlation to domestic stocks include commodities, gold stocks, real estate, and certain alternative investment classes like hedge funds.

All investments should first be analyzed for their risk profile (under what conditions they will zag), and their mathematical expectation (how much they should return over time).

In Summary...

In summary, the game of investing is won or lost on the due diligence battlefield.

You must ask questions until you have the answers you need to make an intelligent decision. A quick review of the five "must ask" due diligence questions follows:

1. How can I lose money with this investment?
2. How will this investment help me achieve my personal and portfolio objectives?
3. What's my exit strategy?
4. Does this investment pass the business common sense test?
5. How does this investment affect the risk profile and mathematical expectancy of my portfolio?

My intention is for the above list of due diligence questions to serve as a basic starting point for your own due diligence process.

> *"The key to wisdom is knowing all the right questions."*
>
> — John A. Simone, Sr.

I don't pretend this list is exhaustive because a whole book could be written on the subject. Other due diligence questions to consider include:

1. How realistic is the expected return?
2. What are the assumptions and drivers behind the expected return?

3. How dependent is the historical return on the time period analyzed?

4. What are the tax consequences of this investment?

5. What's the background and history of each principal involved?

6. And many, many more.

My goal with this article was to arm you with some of the more important due diligence questions that can help you avoid the most obvious and expensive errors on the road to retire early and wealthy.

I hope it helps you.

ABOUT TODD TRESIDDER

Todd Tresidder holds a B.A. in Economics from University of California at Davis. He is a Member of the Economics Honors Society and Deans List.

Todd has been a serial entrepreneur since childhood, building many businesses before retiring at age 35 from his position as a Hedge Fund Investment Manager responsible for a portfolio in excess of $20 million.

He raised his net worth from less than zero at age 23 to being a self-made millionaire 12 years later by "walking the talk", using the same personal finance and investment strategies as he teaches on his website, financialmentor.com.

Todd was an early pioneer and expert in statistical and mathematical risk management systems for investing. He is still an active investor and earns consistent investment returns in both up and down markets.

You can find more of Todd's investment writing at financialmentor.com

Alpha or Assets

BY PATRICK O'SHAUGHNESSY

More and more investors are buying "factor" based strategies which invest using measures like valuation and low volatility, but the most popular strategies are applying factors in the wrong way. **Strategies should be built for alpha, not scale** – but the asset management industry has gone in the opposite direction.

Most factor-based strategies – commonly called Smart Beta – have hundreds of holdings and high overlap with their market benchmark. The far more powerful way to apply factors is to use them first to avoid large chunks of the market and then build more differentiated portfolios of stocks with only the best overall factor profiles. While not as scaleable as smart beta, this alpha-oriented approach has led to much better results for investors.

*   *   *

Professionally managed investment strategies have two components: an investing component (*seeking alpha*) and a business component (*seeking assets*). Outperformance is one goal, scale is another. Factors – like valuation, momentum, quality, and low volatility – have been largely applied by firms with the *business* in mind. In the asset management business, two variables matter: fees and assets. Smart Beta has risen to prominence alongside index funds and ETFs, and indexing has significantly reduced fees across the industry. With fees lower across the board, scale becomes a more important consideration for asset managers when deciding what strategies to offer the investing public. When fees fall, assets need to rise. For assets to rise across a business, the strategies offered need to be able to accommodate more invested money.

More assets may be good for the business, but it's often bad for returns. As the level of assets under management rise, the investable universe of stocks shrinks, trading impact costs rise, and the potential for alpha erodes. In asset management, we find *dis*economies of scale – as mutual funds and hedge funds get larger, their performance tends to suffer.[*]

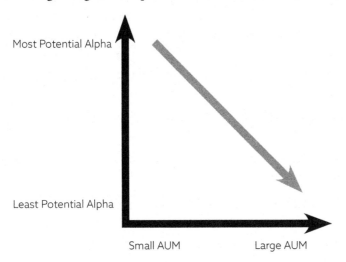

Most Potential Alpha

Least Potential Alpha

Small AUM   Large AUM

Of course, fees matter a great deal, and the nearly free access to broad market index funds is a wonderful thing. But management fees are one thing, and key factors like valuation another. I would rather pay 0.75% for an S&P 500 index fund trading at 12 times normalized earnings than 0.05% for the same market trading at 25 times earnings, which it does as of April 2016. To have a large advantage versus the market – on factors like valuation or shareholder yield – you must build strategies with an emphasis on alpha and the consistency of alpha above all else.

To achieve what we call factor alpha, we believe that investors should use multiple, unique factors to build a more concentrated portfolio of stocks (as few as 50) with the best possible factor profiles. That means *not* owning wide swaths of the market. Relative to Smart Beta, a focus on factor alpha allows for better returns and significantly better factor advantages. In the rest of this post, I explore the dangers of scale and widespread adoption of any strategy and offer an alternative solution for using factors in the investment process.

---

[*]   'Does Fund Size Erode Mutual Fund Performance? The Role of Liquidity and Organization' by Joseph Chen, Harrison Hong, Ming Huang, and Jefffrey D. Kubik; and 'How AUM Growth Inhibits Performance' by Andrea Gentilini.

Watch Scale Eat Returns

The difference between any portfolio and the market is determined by 1) what stocks you own and 2) how you weight those stocks in a portfolio. To show the impact that these two variables have, we start with the constituents of the S&P 500* and create different portfolios based on a single factor that has worked well historically – valuation† – to demonstrate the effect of moving further and further away from the index. We use this basic example not to recommend this as a strategy but rather to show the effects of both concentration and weighting scheme.

What we tested

I show three versions of this strategy.

- The first sorts all stocks in the S&P 500 on each date by valuation and portfolios of between 50–500 stocks (so the 50 stock version would be the 50 cheapest stocks on that date, and so on). Positions are equally-weighted (e.g. 2% each in the 50 stock portfolio or 1% each in the 100 stock portfolio).

- The second takes the same portfolios with the same stocks (between 50–500 holdings) but weights the positions according to market cap. This method can create very top heavy weightings in the more concentrated portfolios (e.g. IBM at 11.3% of the most recent 50-stock portfolio).

- The third forms the portfolios using a market-cap adjusted valuation factor,‡ which multiplies a stock's weight in the index by its relative valuation. This cap-adjusted value factor rewards companies that are big and cheap and penalizes companies that are small and expensive. Again we use the factor to build portfolios between 50–100 stocks. This is the most scaleable version of the value strategy whose holdings look a lot like major value indexes.

---

* Prior to 1990, we use the top 500 stocks by market cap to represent the S&P 500 rather than its actual constituents which are not available.
† Value defined as sales/price, earnings/price, ebitda/ev, free cash flow/ev, and shareholder yield, weighted equally.
‡ Valuation percentile × weight in the S&P 500, think of it like a "contribution to total cheapness".

What we found

Here are the results, highlighting two key variables. **First**, the average forward 1-year excess returns versus the S&P 500 and **second** the average active share (i.e. the percent of the portfolio that is different from the S&P 500; higher means less overlap with the index).

# Stocks	Equal-Weighted Portfolios		Cap-Weighted Portfolios		Cap-Adjusted Value Portfolios	
	% Average Excess Return*	% Average Active Share**	% Average Excess Return*	% Average Active Share**	% Average Excess Return*	% Average Active Share**
50	6.7	91	5.0	91	0.8	61
100	5.8	84	4.3	82	1.5	55
150	4.9	78	3.1	73	1.8	53
200	4.4	73	2.5	63	2.0	51
250	3.9	67	2.1	54	2.2	50
300	3.3	62	1.5	44	2.3	49
350	2.9	57	1.0	33	2.2	48
400	2.6	53	0.7	22	2.3	48
450	2.3	49	0.3	9	2.1	47
500	1.8	45	0.0	0	1.8	45

Closet Index   Very Active   * Average forward 1-year excess return vs. S&P 500.   ** Percent of the portfolio distinct from S&P 500.

Calculations by O'Shaughnessy Asset Management (osamresearch.com).

What we learned

From this simple exercise, we learn the following:

- Concentration and equal weighting lead to portfolios which have better average excess returns and higher active shares.

- The equal weighted portfolios outperform cap-weighted and cap-adjusted value portfolios by an average of 1.8% and 2.0% per year, respectively – a wide margin in the U.S. large cap market.

- More concentrated portfolios have a much better valuation edge: stocks in the portfolio have much cheaper average value percentile scores.

Why this happens

Value (measured by something like a price-to-earnings ratio) is just another way of saying "market outlook." A low relative valuation for IBM means that the market is pessimistic – relative to other stocks – about IBM's future. We believe that value works over time because markets become too pessimistic about these stocks. Pessimism is good – and the lower the P/E, the more pessimistic the market.

Cheapest x # of Stocks	P/E of latest equal-weighted portfolios
50	11.6
100	13.0
150	14.3
200	15.1
250	15.9
300	16.7
350	17.3
400	18.4
450	19.5
500	20.9

Calculations by O'Shaughnessy Asset Management (osamresearch.com).

Now, notice the trend in the price-to-earnings ratios (figure to the right) for the different portfolios today (the equally weighted versions). **If market pessimism (low P/E) signals an opportunity, then the opportunity clearly grows as the portfolio gets more and more different** from the S&P 500.

It helps to see what these simple value portfolios would hold today. Here are the top ten holdings for each of the 50-stock versions of our value strategy, along with each portfolio's weighted average market cap.* You can see, as you move left to right, that the top ten look more and more like the overall market, because the market caps get bigger and bigger.

* Sorted by value ranking for equal weighted and cap-adjusted value portfolios.

Top Ten Holdings

Rank	Equal Weighted 50	Cap Weighted 50	Cap-Adjusted Value 50
1	Valero Energy Corp	Intl Business Machines Corp	Apple Inc
2	Gamestop Corp	Boeing Co	JPMorgan Chase & Co
3	Fluor Corp	Metlife Inc	Exxon Mobil Corp
4	Fossil Group Inc	Target Corp	Wells Fargo & Co
5	HP Inc	Capital One Financial Corp	Microsoft Corp
6	Seagate Technology PLC	Delta Air Lines Inc	Berkshire Hathaway
7	Allstate Corp	Prudential Financial Inc	Verizon Communications Inc
8	Bed Bath & Beyond Inc	LyondellBasell Industries NV	Citigroup Inc
9	Macy's Inc	Travelers Cos Inc	Intel Corp
10	Gap Inc	Valero Energy Corp	Gilead Sciences Inc
Weighted Average Market Cap	$22,299	$45,670	$149,223
Average Historical Excess Return	6.7%	5.0%	0.8%

Calculations by O'Shaughnessy Asset Management (osamresearch.com).

Size vs. Edge

If you are a value investor, or a quality investor, or a yield investor, a key question is: how big is your edge versus the overall market? If you believe in price-to-book, your goal should be to achieve significant portfolio discounts versus the market on that measure.

But the most notable difference across the above portfolios is their size. **When market cap is used as a variable when building a portfolio, it obscures any other edge that exists.** Exxon Mobile has a price-to-book of 1.95x but is a huge company so has a weight of 3.6% in the Russell 1000 Value index. Seadrill – a maligned energy stock – has a price to book of 0.18x. So it is much "cheaper" than Exxon, but it's only a $1.6B company, so its weight in the index is 0.01%, which may as well be zero.

If Exxon went up 40%, it would push the overall index up 1.44%. If Seadrill went up 40%, it would push the index up 0.004%. Seadrill would have to go up 14,400% to have the same impact as Exxon going up 40%.

For the Russell 1000 Value, Exxon is the far more important stock. But if you cared more about value than size, then the weights would be very different. Exxon is the biggest stock, but it's only in the 50th percentile when sorted by price-to-book instead of by market cap. Seadrill is in the cheapest percentile.

From the perspective of an active investor, this is very odd because cheapness should matter much more than market cap when deciding a stock's weight in a portfolio.

Different Means More Potential

If you weight stocks based on market cap – like the Russell 1000 Value does – then your portfolio will always have a lot of overlap with the market (a low active share). With a lot of overlap, there is only so much alpha you can earn.

Active share – our preferred measure of how different a portfolio is from its benchmark – is not a predictor of future performance, but it is a good indicator of any strategy's *potential* alpha. The chart below shows why. On every date through history (1962–2015), we bestow ourselves with perfect foresight so that we can build portfolios that will achieve the highest possible 1-year forward excess return at each level of active share between 0% and 90%. We use only stocks in the S&P 500 itself and allow a maximum position size of 5% in the portfolios, to avoid piling into just a few of the best-performing stocks. This chart shows the maximum possible excess return (average of all historical periods) vs. the S&P 500 by active share level. This potential cuts both ways, so we also show the worst case scenarios by active share level. At any given level of active share, the "potential" excess return skews more to the positive.

Maximum Excess Return by Active Share Level

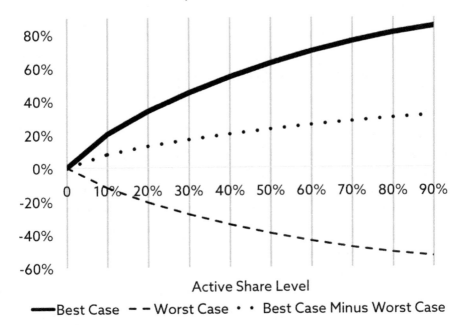

Calculations by O'Shaughnessy Asset Management (osamresearch.com).

More active portfolios have more potential for excess than less active portfolios.* No one has perfect foresight, so nobody achieves alpha like this with any consistency. But these "best case scenarios" show the power of being different.

Factors like value have been a good way of putting yourself on the positive side of this potential curve above. Indeed, we saw the same thing with our different value portfolios: the more concentrated portfolios (higher active share), the better the average results. What is amazing is that in the early 1980s, well over half of mutual funds had an active share above 80%, but as of 2009, only 20% or so of funds were this active. Large, scaled up institutions now control a majority of the market. In 1950, between 7–8% of the market was managed by large institutions. In 2010, that number was 67%.†

---

*   The potential works both ways: more active portfolios also have more potential for underperformance.

†   www.sec.gov/News/Speech/Detail/Speech/1365171515808

Costs Matter

So far we've discussed paper returns only. We saw that – gross of costs – returns to the S&P 500 value strategy get worse as the number of stocks grows. Now let's look at the same issue *net* of trading costs. Simple trading commissions are a real cost, but our focus here is on **market impact** costs, which matter more for big asset managers. Once you start getting too big (trading billions of dollars), your trading moves the price of the names you are buying and selling – you pay a higher price when buying and get a lower price when selling than if you were an individual trading a $100,000 account. Market impact is a cost that doesn't get enough attention, because end investors can't see it, and asset managers don't report it. The table below shows how annualized market impact costs grow with assets (these are estimates, skilled traders can beat these estimates by a little or a lot).

To show the cost drag, we expand our universe to the Russell 3000, which includes small- and mid-cap stocks where market impact is even more important. We again build portfolios based on valuation that have between 50 and 3000 stocks, and assets under management between $50MM and $50B. We rebalance these portfolios on a rolling annual basis, so the holding period is at least one year for each position. It is important to note that the more concentrated equal-weight portfolios have more exposure to smaller-cap stocks, so the impact numbers are higher than if we performed the same analysis on the S&P 500 universe.

Equal-Weighted Portfolios

Assets ($ mil)	50-Stock	100-Stock	250-Stock	500-Stock	1,000-Stock	3,000-Stock
50	0.23%	0.22%	0.19%	0.17%	0.13%	0.00%
100	0.29%	0.25%	0.21%	0.19%	0.14%	0.01%
250	0.41%	0.33%	0.25%	0.21%	0.15%	0.01%
500	0.56%	0.43%	0.31%	0.25%	0.17%	0.01%
1,000	0.80%	0.59%	0.40%	0.31%	0.21%	0.01%
2,500	1.29%	0.94%	0.60%	0.45%	0.28%	0.01%
5,000	1.81%	1.33%	0.85%	0.62%	0.37%	0.01%
10,000	2.44%	1.84%	1.20%	0.88%	0.52%	0.02%
20,000	3.13%	2.43%	1.64%	1.23%	0.73%	0.03%
30,000	3.53%	2.80%	1.94%	1.48%	0.89%	0.03%
40,000	3.83%	3.07%	2.16%	1.67%	1.02%	0.03%
50,000	4.06%	3.27%	2.34%	1.83%	1.13%	0.04%

Market Cap-Weighted Portfolios

Assets ($ mil)	50-Stock	100-Stock	250-Stock	500-Stock	1,000-Stock	3,000-Stock
50	0.07%	0.05%	0.04%	0.02%	0.01%	0.00%
100	0.09%	0.07%	0.05%	0.02%	0.01%	0.00%
250	0.12%	0.09%	0.07%	0.03%	0.01%	0.00%
500	0.16%	0.12%	0.09%	0.04%	0.02%	0.00%
1,000	0.23%	0.15%	0.13%	0.05%	0.03%	0.00%
2,500	0.36%	0.24%	0.19%	0.08%	0.04%	0.00%
5,000	0.47%	0.34%	0.26%	0.11%	0.05%	0.00%
10,000	0.62%	0.44%	0.36%	0.16%	0.07%	0.00%
20,000	0.83%	0.58%	0.48%	0.22%	0.10%	0.00%
30,000	1.00%	0.69%	0.56%	0.27%	0.12%	0.00%
40,000	1.15%	0.79%	0.63%	0.30%	0.14%	0.00%
50,000	1.29%	0.87%	0.68%	0.33%	0.16%	0.01%

Calculations by O'Shaughnessy Asset Management (osamresearch.com).

The cost estimates reported in the table[*] are based on five years of simulated trading in the actual value portfolios between 2010 and 2015. These are based on actual market conditions, not hypotheticals. We've highlighted the point at which impact (annualized) crosses 1%. For cap-weighted portfolios, you reach $30 billion in the most concentrated portfolio before crossing 1% impact costs. But in the equal weighted portfolios, you reach the 1% threshold much more quickly in the more concentrated portfolios. We've already seen that equal weighting and concentration have delivered better results. This table proves that the more concentrated value portfolios *cannot accommodate the kind of scale that large asset managers are after*. If you are seeking alpha, you'd equal weight and you'd be willing to have fewer names in the portfolio. If you were seeking assets, you'd do what the industry has done: build broader smart beta indexes that focus on the large cap market or weight based on market cap.

Back to Smart Beta

We've seen that scale and excess return are mortal enemies. As Buffett said in his 1994 letter to shareholders, in which he warned of lower future growth rates for Berkshire Hathaway, "a fat wallet…is the enemy of superior investment results." Price-to-book was arguably the first smart beta factor and has likely suffered from its own popularity as a measure of value. Hundreds of billions are invested based on price-to-book, but we've

---

[*]   ITG TCI analysis

watched it deteriorate since 1993, when Fama and French first held it out as the defining value factor:

Value Factors – Cumulative Excess Return

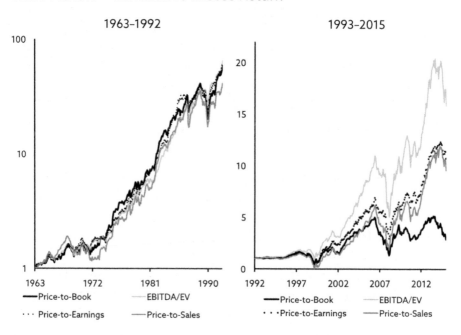

Calculations by O'Shaughnessy Asset Management (osamresearch.com).

Science fiction master William Gibson wrote in his book *Pattern Recognition* that **"commodification will soon follow identification."** In another passage, also from *Pattern Recognition*, Gibson is talking about clothes, but he could be talking about Smart Beta ETFs:

> This stuff is simulacra of simulacra of simulacra. A diluted tincture of Ralph Lauren, who had himself diluted the glory days of Brooks Brothers, who themselves had stepped on the product of Jermyn Street and Savile Row, flavoring their ready-to-wear with liberal lashings of polo knit and regimental stripes. But Tommy surely is the null point, the black hole. **There must be some Tommy Hilfiger event horizon, beyond which it is impossible to be more derivative, more removed from the source, more devoid of soul.**

Smart Beta is the commodification of the most common historically proven factors. By definition, a commodity must be widely available. In asset management, that means it must be able to accommodate lots of invested money. We haven't seen many active strategies with hundreds of billions of dollars behind them consistently beat a simple market index. Even Warren Buffett has been slowed – though not stopped by – scale.

Factor investing has huge potential benefits. Factor investing strategies tend to be cheaper than traditional active management. Properly managed, factor-investing strategies are also very disciplined. But, if a given strategy can accommodate $100 billion in assets, you may want to look elsewhere. Always avoid saturated strategies. For most of history, the factors behind Smart Beta strategies weren't big targets. Now they are. Beware of popularity, beware scalability, and beware newly accepted "measures" of a strategy or idea. Too often, popular measures become targets and then lose their meaning and their edge.

Factor Alpha

The philosophical roots of the factor-alpha approach are notably different than those of Smart Beta.

First, what you don't own matters. If Apple or Microsoft don't look attractive, we believe you should own none of either in your portfolio. We start with a weight of zero in every stock, not with the market weight. **Stocks are guilty until proven innocent.** This naturally leads to higher active share and a portfolio with a greater overall potential for alpha.

Second, alpha comes from the relative advantage a portfolio has versus the market measured across key factors. Greater spreads – like bigger discounts or higher shareholder yields* – have led to better excess returns through time. Portfolios should focus on just the stocks with the best factor profiles. To achieve these big factor advantages, portfolios should be more concentrated than has become typical for smart beta strategies.

Sample the most popular Smart Beta ETFs and you'll find the opposite: high overlap with the S&P 500 or Russell 1000. USMV, the popular "low volatility" ETF has an active share of 46% to the S&P 500. That means

---

* Shareholder yield = dividend yield + net buyback yield (percent of shares outstanding repurchased, net of any issuance, over the past one-year period).

it has more in common with the S&P 500 than does an equal-weighted version of the S&P 500 with an active share around 50%. Strategies designed for factor alpha often have active shares higher than 80%. They are still well diversified, but more diversification is not always better. In the case of factor investing, diversification often means diluted factor exposures. If factors work best at their extremes, then diversification means moving away from your edge and towards the market return.

Often, a picture tells the story better than words can. Below, we show the unmistakable difference between popular smart beta approaches vs. the factor alpha approach. We recreate the spirit of a Morningstar style box, but instead of using market cap and value vs. growth as the dimensions on the chart, we instead use the factors that we've found to be most predictive of future excess return: shareholder yield and quality (where quality is a combination of valuation, earnings growth, earnings quality, and financial strength).

The goal is to show where the different portfolios plot on the yield and quality continuum. A portfolio in the lower left would have the strongest relative readings on both quality and yield. The central dot in each circle represents the average current shareholder yield and quality readings for the portfolio, and the surrounding circle encompasses 75% of the portfolio's weight. The trend is clear. As you move from the broad Russell 1000, to the Russell 1000 Value, to the biggest "fundamental index" smart beta approach, what you see is a tilt towards factors, but with very broad exposure. The factor alpha approach is entirely different, by design: a much better and tighter exposure to the key factors.

Measuring the Factor Advantage – Smart Factor Alpha vs. Smart Beta

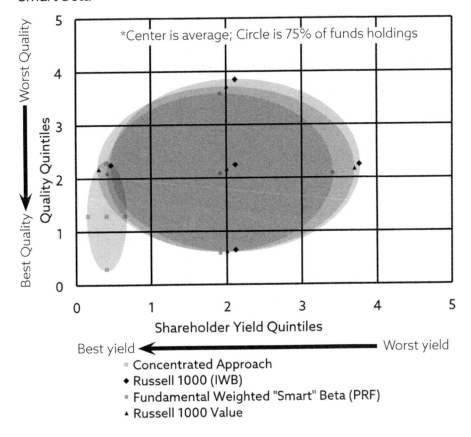

*Center is average; Circle is 75% of funds holdings

Quality Quintiles (vertical axis: Best Quality → Worst Quality)

Shareholder Yield Quintiles (Best yield ← → Worst yield)

- Concentrated Approach
- Russell 1000 (IWB)
- Fundamental Weighted "Smart" Beta (PRF)
- Russell 1000 Value

Calculations by O'Shaughnessy Asset Management (osamresearch.com).

We can get even more granular a visualization: by plotting the position (good to bad on quality, vertical axis, and shareholder yield, horizontal axis) and portfolio weight (size of the circle) of every stock in a variety of popular ETF smart beta strategies: S&P 500 (SPY), Russell 1000 Value (IWD), Fundamental Index (PRF), and Minimum Volatility (USMV). Compare these with the final chart: the factor-alpha approach, and you can see the clear difference in portfolio construction and position in the shareholder yield and quality themes.

S&P 500 (SPY)

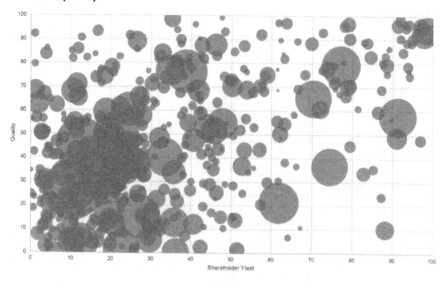

Calculations by O'Shaughnessy Asset Management (osamresearch.com).

Russell 1000 Value (IWD)

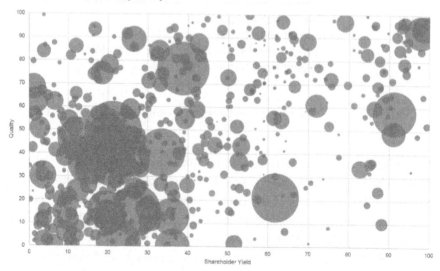

Calculations by O'Shaughnessy Asset Management (osamresearch.com).

Fundamental Index (PRF)

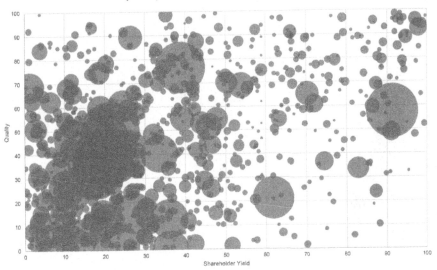

Calculations by O'Shaughnessy Asset Management (osamresearch.com).

USA Minimum Volatility (USMV)

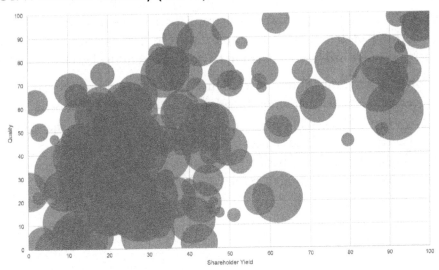

Calculations by O'Shaughnessy Asset Management (osamresearch.com).

"Factor Alpha" Portfolio

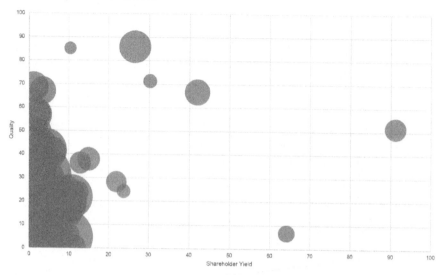

Calculations by O'Shaughnessy Asset Management (osamresearch.com).

There are some outliers in the factor-alpha approach: these are positions whose factors profiles are deteriorating. The one of the far right, for example, is XL group, which had a strong shareholder yield until it issued a big chunk of shares for an acquisition last year. As the strategy rebalances, these positions will be sold down in favor of stocks in the lower left corner.

Wonky calculation note: these all use different starting universes, so percentiles are calculated on the broadest set of investable U.S. stocks, about 2,500 or so. This is why you see a slight skew towards higher shareholder yield everywhere in these charts: these are all large cap-ish strategies which have higher dividend and buyback yields than smaller cap companies which are included when calculating the percentages but often not shown on the chart.

Into the Future

Indexes and Smart Beta factors are affected and changed by asset flows into strategies which target those indexes. Hundreds of billions of dollars flowed into low price-to-book strategies, and price-to-book has suffered as a result.[*] Fund flows affect everything.

Mark Twain said, "I was seldom able to see an opportunity until it had ceased to be one." We often become aware of market strategies only after they've been identified, commodified, and scaled away. Smart Beta factors are a commodity. There is an ETF for everything, from value, to obesity, to put writing. When making an investment, consider the motivations of the manager or sponsor company – are they oriented toward gathering assets or earning alpha over time? If you believe in value, is a market-cap weighted value portfolio – where, for example, Exxon is your top holding despite being in the 50th percentile by price-to-book – really the best expression of that factor? Factor alpha has won for investors in the past.

Nothing is perfect. Other quants will disagree, citing the fact that fewer positions likely means higher tracking error, lower information ratios, and so on. I believe that as asset managers continue to put out hundreds of smart beta strategies, that a more differentiated approach will continue to win in the future. My suggestion is: if you believe in factors enough that you are willing to move away from the simple, cheap, market portfolio, don't do it via tilt. Do it in a way that gains true exposure to factors. A neat parting idea: consider blending a 5-basis point S&P 500 or Russell 1000 fund with a truly deep value portfolio (or some other factor). The combination might get you similar overall factor exposures as a smart beta option, but at a cheaper price.

Always always always, ask yourself: is this strategy about alpha, or about assets?

ABOUT PATRICK O'SHAUGHNESSY

Patrick O'Shaughnessy is a Principal and Portfolio Manager at O'Shaughnessy Asset Management (OSAM). Patrick is the author of *Millennial Money: How Young Investors can Build a Fortune*, published by Palgrave Macmillan. He is also a contributing author to the Fourth Edition of *What Works on Wall Street* and the author of several white papers such as 'Alpha or Assets? – Factor Alpha vs. Smart Beta', the subject of which was a keynote presentation at the 2016 Morningstar annual ETF conference.

---

[*] There are, or course, issues beyond flows that affect factor performance.

Patrick's podcast Invest Like the Best recently passed 700,000 listeners and was named among '5 Investment Podcasts You Should Listen To' by *The Wall Street Journal.* He is also the author of The Investor's Field Guide blog.

Patrick holds a B.A. in Philosophy from the University of Notre Dame and is also a Chartered Financial Analyst. He lives with his wife and two children in Greenwich, Connecticut.

50% Returns Coming for Commodities and Emerging Markets?

BY MEB FABER

If history is any guide, we're standing at the edge of 40%–96% returns over the next two years.

This isn't wishful thinking or wild speculation. I'm not selling anything. Rather, I'm just reporting historical gains from a market set-up that's repeating itself right now.

So what's going on?

Well, imagine a rubber band. If you stretch it only slightly then let it go, it's not going to shoot very far. On the other hand, if you stretch the rubber band to its full elasticity then release it, it's going to rocket across the room.

History suggests we're about to see some asset classes rocket across the room.

Back in 2008, I wrote my first book *The Ivy Portfolio*. While the focus of the book was asset allocation and basic trend following models, I also touched upon mean reversion strategies. For anyone who's unaware, mean reversion is the idea that markets tend to have a general equilibrium level. And though their values will rise and fall, sometimes to extreme levels for long periods, eventually they tend to gravitate back toward their unique equilibrium level. And like a rubber band, the more stretched markets get, and the longer they stay stretched, the faster they'll race back to equilibrium when they finally start moving.

Below is a chart from *The Ivy Portfolio* that shows some historical returns associated with mean reversion.

Table A: Country Mean Reversion 1903–2007

	All Years	After Two Down Years in a Row	After Three Down Years in a Row
Average Return	13.02%	19.03%	30.30%
Median Return	10.65%	14.97%	19.57%
Frequency	100%	9.26%	2.59%

Table B: Asset Class Mean Reversion 1975–2007

	All Years	After Two Down Years in a Row	After Three Down Years in a Row
Average Return	12.97%	23.19%	33.93%
Median Return	12.18%	28.68%	33.93%
Frequency	100%	7.27%	1.21%

Before we get to the opportunity before us right now, I'll provide a bit more context to help you see how "stretched" we really are.

As it has been eight years since writing *The Ivy Portfolio*, I wanted to re-run the numbers and expand the data set. So I started by taking the asset class set above and increasing it to ten broad assets classes, and extending the tests back to 1972.

But this time, I did something different. When I originally ran these tests for *The Ivy Portfolio*, I looked at only the one-year returns after the asset began reverting. But I realized there's no reason to believe the gains should stop after just one year. So this time, I expanded the hold period to two years. The results are very interesting:

1. Three down years in a row from one asset class is still quite rare. It has only happened six times across 378 total years, or less than 2% of the time. But when it happens the returns are impressive:

   - 30 Year Bonds 1978–1980. A two-year return of 48%.

   - US, Foreign, Emerging Stocks 2000–2002. Two-year returns of 43%, 69%, 96%, respectively.

- (For those of you counting, yes, that's just four of the six occurrences. The remaining two are happening now, which we'll get to in just a moment.)

2. We can run similar studies that analyze countries, sectors, and industries rather than asset classes. But since they are more concentrated and more volatile, it makes sense to increase our "down years" time-frame from two to three years to three, four, and five years. Dating back to the 1920s, these are still rare occurrences. Down three years in a row only occurs about 3% of the time; down four about 1% of the time, and down five straight years happens almost never. But the returns are just as impressive as those we found with asset classes.

   - Countries down three years in a row returned 56% over the ensuing two years. If down four years in a row, it bumps to 74%. Five years in a row? 135%.

   - For sectors, we find three down years returns 60% over the ensuing two years. Four years jumps to 91%. Five years returns, 138%

   - For industries, down three years = 59% returns; down four years = 80% returns; and five straight down years returns 105% over the ensuring two years.

3. A basic rule of thumb is that if the asset is down two, three, four, and five years in a row you can expect future two year total returns of 40%, 60%, 80%, and 100%. (So multiply the number of years down in a row by two.)

The following chart shows the average two year total returns across asset class, sector, country, and industry.

So, with all this in mind, we have some exciting opportunities at this very moment.

On the large asset class level, we have two assets that are down three years in a row. As mentioned above, this is just the fifth and sixth times across 378 years that this opportunity has existed. What are they?

Emerging stocks and commodities.

We've written at length on cheap valuations for emerging stocks and foreign stocks in general, and we believe you could see strong returns in the coming years for both. As I wrote above, the last time today's set-up occurred in emerging stocks, two-year returns were 96%. We've never seen this from commodities over the past 40 years – who knows what the returns could be?

Two Year Total Returns

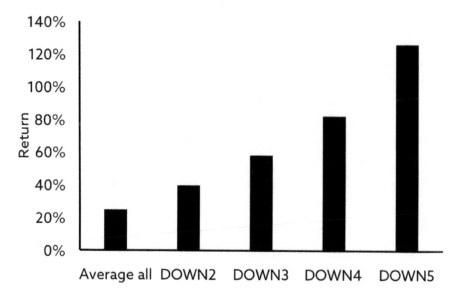

As far as opportunities from smaller sectors, countries, and industries, we wrote about this trend in the fall, mentioning coal stocks specifically. But other industries currently down five years in a row include gold miners and the yen. And all three of these assets are having monster years in 2016. Coal is up 40%, gold miners up 66%, and the yen up 10%.

As far as countries go, Brazil, which we wrote about as being the cheapest country in the world at the beginning of the year, is up a staggering 36%.

Even though these 2016 gains are already big, history suggests the rubber band has been so stretched there's still major gains ahead.

Will check back in 2018!

ABOUT MEB FABER

Meb Faber is a co-founder and the Chief Investment Officer of Cambria Investment Management. Faber is the manager of Cambria's ETFs, separate accounts and private investment funds. Mr. Faber has authored numerous white papers and five books. He is a frequent speaker and writer on investment strategies and has been featured in *Barron's, The New York Times,* and *The New Yorker*. Mr. Faber graduated from the University of Virginia with a double major in Engineering Science and Biology.

MARKET
CONDITIONS,
RISKS
&
RETURNS

Estimating Future Stock Returns

BY DAVID MERKEL

There are many alternative models for attempting to estimate how undervalued or overvalued the stock market is. Among them are:

- Price/Book

- P/Retained Earnings

- Q-ratio (Market Capitalization of the entire market / replacement cost)

- Market Capitalization of the entire market / GDP

- Shiller's CAPE10 (and all modified versions)

Typically these explain 60–70% of the variation in stock returns. Today I can tell you there is a better model, which is not mine. I found it at the blog Philosophical Economics. The basic idea of the model is this: look at the proportion of US wealth held by private investors in stocks using the Fed's Z.1 report. The higher the proportion, the lower future returns will be.

There are two aspects of the intuition here, as I see it: the simple one is that when ordinary people are scared and have run from stocks, future returns tend to be higher (buy panic). When ordinary people are buying stocks with both hands, it is time to sell stocks to them, or even do IPOs to feed them catchy new overpriced stocks (sell greed).

The second intuitive way to view it is that it is analogous to Modiglani and Miller's capital structure theory, where assets return the same regardless of how they are financed with equity and debt. When equity is a small component as a percentage of market value, equities will return better than when it is a big component.

What it Means Now

Now, if you look at this graph, which was estimated back in mid-March off of year-end data, you can notice a few things:

- The formula explains more than 90% of the variation in return over a ten-year period.

- Back in March of 2009, it estimated returns of 16%/year over the next ten years.

- Back in March of 1999, it estimated returns of -2%/year over the next ten years.

- At present, it forecasts returns of 6%/year, bouncing back from an estimate of around 4.7% one year ago.

Estimating Future Stock Returns – Total returns of the S&P 500 for the next ten years

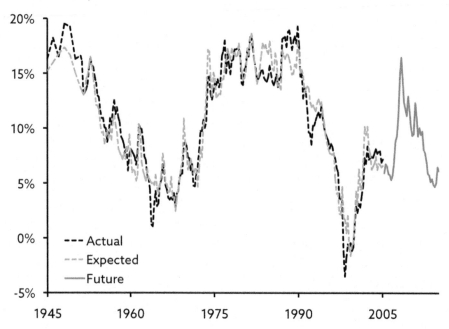

Idea Credit: Philosophical Economics (www.philosophicaleconomics.com), but I estimated and designed the graphs.

I have two more graphs to show on this. The first one below is showing the curve as I tried to fit it to the level of the S&P 500. You will note that it fits better at the end. The reason for that it is not a total return index and so the difference going backward in time is the accumulated dividends. That said, I can make the statement that the S&P 500 should be near 3000 at the end of 2025, give or take several hundred points. You might say, "Wait, the graph looks higher than that." You're right, but I had to take out the anticipated dividends.

Estimating Future Stock Returns – Predicting the level of the S&P 500 (but what about dividends?)

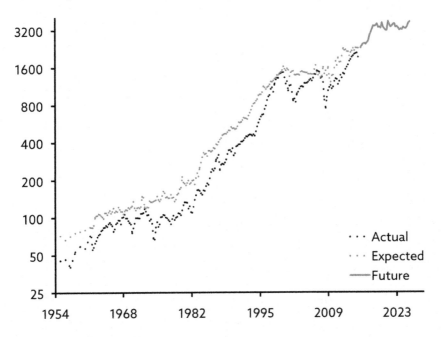

The next graph shows the fit using a homemade total return index. Note the close fit.

Estimating Future Stock Returns – How the model fits on a total return basis

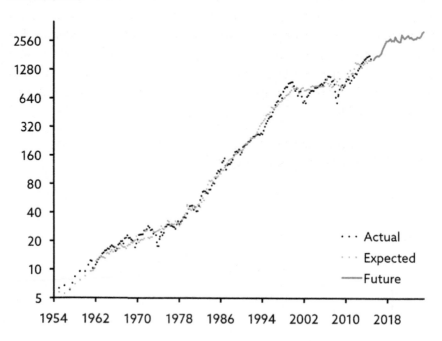

Implications

If total returns from stocks are only likely to be 6.1%/year (w/ dividends @ 2.2%) for the next ten years, what does that do to:

- Pension funding / Retirement
- Variable annuities
- Convertible bonds
- Employee Stock Options
- Anything that relies on the returns from stocks?

Defined benefit pension funds are expecting much higher returns out of stocks than 6%. Expect funding gaps to widen further unless contributions increase. Defined contributions face the same problem, at the time that the tail end of the Baby Boom needs returns. (Sorry, they *don't* come when you need them.)

Variable annuities and high-load mutual funds take a big bite out of scant future returns – people will be disappointed with the returns. With convertible bonds, many will not go "into the money." They will remain bonds, and not stock substitutes. Many employee stock options and stock ownership plans will deliver meager value unless the company is hot stuff.

The entire capital structure is consistent with low-ish corporate bond yields, and low-ish volatility. It's a low-yielding environment for capital almost everywhere. This is partially due to the machinations of the world's central banks, which have tried to stimulate the economy by lowering rates, rather than letting recessions clear away low-yielding projects that are unworthy of the capital that they employ.

Reset Your Expectations and Save More

If you want more at retirement, you will have to set more aside. You could take a chance, and wait to see if the market will sell off, but valuations today are near the 70th percentile. That's high, but not nosebleed high. If this measure got to the level implying 3%/year returns, I would hedge my positions, but that would place the S&P 500 at around 2500. As for now, I continue my ordinary investing posture. If you want, you can do the same.

ABOUT DAVID MERKEL

David J. Merkel runs his own equity asset management shop, called Aleph Investments. He manages separately managed stock and bond accounts for upper middle class individuals and small institutions. His minimum is $100,000. More of his writing can be found on his blog at alephblog.com.

Previously, David was Chief Economist and Director of Research of Finacorp Securities, senior investment analyst at Hovde Capital, a leading commentator at the investment website RealMoney.com, and a corporate bond manager for Dwight Asset Management.

David holds bachelor's and master's degrees from Johns Hopkins University.

Predicting Stock Market Returns Using Shiller-CAPE and PB

BY NORBERT KEIMLING

Summary

- Shiller-CAPE and price-to-book ratio enable reliable forecasts on subsequent stock market returns.

- In countries with structural breaks, price-to-book ratio even exhibits some advantages compared to CAPE.

- Long-term market potential based on findings: US 4.3%, Europe 8.0%, and Emerging Markets 8.4%.

Over the past 100 years, investors in US stocks have been able to realize real capital gains of around 7% per annum. No other asset class – neither bonds, cash, gold nor real estate – has offered comparable return potential. Nevertheless, stock markets are subject to very strong fluctuations, and the achievable returns largely depend on the time of investment. Thus, the question for investors is how they can most accurately forecast long-term stock market developments.

The standard approach – forecasting a company's earnings development based on the economic development of a market and using the resulting stock market valuation to forecast the short- to medium-term stock market performance – is rarely successful in practice. At best, economic developments can only be estimated roughly. The earnings growth of internationally-oriented companies is more and more decoupled from the economic cycle of their countries of origin, and short- to medium-term earnings growth correlates only very weakly with stock market developments. Unforeseeable developments such as terrorist attacks, oil price shocks or central bank statements, and the resultant market sentiment have a much greater impact on capital market developments in the short to medium term than calculable fundamental data.

Traditional price-earnings ratios are unreliable

Given this fact, valuation metrics such as the commonly used price-to-earnings ratio (PE), which looks at a market's corporate earnings in relation to current market prices, would not provide a reliable correlation to the next year's stock market earnings even if it were possible to make an exact forecast (Figure 1). Rather a pity, given the hordes of analysts who compete on a daily basis to get the most accurate earnings forecasts!

Figure 1: Relationship between PE, using correctly forecast earnings for the following year, and the real S&P 500 Performance Index in USD for the period 01/1871–04/2016 – PE unreliable even with accurate earnings forecasts

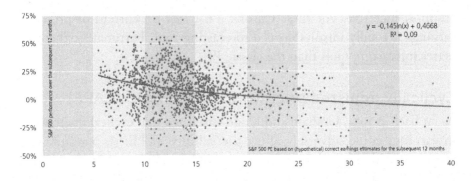

Source: Shiller, StarCapital

There are also two reasons why classic PE is of almost no use in long-term forecasting. On the one hand, corporate earnings are extremely volatile – in practice, they can at best be predicted roughly. S&P 500 earnings, for example, fluctuated between 7 and 77 points between 2009 and 2010 (Figure 2). Thus, the level of profit in any one year is not necessarily representative of the future development.

Figure 2: Inflation-adjusted earnings of S&P 500 companies from 01/1871–04/2016

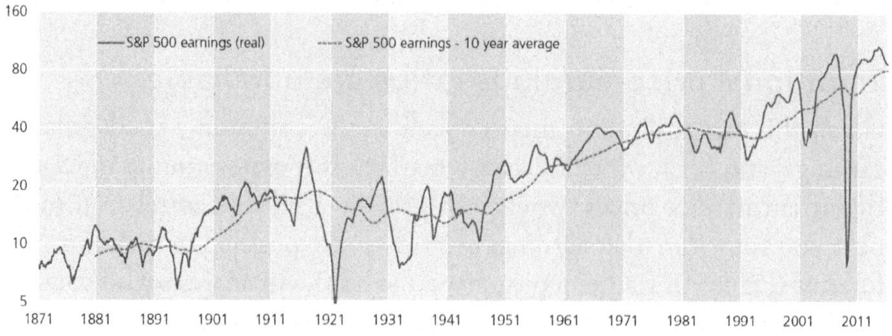

Source: Shiller, StarCapital

Furthermore, PE always looks unattractive in times of crisis because of the lower corporate earnings, yet this is when the buying opportunities are most lucrative. For these reasons, PE based on current or projected earnings is totally unsuitable as a forecasting tool. Fortunately, there are better forecasting tools than the classic PE.

Cyclically adjusted price-to-earnings ratio (CAPE)

As far back as 1934, Graham and Dodd suspected that cyclical fluctuations in earnings could adversely affect the validity of PE. As a result, they recommended using a long-term average of historical earnings to calculate the PE. In 1998, Robert J. Shiller, winner of the Nobel Prize in Economic Science, and John Campbell acted on this suggestion. The professors were able to prove that inflation-adjusted corporate earnings in the US S&P 500 had grown relatively steadily since 1871, increasing by just under 2% annually. As both above-average corporate earnings in economically strong years and high corporate losses in periods of recession are not sustained over longer periods of time, they developed a cyclically-adjusted price-to-earnings ratio. CAPE puts the current market price in relation to the average inflation-adjusted earnings of the previous ten years. Adjusted for an economic cycle, it duly measures whether the value of an equity market is high or low compared to its earnings level, to which it will very probably return.

Attractive CAPE indicates investment opportunities

The cyclically adjusted CAPE actually permits much more reliable long-term return forecasts than the classic PE. Over the past 135 years, for example, the CAPE for the US stock market remained in the range of 10 to 22 in all but a handful of cases, often returning to its historical average of about 17 (Figure 3).

Figure 3: Relationship between CAPE and the S&P 500 Total Return Index in USA from 01/1881–04/2016

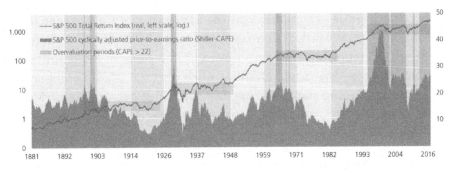

Periods with CAPE-levels greater than 22 are shaded with vertical grey bars, the following stagnation periods are shaded with horizontal bars. Source: Shiller, StarCapital.

The CAPE has significantly exceeded this range just four times: 1901, 1928, 1966 and 1995. For each of these years, plausible reasons were given for why long-standing methods of evaluation should no longer apply, such as the introduction of mass production or the telephone, the departure from the gold standard or globalization. Authors such as Siegel also provide a strong rationale for the current, significantly higher CAPE levels. For example, extremely negative interest rates may be the reason for lower risk premiums, changes to accounting rules may underestimate the earnings potential of the S&P 500 companies and, adjustments to dividend policies, with increased buybacks, could lead to a permanently higher earnings growth. All of these factors provide good reason for higher CAPE levels and only the future will reveal whether they actually herald a new era in evaluation terms, or whether Templeton's dictum once again holds true: "The four most expensive words are 'this time it's different'."

One thing is certain: All the reasons given for higher valuations over the last 135 years, no matter how plausible, have proven wrong: The S&P 500 marked record highs in all of these overvaluation periods. As a general rule, those who invested in these overvaluations experienced real losses over periods of 10–20 years. In contrast, those who invested during periods of attractive CAPE and pessimistic market sentiment always benefited from above-average returns in the long term.

CAPE enables international return forecasts

This correlation is not exclusive to the US market. In our recent study, 'Predicting Stock Market Returns Using the Shiller-CAPE', we found evidence of comparable relationships in all the country indices surveyed for the period 1979–2015. Despite much shorter assessment periods, different accounting standards and regional differences, the same applies to all countries: attractive valuations were followed by high returns while overvaluations led to low returns (Figure 4).

Figure 4: Relationship between CAPE and average real returns of the subsequent 10–15 years

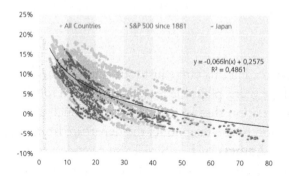

The left chart shows the relationship between CAPE and the returns of the subsequent 10-15 years for the periods 01/1881–05/2015 (S&P 500) and 12/1979–05/2015 (other MSCI countries). All return data is adjusted for inflation, in local currency, incl. dividend income annualised. The regression function applies to "All Countries". The right table shows the average returns (median) over the subsequent 10-15 years depending on the CAPE in each country. Source: S&P 500: Shiller, other countries: MSCI, calculations: StarCapital.

In Germany, for instance, attractive CAPE valuations of less than 10 were followed by real average (median) earnings growth of 10.2% p.a. over the following 10–15 years. In contrast, investors who chose to commit funds at times when the markets were expensive, with a CAPE of over 30, would have posted gains of just 0.7% in the following years. The Japanese stock market, with its low correlation to other stock markets, stands out both because of its above-average CAPE – at times well above 50 – and its extremely negative subsequent returns. Japan thereby improves the international relationship between CAPE and subsequent long-term returns. Assuming that this correlation holds for the future, current CAPE values can be used to make rough estimates of possible returns over the next 10–15 years.

Flaws in the CAPE approach

Investors need to note that the CAPE approach is based on the assumption that stock market earnings reverse to their ten-year mean. This cannot be assumed in small markets subject to structural breaks or in markets where earnings growth diverges significantly from the past. This is illustrated by the MSCI Greece, which currently has an extremely low CAPE of below 2: Over the past ten years, the number of shares in the MSCI Greece has fluctuated between a low of 2 in 2013 and a high of 20 in 2006. In the face of such variations, the question is whether the aggregate corporate profits of these different companies adequately reflect the earnings strength of the 10 companies currently represented in the index. Also, to what extent is a return to the ten-year mean realistic, given that it was greatly determined by the high profits of a now defunct financial industry? A comparison with the broader and more structurally stable MSCI Greece Investable Market Index (IMI), with a CAPE valuation that is several times higher, gives reason for doubt (Figure 5).

Figure 5: Structural breaks may dampen explanatory power of CAPE

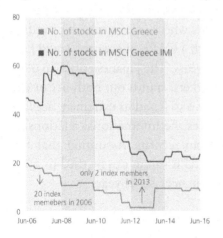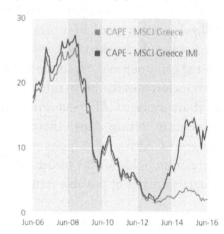

The left chart shows the number of constituents of the MSCI Greece since 06/2006. The right chart shows the CAPE of the MSCI Greece and the MSCI Greece Investable Market Index (IMI). The more stable Investable Market Index (IMI) had more than 20 constituents at all times. Source: MSCI, StarCapital.

Price-to-book ratio (PB) improves return forecasts

In view of the above, it seems advisable to take a look at other key figures used for making long-term return forecasts, not just CAPE. The price-to-book ratio lends itself well to this since book values are less volatile than profits and cash flows, and require no ten-year smoothing. This also eliminates the (not unproblematic) assumption of a comparable market structure over the preceding ten years. PB is also a good option because it brings a net asset value component to the table beyond CAPE's focus on earnings.

Our results support this research not just in theory. Empirically, PB has been providing return forecasts of comparable accuracy to CAPE forecasts since 1979 (Figure 6). It seems logical that an indicator frequently used as a value proxy at the stock level also correlates to future returns at market level. Probably, the only reason why PB is not used in practice as much as CAPE is because of missing data and the resulting inability to verify it empirically (results for other indicators are shown here:

www.starcapital.de/files/publikationen/Research_2016-01_Predicting_Stock_Market_Returns_Shiller_CAPE_Keimling.pdf).

Figure 6: Relationship between PB and long-term stock market returns

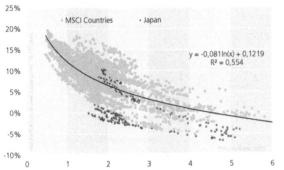

The left chart shows the relationship between PB and the returns of the subsequent 10–15 years for the period 12/1979–05/2015. All return data is adjusted for inflation, in local currency, incl. dividend income and annualised. The regression function applies to all observed "MSCI Countries". The right table shows the average returns (median) over the subsequent 10–15 years depending on the PB in each country. Source: MSCI, StarCapital.

The coefficient of determination (R^2), which measures the strength of the relationship between the predicted values and the subsequent long-term returns, is similarly conclusive with both indicators. With an R^2 of about 0.5 and a correlation of just under –0.7, the relationship between these indicators and the subsequent long-term returns is statistically comparable to the relationship between annual returns of the DAX and the S&P 500 in the period from 1973 to 2015 (R^2 0.47 – correlation 0.68).

A further comparison: In the period between 1871 and 2016, earnings growth in the S&P 500 and the returns of the following 15 years showed a much lower correlation (R^2 0.16 – correlation 0.40, Figure 7). This shows that CAPE and PB enable significantly more reliable long-term forecasts than correctly estimated long-term earnings growth rates for the subsequent 15 years.

Figure 7: Relationship between long-term earnings growth and stock market returns

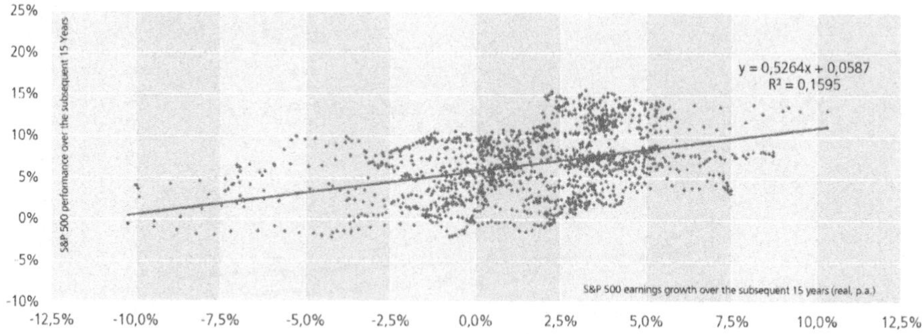

The chart displays the relationship between real earnings growth and real returns of the S&P 500 over the subsequent 15 years for the period 01/1871–04/2016. Source: Shiller, StarCapital.

What level of stock market returns can investors expect?

Assuming that the relationships of the past 135 years continue to hold true, current CAPE and PB values can be used to make long-term forecasts for international stock markets. The US stock market, for example, has a current CAPE value of 24.7 and a PB of 2.8. In the past, valuations at these levels were followed by returns of on average 4.3% p.a. over the subsequent 10–15 years (Figure 8). As such, those investing in the US market in the hope of achieving high long-term returns need to have good reason for doing so, because this kind of growth would be at odds with the stock market experience of the past 130 years.

In some European markets, however, including Germany, higher stock market returns can be expected. The German stock market, for example, currently has a CAPE of 16.0 and a PB of 1.6. In the past, periods with comparable valuations were followed by average long-term annual returns of 7.9%.

At present, the emerging markets offer even higher expected long-term returns. After over five years of underperformance, long-term returns of over 8% p.a. seem probable. Details and updates can be found in my article, 'Long-Term Stock Market Expectations':

www.starcapital.de/research/CAPE_Stock_Market_Expectations.

Figure 8: What returns can investors expect in the long term?

Country	CAPE	PB	Forecast (%)
Australia	15.4	1.8	7.4
Belgium	20.6	2.2	5.8
Canada	18.4	1.8	6.9
Denmark	36.6	3.0	2.7
France	15.5	1.4	8.3
Germany	16.0	1.6	7.9
Hong Kong	14.4	1.2	9.1
Italy	10.1	1.0	11.2
Japan	20.7	1.1	8.1
Netherlands	17.3	1.7	7.3
Norway	11.3	1.3	9.7
Singapore	11.4	1.1	10.3
Spain	9.9	1.3	10.3
Sweden	18.1	1.9	6.7
Switzerland	20.5	2.4	5.5
United Kingdom	13.2	1.8	8.1
United States	24.7	2.8	4.3
World AC	19.1	1.8	6.7
Developed Markets	20.0	1.9	6.4
Emerging Markets	13.6	1.6	8.4
Developed Europe	14.7	1.6	8.0

This table shows the valuations of Datastream Market Indexes as of 30/06/2016, as well as the resultant estimates based on equally weighted CAPE and PB regression functions for real stock market returns in the coming 10–15 years in local currency and incl. dividends.

Which uncertainties cloud these forecasts?

Generally, however, the predicted performance is achieved not through a stable upward trend, but with strong fluctuations which can be described in terms of scenario analyses. Looking at the S&P 500 and taking valuations comparable to those of today, Figure 9 shows the course taken by past equity markets over the following 1 to 15 years.

Historically, returns of between 1.9% and 6.4% followed on from valuations similar to those we see today. Transposed onto the S&P 500, this would put it at about 3,200–6,100 points in 2031, assuming reinvestment of dividends and a conservative inflation rate of 1%. The light grey corridor in Figure 9 thus shows the most likely future development of the S&P 500 based on comparable historical values. The sideways tendency of the corridor suggests that investors should not necessarily expect the real returns of about 7% seen in the past to be repeated over the next 15 years.

Figure 9: Analysis suggests increase in S&P 500 to over 3,200 points by 2031

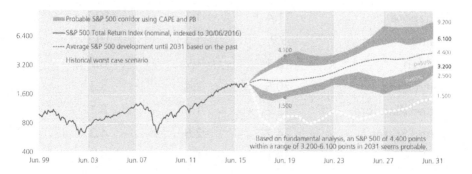

This chart shows the nominal S&P 500. As of 06/2016, the US market has a CAPE of 24.7 and a PB of 2.8. The diagram shows the average subsequent returns (which followed a comparable valuation worldwide) over 1 to 15 years. The light grey corridor (p=50%) reflects 50% of all observed values, the dark grey 80%. The worst case scenario corresponds to the lowest subsequent return for a comparable value. The average S&P 500 development line shows the average of the average subsequent returns using CAPE and PB. All calculations assumed an inflation rate of 1% and reinvestment of dividends.

The scenario corridor depicted in the chart does not just enable us to draw conclusions about possible long-term returns. It also provides information about medium-term risks and rewards, as well as the limits of fundamental subsequent return estimates. If you exclude outliers – that is, the highest and lowest 10% of the historical extreme periods – it is clear that the S&P 500 could fall to 1,500 points or climb to 4,100 points over the next three years.

The "worst case scenario" in the chart, showing the potential to correct down to 700 points, corresponds to the lowest subsequent return ever measured for a comparable valuation. Although such a scenario – based on negative outliers – is highly unlikely, it does give us an insight into the impact of extreme events, such as world wars or severe depressions, as in 1929, and the effect they can have on price developments. Needless to say, it is just as unlikely that the S&P 500 will reach 6,700 points within the next three years (as an outlier, this "best case scenario" is not depicted in the chart).

Scenario analysis for the German stock market

The distribution of returns in the German market is far more upbeat. In the past, subsequent returns of between 5.4% and 9.5% were generally measured on values comparable to today's for the following 15 years. This would correspond to a DAX level of approximately 24,000–43,000 points.

Figure 10: Analysis suggests increase in German DAX to over 24,000 points by 2031

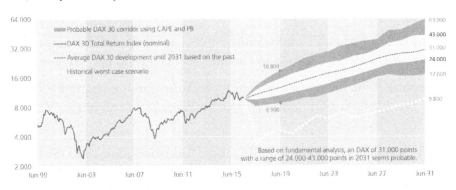

This chart shows the nominal DAX 30 Index. As of 06/2016, the German market has a CAPE of 16.0 and a PB of 1.6. The diagram shows the average subsequent returns (which followed a comparable valuation worldwide) over 1 to 15 years. The light grey corridor (p=50%) reflects 50% of all observed values, the dark grey 80%. The worst case scenario corresponds to the lowest subsequent return for a comparable value. The average DAX development line shows the average of the average subsequent returns using CAPE and PB. All calculations assumed an inflation rate of 1% and reinvestment of dividends.

The chart shows that the DAX could fall to 8,900 points within the next three years, or rise to 18,800 points. The worst-case scenario, showing the DAX at 9,800 in 2031, corresponds to an annual return of +0.1%. Looking at a more probable return of 5–9% p.a., it is unlikely that this worst-case risk would be as upbeat for other investment forms, such as government bonds, given the already negative interest rate environment and current national debt.

Conclusion

Equity investment is not just the most lucrative long-term form of investment; taking inflation and liquidity into account, it is also one of the safest. This is especially true of times when valuations are attractive, as is currently the case in Europe and emerging markets in particular. Strategic investors, who decide not to position themselves along with the masses who stick close to the benchmark with high US weightings, can therefore expect long-term gains of about 8% p.a. above inflation. At the moment, no other asset class can offer comparable potential.

Bibliography

Campbell, John, and Robert Shiller. 1988. 'Stock Prices, Earnings, and Expected Dividends'. *Journal of Finance*, Vol. 43, No. 3, pp. 661–676.

Campbell, John, and Robert Shiller. 1998. 'Valuation Ratios and the Long-Run Stock Market Outlook'. *Journal of Portfolio Management*, Vol. 24, No. 2, pp. 11–26.

Campbell, John, and Robert Shiller. 2001. 'Valuation Ratios and the Long-Run Stock Market Outlook: An Update'. National Bureau of Economic Research Working Paper 8221.

Dimson, Elroy, Paul Marsh, Mike Staunton, Jonathan Wilmot, Paul McGinnie. 2012. 'Credit Suisse Global Investment Returns Yearbook 2012'. Credit Suisse Research Institute.

Graham, Benjamin, and David Dodd. 1934. *Security Analysis*. 1st Edition, McGraw Hill, New York.

Keimling, Norbert. 2016. 'Predicting Stock Market Returns Using the Shiller CAPE – An Improvement Towards Traditional Value Indicators?'. StarCapital. SSRN 2736423.

Philosophical Economics. 2014a. 'Forecasting Stock Market Returns on the Basis of Valuation: Theory, Evidence, and Illusion'.

Philosophical Economics. 2014b. 'Dilution, Index Evolution, and the Shiller CAPE: Anatomy of a Post-Crisis Value Trap'.

Shiller, Robert. 2000. *Irrational Exuberance*. Princeton University Press, Princeton, New Jersey.

Shiller, Robert. 2016. Online Stock market data used in *Irrational Exuberance*.

Siegel, Jeremy. 2014. *Stocks for the Long Run*. 5th Edition, McGraw-Hill.

Note: MSCI. Neither MSCI nor any other party involved in or related to compiling, computing or creating the MSCI data makes any express or implied warranties or representations with respect to such data (or the results to be obtained by the use thereof), and all such parties hereby expressly disclaim all warranties of originality, accuracy, completeness, merchantability or fitness for a particular purpose with respect to any of such data. Without limiting any of the foregoing, in no event shall MSCI, any of its affiliates or any third party involved in or related to compiling, computing or creating the data have any liability for any direct, indirect, special, punitive, consequential or any other damages (including lost profits) even if notified of the possibility of such damages. No further distribution or dissemination of the MSCI data is permitted without MSCI's express written consent.

ABOUT NORBERT KEIMLING

Norbert Keimling leads the capital markets research section of StarCapital AG. After studying business informatics, he worked for the quantitative research division of AMB Generali in Cologne. Since 2004, he has been working for StarCapital which provides complete asset management services based on mutual funds.

Risk Parity and the Four Faces of Risk

BY ADAM BUTLER

Benjamin Graham famously said that "In the short run, the market is a voting machine but in the long run, it is a weighing machine." But this is not quite correct. Rather, in the short term, the market is a machine where investors "vote" about what the market will "weigh" in the future. Of course, when Benjamin Graham referred to "weighing", he was actually referring to how investors "value" an asset.

The goal of this article is to summarize the complex dynamics that drive asset returns. You'll discover that asset returns are impacted by four sources of risk. Two of these risks affect all assets in the same way, and therefore are undiversifiable. The other two risks impact different kinds of assets in different ways. Since some assets respond positively to changes in these risks while others react negatively, these latter two risks can be diversified away. In other words, investors who take an informed view of diversification can almost eliminate fully half of the sources of risk in their portfolio.

Prices always reflect investor expectations

Before investigating the four sources of risk, it's important to understand that markets are constantly adjusting prices to reflect investor expectations about the future. As a result, meaningful changes in prices will only occur if investors receive new information that is inconsistent with current expectations. When this happens, investors experience a *shock*, which causes them to adjust the price of assets higher or lower to reflect this new reality.

To make this concept more concrete, imagine that investors are currently expecting a poor environment for a certain asset. To reflect these pessimistic expectations, investors will have acted accordingly to lower the price of the asset. If the future environment is unfavorable for the asset, the price of the asset should not change. That's because investors have already priced the asset appropriately for an unfavorable future. The price of the asset will only be reset higher or lower if investors receive new information that causes a meaningful change in expectations.

To summarize this critical point, asset prices do not change in response to favorable or unfavorable environments. Rather, asset prices reflect investors' current expectations about a favorable or unfavorable environment. Prices will only experience meaningful change if investors receive new information that represents a shock to their current expectations.

Asset classes

Asset classes refer to the broadest categories of financial assets. Few investors think about investing from this perspective, but in fact most of the important things that happen in markets are driven by what happens at the asset class level.

When we refer to asset classes, we are talking about global stocks, bonds, currencies, commodities, inflation protected securities, and traded real-estate. These asset class categories have very different underlying mechanics, which cause them to react in different directions to certain types of shocks. In other words, a given shock may cause stocks to be repriced in one direction while bonds are repriced in the opposite direction.

In some cases, stocks and bonds in different regions of the world will also react to shocks in different directions for intuitive fundamental reasons. For example, some regions are primarily exporters while others are primarily importers. Some regions produce a surplus of commodities, while other economies produce few commodities. As a result, it is sometimes useful to divide global stocks and bonds into regional baskets to capture this diversity. Figure 1. describes the major asset classes that matter to this discussion.

Figure 1. Asset class behavior in different inflation and growth environments

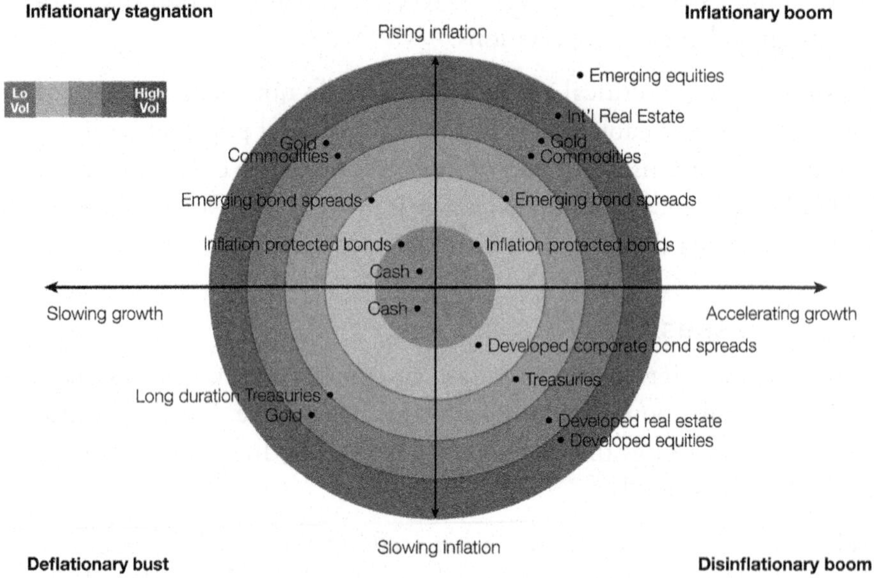

Inflationary stagnation

Inflationary boom

Rising inflation

Lo Vol   High Vol

• Emerging equities

• Int'l Real Estate

Gold •
Commodities •

• Gold
• Commodities

Emerging bond spreads •

• Emerging bond spreads

Inflation protected bonds •

• Inflation protected bonds

Cash •

Slowing growth

Cash •

Accelerating growth

• Developed corporate bond spreads

• Treasuries

Long duration Treasuries •
Gold •

• Developed real estate
• Developed equities

Slowing inflation

Deflationary bust

Disinflationary boom

Source: ReSolve Asset Management

There are other ways to segment stock and bond markets, such as by industry sector or credit rating. While these categories are useful for certain investment activities, they are not meaningful distinctions in the context we will discuss here. At root, stocks of all industries within a given regional economy will react in the same direction to the same fundamental shocks. For this reason, thinking about asset classes in terms of sectors adds little incremental value in terms of diversity.

A Fundamental Pricing Model

All things equal, investors prefer to hold cash because it is available for immediate consumption. Most investors don't hold cash on hand directly, but rather hold their savings in bank accounts. Larger investors hold cash in Treasury bills. As a result, cash actually earns a small return. As Treasury bills mature, they are rolled over at different rates. Savers have a good sense of what cash will earn at each point in the future by observing the yield curve, which signals investors' expectations about future cash rates.

Why would an investor abandon a safe cash investment, which can be used for guaranteed consumption at any time, for a risky investment which may produce an uncertain amount of consumption in the future? The answer is that in return for accepting the risk of uncertain future consumption, including the possibility of loss in the short term, investors expect to produce higher returns to fund a larger amount of consumption in the long term. But how do investors decide how much cash they should pay today for the opportunity for higher future consumption?

Perhaps the most fundamental principle in finance is that the value of an asset today is the sum of all the future cash flows that we expect the asset to produce in the future. For most assets, these cash flows are distributed in two forms: dividends or interest payments, which are made at regular intervals, and; the cash we expect to receive on the sale (or maturity) of the asset.

In order to entice an investor out of cash and into an investment, the investor must believe its future cash-flows will be larger than what he would otherwise earn on cash invested in Treasury bills. Each future cash flow on the investment is compared against the expected return on cash, which is forecast by the yield curve. So as a useful simplification, investors actually price an investment as the sum of its future cash-flows *in excess of* what they would otherwise earn on cash.

For practical purposes, the asset classes in Figure 1. can be divided into three fundamental groups. Stock-like assets, which include all global equity markets and real estate, have highly variable cash-flows. Bond-like assets, including inflation protected securities, have guaranteed cash-flows. The third category consists of assets with no cash-flows, such as commodities and gold. The nature of an asset's cash-flows will dictate how it should react to different types of shocks.

With these simple concepts in mind, let's turn our attention to how the four risks described above impact the price of investments by *shocking* investors' expectations about future cash flows from investments versus future returns on cash itself. Importantly, the framework below ignores complex feedback dynamics that cause some types of risk to impact other types of risk. For simplicity, we also discuss risks as primarily affecting certain asset classes. While the forces we describe below are important drivers of asset returns, it is easier to understand the four types of risks in isolation. We spend some time at the end of this article describing their interactions.

Diversifiable Risk #1: Growth Risk

The prices of stock-like investments are primarily influenced by investors' expectations about the *size* and *timing* of future cash-flows. Cash-flows from stocks are produced from corporate earnings. All things equal, when sales growth is strong, earnings growth is strong. In aggregate, corporate revenues are ultimately driven by economic growth. When economic growth exceeds expectations, revenues also exceed expectations, and this results in better-than-expected corporate cash-flows. When economic growth is weak, this dynamic flows in reverse, resulting in lower than expected cash-flows.

Stock prices are thus very sensitive to expectations about future economic growth. If a series of new data points leads investors to increase expectations about future economic growth, investors are likely to increase their expectations about future cash-flows. This should result in higher stock prices. On the other hand, where investors observe a series of underwhelming economic data, they will reduce their expectations about future cash flows, and price stocks lower.

Diversifiable Risk #2: Inflation Risk

The prices of bond-like investments, and hard assets like commodities and gold, are primarily impacted by changes in inflation expectations. Inflation impacts the cost of future consumption. If inflation is expected to be high, investors expect that they will have to pay much more in the future for important goods and services. That is, the price of consumption is expected to rise. If inflation is expected to be low, investors expect that the price of consumption is expected to remain relatively stable. Sometimes, investors expect negative inflation – deflation – in which case they expect prices in the future to fall.

Inflation affects the rate that investors require to hold cash rather than consume. If investors believe that prices will be much higher in the future, they have high incentives to consume today. As a result, they require a higher return on cash to offset their rational desire for immediate consumption. This higher return on cash will be reflected at each future point on the yield curve. In other words, all things equal high inflation means high interest rates. The opposite is also true: low inflation expectations typically result in low interest rates.

Recall however that asset prices do not change because of investor expectations. Prices at all times are consistent with investor expectations. Rather, asset prices change because of unexpected shifts in investor expectations that occur as a result of new information.

Bonds and hard assets would be expected to react in opposite ways to changes in inflation expectations. When a bond is issued, its interest payments are fixed at the rates that prevailed at the time. The size of these interest payments are known in advance, and do not change over the life of the bond. The price of a bond is simply the sum of its future interest payments, in excess of what an investor would expect to earn on cash over the same period.

When fixed interest payments on a bond are exactly in line with what an investor would expect to earn on cash over the same investment period, the bond trades at 'par'. (We will, for now, ignore the fact that bond investors also require a premium return because they must either lock-up their savings for several years, or accept the possibility of having to sell the bond before it matures at a lower price.) Now imagine that there is an upside inflation shock, such that investors become more concerned about higher costs of consumption in the future. Investors feel pressure to consume now rather than later, so holding onto cash becomes less attractive. As a result, higher yields on cash are required at each point in the future to entice savers to remain in cash.

Now the fixed interest payments on the bond are below what an investor could expect to earn on their cash over the same horizon. An investor would no longer be willing to price the bond at par. Rather, investors would only be willing to purchase the bond at a lower price, so that their expected return on the bond (relative to the price they pay) is once again attractive relative to the choice of holding cash.

In this way, the price of bonds is directly impacted by inflation shocks in either direction. Upside inflation shocks cause interest rates to rise, which makes the fixed interest payments on existing bonds less attractive, causing bond prices to fall. Downside inflation shocks cause future interest rates to fall, which makes the fixed interest payments on bonds relatively more attractive, pushing bond prices higher.

Bonds react positively to negative inflation shocks, but fall on rough times in periods of unexpectedly high inflation. Which prompts the question, what assets should offer protection against upside inflation shocks?

By their fundamental nature, inflation protected bonds, commodities and gold should produce strong returns during periods of unexpectedly high inflation. For this reason, they perform an important duty in portfolios, acting as ballast to falling bond prices in the event of upside inflation shocks. To understand why, and when each of these asset classes might be expected to flourish, we need to understand the three fundamental causes of inflation.

Inflation can be caused by a demand shock, a supply shock, or a monetary shock. A demand shock results when consumption growth is stronger than expected, and producers can't keep up with demand, which causes the prices of goods and services to increase. This type of inflation is often broad-based, and directly impacts people's daily consumption basket. This is picked up using measures of price increases such as the Consumer Price Index (CPI). Inflation protected bonds, such as Treasury Inflation Protected Securities are designed so that their interest payments are adjusted regularly to reflect changes in the CPI. As a result, this special type of bond becomes valuable during demand led inflation shocks, as investors seek ways to preserve their purchasing power.

A supply-led inflation shock occurs when a fundamental input to the economy – for example oil or iron ore – experiences an unexpected change in supply. For example, in the 1970s two Middle-Eastern conflicts – the Yom Kippur War in 1973, and the Iranian Revolution in 1979 – triggered interruptions in oil exports, causing major oil shortages in major industrial countries and triggering large increases in energy costs. On the other hand, rapid unexpected on-stream supply of unconventional petroleum in the United States as a result of 'fracking' technology may have contributed to the large drop in oil prices observed in 2014–2015. It's clear that commodities do well during supply-led inflation shocks.

Lastly, monetary inflation shocks occur because central banks of the world enact policies that have the goal of altering currency exchange rates. When a country's currency exchange rate declines relative to other currencies, it costs that country more to import goods and services, while its exported goods and services get cheaper. When a country's central bank acts to set exchange rates far below what might be warranted on the basis of economic competitiveness, investors may seek to preserve their global purchasing power by purchasing assets that are outside the reach of central banks. For several thousand years, gold has been a primary recipient of these capital flows. As a result, gold often does quite well during monetary led inflation shocks.

The Interplay Between Growth and Inflation

So far we have presented a framework where asset prices are impacted by unexpected shifts in expectations about *either* growth *or* inflation *in* isolation. We positioned stocks as being particularly sensitive to economic growth, while bonds and commodities are sensitive to inflation expectations. But in economics, few things happen in isolation.

The fact is, changes in expectations about growth are typically coincident with changes in expectations about inflation. Consider a situation where a confluence of unexpectedly negative economic data causes investors to reduce their expectations about future economic growth. Clearly this will impact expectations about corporate earnings, with predictable effects on stocks.

But lower growth rarely happens in isolation. Slower than expected growth means that there will not be as much demand for goods and services as companies were expecting. Companies may end up with a surplus of inventory, and have to lower prices to entice greater consumption. Lower than expected prices means a negative inflation shock. Lower than expected inflation means a downward revision to interest rates, which benefits bond prices.

On the other hand, lower growth may be the result of a large potential supply shock emanating from a primary economic input, such as a large spike in the prices of basic necessities like oil or food. The cost of basic necessities competes with discretionary consumption, so if consumers end up spending more at the gas station or the supermarket, they have less money left in their pocketbook for discretionary consumption. In this case, commodity prices (oil and food) will have been steadily rising as investors were adjusting stocks lower in anticipation of slower than expected economic growth.

You can see that changes in asset prices are driven by interactions between the forces of inflation and growth. Investors are constantly adjusting their expectations about these dynamics, and repricing asset prices accordingly. Moreover, each asset class responds in a predictable way to different combinations of shocks. But as we will now see, investors who are mindful of these relationships between asset pricing and economic shocks have the ability to diversify away the risks of potentially adverse economic outcomes.

Growth and Inflation Risks Can Be Diversified Away

Figure 1. above provides a theoretical framework for how a wide variety of assets should react to different types of economic shocks. You'll note that stocks and bonds only really do well in certain economic environments. Specifically, portfolios of stocks and bonds thrive when growth is stronger than expected, and changes in inflation expectations are benign or decelerating.

Unfortunately, most investors' portfolios are composed almost entirely of these two asset classes. Since the global economy can spend decades experiencing negative growth shocks and large inflation shocks in either direction, these traditional portfolios can struggle for long stretches of time during unfavorable regimes.

The following chart and table describe how a typical US "balanced" portfolio (light gray line in the chart) consisting of 60% stocks and 40% intermediate Treasury bonds would have fared during major economic environments over the past half century. Pay special attention to the 1970s, where both stocks and bonds struggled under a stagflationary regime. Also note the extended periods of 20–30% losses, in some cases lasting several years, during the brutal bear markets of 1974, 1987, 2000 and 2008. These episodes are symptomatic of inadequate portfolio diversification.

Figure 2. Cumulative growth of US 60/40 portfolio vs. Global Risk Parity portfolio scaled to similar volatility

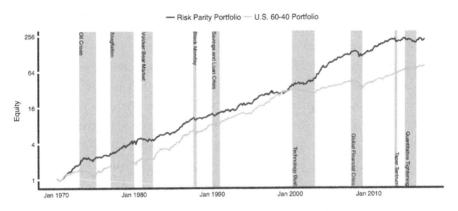

	Risk Parity Portfolio	US 60-40 Portfolio
Compound Return	12.09%	9.73%
Volatility	9.99%	9.99%
Sharpe Ratio	0.71	0.49
Max Drawdown	−19.72%	−29.28%
Positive Rolling Yrs	87.00%	82.00%
Growth of $1	$218.54	$80.15

Source: ReSolve Asset Management. Data from MSCI, CSI, Deutsche Bank, Bloomberg, S&P Dow Jones, Global Financial Data. Simulated Performance. Past performance is not necessarily indicative of future results. It is expected that the simulated performance will periodically change as a function of both refinements to our simulation methodology and the underlying market data. Please review disclaimers at www.investresolve.com/us/general-information-regarding-hypothetical-performance-and-simulated-results.

Sadly, investors in traditional portfolios of stocks and bonds endure unnecessary financial risk because they think too narrowly about diversification. Worse, this extra risk is not rewarded with excess returns, because it can be diversified away.

A truly diversified portfolio would hold assets, such as the entire universe described in Figure 1, that are designed to thrive in a wide variety of economic environments. Of course, among these assets there are some that are quite volatile, and others that are much more stable. In order to maximize the diversification properties of all the assets, they must all contribute an equal amount of volatility to the portfolio. This maximally diversified portfolio has a name: Global Risk Parity. The darker line in Figure 2 illustrates the performance profile of a Global Risk Parity portfolio that has been scaled to the same volatility as the US balanced portfolio. Notice how this diversified approach produced steady returns in virtually all market environments from 1970, with stronger performance, lower volatility, and relatively minor peak-to-trough losses (drawdowns).

It's clear that shifts in inflation and growth expectations pose a meaningful risk to investors in any major asset class. Fortunately, it is possible to assemble a portfolio that neutralizes exposure to these risks. By expanding into assets that respond in predictably diverse ways to positive or negative shocks to growth and inflation expectations, and equalizing risk exposures, it is possible to manage economic uncertainty through diversification. In fact, this very concept is the primary feature of Global Risk Parity portfolios.

Undiversifiable Risk #1: Policy Risk

It is sometimes rational for investors to reprice assets even if there is no change in expectations about economic variables. In other words, assets can be repriced even if there is no change to investor expectations about growth or inflation.

Consider that a rational investor will only be enticed out of a safe cash position to invest in a risky asset, such as a stock or bond, if he expects to earn a higher return on that asset than he could earn from cash. Investors will pay a high premium for an asset when its expected return is substantially higher than that of cash over the term of the investment.

As a simplification, central banks are largely responsible for setting the return on cash. And through their communications, they not only set the expected returns on cash at the current moment, but they also can communicate their intentions about cash rates in the future. Sometimes – for example, when central bankers are concerned about the prospects of overheated inflation – they communicate that their intent is for cash rates to rise over the next few years. At other times, and for other reasons, they signal their intent for cash rates to go lower.

Consider a stock market index that is trading at $1000. Assume that at this price, the market is expected to produce a compound return of 7% over the next few years. Meanwhile, central banks have been communicating their intent for cash rates to remain below 5% for the foreseeable future. In this case, the current market price of $1000 is reflecting that, at equilibrium, investors are prepared to accept stock-market risk in return for at least a 2% premium return over cash.

Now imagine that the central bank signals that they are going to move their target for cash rates from 5% to 7% over the next few years. Critically, this move was not anticipated by the market. This may be because the possibility of a shift in policy was not well communicated by the central bank in previous announcements. Or perhaps the move is inconsistent with how the central bank has traditionally behaved in response to the type of economic conditions that currently prevail.

Whatever the reason, stock market investors are now faced with a very different economic equation. They can invest in risky stocks and expect to earn 7%, but with a chance of extreme losses in the short and intermediate term. Alternatively, they can invest in safe cash and expect to earn 7% with essentially no risk of loss.

Investors had previously signaled that they were willing to accept a 2% premium for investing in stocks over cash. Now they are faced with earning a 0% premium. The natural consequence is for investors to reprice the market lower so that, if investors were to purchase the market at the new lower price, they would expect to earn the same 2% excess return that they required before the rate shock. This might require that the market should be priced to $800, or $500.

This example highlights that unanticipated changes to expected future cash rates represents a very significant driver of asset class returns. Importantly, the market in the example above could be any market – stocks, bonds, REITs, etc., as all assets respond in the same way to this type of shock. This fact has profoundly important consequences. That's because, since all risky assets respond in the same way to the same shock, this type of risk cannot be diversified away. In other words, all portfolios everywhere – no matter how diversified – will be impacted by this risk, and there is no costless way to hedge the risk away.

Undiversifiable Risk #2: Sentiment Risk

It is critical to understand that markets are nothing more than the collective expression of all investors' fears and hopes at any particular time. Sometimes investors are optimistic and hopeful in aggregate, while at other times they are pessimistic and fearful. An investor who is fearful about economic uncertainty will require a larger potential return to entice them out of safe cash and into a risky investment. Greedy investors, on the other hand, will be willing to accept a high degree of risk for the chance to earn a small excess return.

This dynamic is complicated by the fact that investors' feelings of hope and fear are to a very large extent informed by the market's behavior itself. When the market rises, investors perceive that other investors are feeling more optimistic about the future, and this prompts feelings of optimism, greed and envy. Optimistic investors who are greedy for returns are more likely to move capital from cash into risky assets for the promise of greater returns. This in turn causes markets to rise further, bolstering aggregate confidence. When markets fall investors perceive that risks were larger than they thought, and this provokes feelings of pessimism and fear. Fearful investors are less likely to deploy cash assets into the market, and are more likely to move capital out of markets and into safe cash. This causes prices to fall, invoking more fear and commensurate selling.

A meaningful portion of changes in investor risk appetite stems from changes in expectations about growth and inflation. As a result, it is challenging to observe this type of risk in isolation. Moreover, when changes in risk appetite do manifest independent of genuine fundamental shifts in investor expectations about economic conditions, markets tend to normalize quickly. As a result, while this risk is real, and can't effectively be diversified away, the practical effects of this risk are likely to be relatively small.

Setting Expectations

It is useful to decompose expected returns on risky assets into the returns that investors are guaranteed to receive on cash plus a premium that investors expect to receive for bearing market volatility. As we've seen, this volatility is derived from three fundamental sources, as illustrated in Figure 3.

Figure 3. Decomposition of Risk

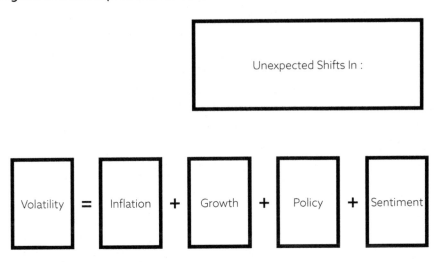

Source: ReSolve Asset Management with reference to *Balanced Asset Allocation* by Alex Shahidi (Wiley, 2014)

What does this all mean for investors? First, investors in diversified portfolios *should* expect to be compensated for accepting the risk of unanticipated shifts in expectations about future cash rates. That's because this risk affects all assets *in the same direction*, so it cannot be diversified away. Indeed, all investors everywhere are susceptible to this one source of risk.

Second, investors should not expect to be compensated for taking risks that can be easily neutralized through better diversification. For a humble investor with neutral views on the future, a diversified portfolio like Global Risk Parity almost always has a higher expected risk-adjusted return, with less exposure to major economic risks, than any other more concentrated portfolio.

ABOUT ADAM BUTLER

Adam Butler, CFA, CAIA, is Co-Founder and Chief Investment Officer of ReSolve Asset Management. ReSolve manages funds and accounts in Canada, the United States, and internationally. The firm employs quantitative methods in the management of three multi-asset factor strategies in including Systematic Global Macro and Global Risk Parity strategies. Adam has 14 years of experience in investment management including 11 years as a Portfolio Manager, and is a sub-advisor for the ReSolve Adaptive Asset Allocation Fund (Canada), the Horizons Global Risk Parity ETF, and the ReSolve Online Advisor. Adam is lead author of the book *Adaptive Asset Allocation: Dynamic Global Portfolios to Profit in Good Times – And Bad* (Wiley, 2016), and many investment related articles and whitepapers.

The Biggest Challenge for
Hedge Funds in 2017

BY STAN ALTSHULLER

A billion dollars a day. That, according to Jack Bogle, is the rate at which money leaves managed funds and pours into index funds. "Wall Street hates it. Mutual fund managers don't like it either." Hedge Funds are likely to feel this and see outflows this year for the first time since 2008. The reason? Investors lament transparency, liquidity, complexity, and – most of all – fees. But I think it's mainly this:

Hedge Fund Alpha: Five-Year Rolling Alpha of HFRI Equity Hedge to S&P 500 (Annualized)

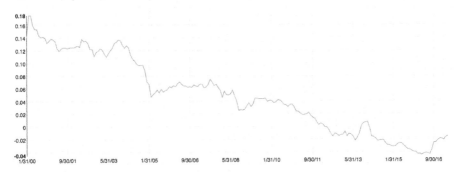

Alpha is a performance measure adjusted for risk. Though hedge funds are meant to generate alpha, it's been declining for two decades. Even if you change your definition of alpha, this is still bad. Thus some investors are packing their bags and investing in index trackers or liquid alternatives. Hedge funds won't retain assets unless alpha goes up.

Why is alpha declining? Partially due to the market, partially due to managers.

Market

Making alpha is easier when there's high dispersion, low correlation, and a lot of volatility in the market. Recently, this hasn't been the case. Generating alpha is also easier when markets have good breadth – ie, when many stocks share the market's gains. These days, technology shapes consumer trends, making it possible for companies like Amazon and Uber to gain dominance quickly. In 2015 only 28 stocks out of the S&P 1500 made up half the gains of the whole index, and 49 stocks made up half the losses. That's low breadth for the winners, high for the losers. Here's what that's looked like in other years:

Number of stocks with 50% share of total gain (dark gray) / loss (light gray) for S&P 1500

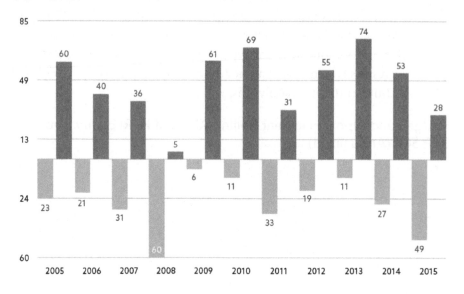

Low breadth indicates less opportunity for alpha-yielding trades that can handle large amounts of assets. (I wrote more about breadth in my piece 'Market Breadth Nearing Record Lows'). This coupled with a large increase in hedge fund assets means managers must put more dollars into the same stocks to generate alpha.

Managers

Managers also shoulder some blame. We've found that overlap – the percentage of a portfolio that's identical for two managers – has grown.

Below we've calculated a matrix of overlap values for 50 of the largest (non-quant) hedge fund managers and then took the average over time:

Top 50 HF Historical Average Overlap

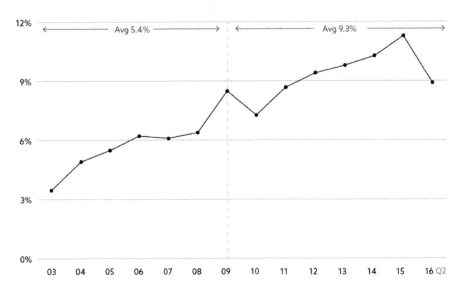

Per the above chart, if you chose two managers at random in 2003, only 3% of their portfolio would be identical. Now that number is closer to 10%.

Investing in the same securities isn't a problem for performance, per se. It only becomes an issue when the securities are crowded. A security's crowdedness is determined by the number of invested managers and the percent of trading volume they represent. The most crowded securities underperformed the markets by 23 percentage points since 2015 – this is the worst relative performance since we started tracking the data in 2003.

Crowdedness has hit record highs. More managers are invested in the same securities, representing higher portions of ADV than ever before. Crowding is likely the biggest risk factor to drive performance in the years to come, yet few traditional risk models track it.

Most models focus on factors like Fama-French. While interesting, these models don't fully explain the recent decline in alpha. Taking crowding and liquidity into account helps explain a lot more.

Take the particularly turbulent period of July 2015–June 2016: We ran an attribution analysis on our HFU consisting of individual holdings across

1,300+ managers' public regulatory filings representing over $2 trillion of assets.

Below are the largest winners and losers for the period. The numbers shown are the P&L (in bps for the HFU) not explained by market and sector trends.

Top Winners / Losers by Trailing 12M Active Contribution (July 2015–June 2016)

Total contribution from top 10 winners / losers

Valeant	-117		25	Amazon
Williams	-28		12	Facebook
Allergan	-26		10	Time Warner
Apple	-20		10	Microsoft
SunEdison	-20		8	Equinix
Cheniere Energy	-19		8	Google
JD.com	-19		7	Constellation Brands
Community Health	-16		6	McDonald's
Icahn Enterprises	-15		6	Barrick Gold
Endo	-14		6	Charter Comm.
Total	-293 bps		+99 bps	

Without understanding the impact of crowding in Valeant, Sun Edison, Allergan, and others, it's impossible to discover the source of this negative alpha.

What Can You Do About Crowding?

Some of our clients, like us, are uneasy about crowding and are careful not to invest in a crowded stock without buying protection. To make their decisions easier, we calculate a crowding score for every single security and provide a weighted score for their portfolio. This information explains performance and helps the client avoid (or protect from) the most crowded situations.

ABOUT STAN ALTSHULLER

Stan Altshuller is Co-Founder and Chief Research Officer at Novus. At Novus, he spearheads research and content initiatives and contributes to product development. His cutting-edge research is followed by nearly 50,000 investment management professionals, spanning across hedge funds, foundations and endowments, pensions, and other asset owners. To follow his work, visit Novus' research library at www.novus.com/research-library.

Before co-founding Novus in 2007, Stan worked in Ivy Asset Management's Portfolio Management Group as part of a team responsible for constructing, monitoring and managing all of Ivy's portfolios. At Ivy, he designed and implemented a set of tools and processes for analyzing multi-manager portfolios focusing on key drivers and risks across the entire product line. Prior to Ivy, Stan served at Lyster Watson & Co., where he was responsible for quantitative analysis, manager screening and portfolio modeling. Stan holds a B.S. in Mathematics and a B.A. in Economics from Brandeis University.

Bond Market Knows What Fed Should Do

BY TOM MCCLELLAN

We have an unblemished 21-year track record of predicting what the Fed should do, with 100% accuracy. What the FOMC actually does is often different from what it should do. As of the Sep. 21, 2016 FOMC meeting announcement, the Fed has missed another chance to do the right thing.

There is only one reason why the FOMC should ever change the Fed Fund target rate, and that is if the rate is in the wrong place. Deciding what is the right or wrong rate is really difficult to do if all you do is look at economic data and complex models with Greek-letter math. It is a lot easier if you just look at the bond market.

We have long held the belief that the FOMC should just outsource the task of setting the Fed Funds rate, and give that job over to the 2-year T-Note yield. The first chart compares those two, and makes the point that the further apart they are, the bigger the problems that the Fed is creating. Problems can result from being too restrictive, or too stimulative. Right now, they are being too stimulative (and punishing savers).

This point is perhaps easier to see in the second chart. It looks at the raw percentage point spread between the 2-year T-Note yield and the Fed Funds target. Right now the 2-year is above Fed Funds, and so it is a positive spread.

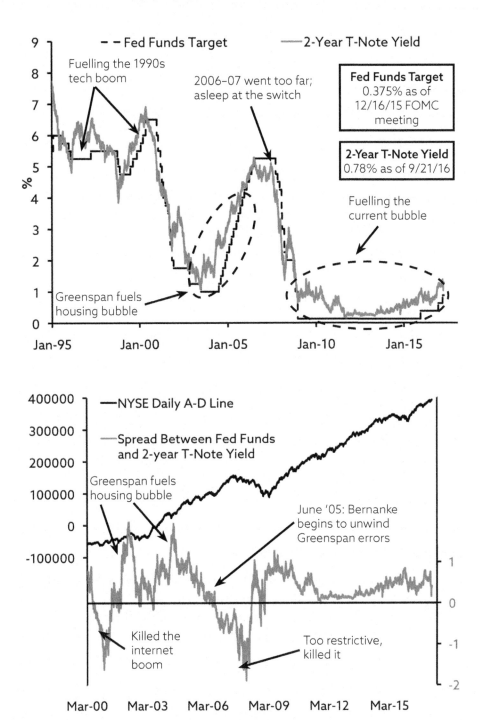

Charts © 2016 McClellan Financial Publications, www.mcoscillator.com

To reveal the effect of that stimulus, we compare it to the NYSE's A-D Line, which is the best indicator of market liquidity that we know of. When the Fed is being stimulative by keeping the Fed Funds target below where it ought to be, that tends to create excess liquidity and push up the A-D Line. But when we get conditions like 2000–01 and 2006–08, when the Fed is being overly restrictive, then that creates a rough time for the A-D Line, and for the economy overall.

There is one period in both charts when the Fed appears to have been "just right" about setting the Fed Funds target very close to the 2-year T-Note yield, and that was in 2011–13. But this seemingly correct interest rate policy was more of a case of QE pushing the 2-year T-Note yield down far below where it rightfully should have been, thus shooting the messenger and losing the message about what interest rate policy should be.

The Fed now seems to be done with QE, and the 2-year rate has been rising. The FOMC should follow suit, and move the Fed Funds target closer to where the 2-year T-Note yield is saying is an appropriate rate. The Fed should then adjust further as the 2-year rate moves around.

The downside of adopting this policy would be that the various Fed officials would not get to feel as self-important, and perhaps we would not have to pay for their travel expenses to visit Washington, DC 8x per year for the critical FOMC meetings. Missing out on that expenditure, and taking down their sense of self-worth, is a small price to pay in order to get the Fed to stop jerking around the economy and markets.

I am willing to allow them to pay that price.

ABOUT TOM MCCLELLAN

Tom McClellan is a graduate of the US Military Academy at West Point where he studied aerospace engineering, and he served as an Army helicopter pilot for 11 years. He began his own study of market technical analysis while still in the Army, and discovered ways to expand the use of his parents' indicators to forecast future market turning points. Tom views the movements of prices in the financial market through the eyes of an engineer, which allows him to focus on what the data really say rather than interpreting events according to the same "conventional wisdom" used by other analysts.

In 1993, Tom left the Army to join his father Sherman in pursuing a new career doing this type of analysis. Tom and Sherman spent the next two years refining their analysis techniques and laying groundwork.

In April 1995 they launched their newsletter, The McClellan Market Report, an eight-page report covering the stock, bond, and gold markets, which is published twice a month. They utilize the unique indicators they have developed to present their view of the market's structure as well as their forecasts for future trend direction and the timing of turning points. A Daily Edition was added in February 1998 to give subscribers daily updates on their indicators and also provide market position indications for stocks, bonds and gold. Their subscribers range from individual investors to professional fund managers. Tom serves as editor of both publications, and runs the newsletter business from its location in Lakewood, WA.

The Interest Rate Issue

BY JARED DILLIAN

F act: interest rates have pretty much gone down for 35 years straight (up until recently). There were a few blips along the way, like 1994, but not many.

10yr Yields

Source: Bloomberg

There was one obvious reason why interest rates were so high:

1) Inflation

Which was primarily due to:

1) Energy prices

At least in the public consciousness. But people in the know really know that it was due to:

2) Regulation

Which was totally out of control. The pre-eminent example was airlines, where the government was setting fares throughout the system. You might not be surprised to learn that these fares were higher than when the free market was allowed to do its thing.

So for pretty much all of the 70s we had lots of inflation, that eventually got out of control, which required some emergency action.

So Paul Volcker took over for G. William Miller and jacked up interest rates massively, which:

1) Caused a giant recession, right in the beginning of Reagan's term

But succeeded in reversing inflationary psychology.

So Volcker gets all the credit here, but Reagan deserves an equal amount of credit, because when you deregulate (and trade), you allow the deflationary effects of capitalism to take hold.

Using airlines as the example again, fares dropped by (guessing) 7080% in real terms over 30 years.

And that is the interesting thing about what Reagan and Volcker did – the effects of taming inflation were not short term. They were very long term. They set into motion very powerful deflationary forces that continue to this day, powerful enough that the BS artists in positions of power started to wonder if too much of a good thing was bad. (It's not.)

Just one more time for those of you at home: capitalism = deflation. Something other than capitalism = inflation.

If you wondered why I have been so bulled up on inflation, it's because I haven't seen a lot of capitalism. Not even on TV.

*   *   *

That is all the history of it. So fast forward to today.

1. Central banks think we need more inflation

2. For the last eight years they have been trying to cause inflation

3. Unsuccessfully

4. Until maybe now?

You have seen the charts of bank excess reserves, I am not going to show it here (besides, the Fed spiked the statistic a few years ago). Now that Trump has inspired "animal spirits," what do you think is going to happen?

My guess:

1. Money velocity picks up

2. Banks won't care about 0.25 IOER and will start lending out those reserves

Inflation will rise. No doubt about it.

Throw in:

1. Trump starts a trade war

Inflation rises further.

Back to the bond market. **Interest rates go up for three reasons**:

1. **Supply of bonds increases as we run deficits**

2. **Real rates rise (supply and demand for loanable funds)**

3. **Nominal rates rise (inflation)**

All of these things have one catalyst:

1. Trump

I will concede this: for all my talk about higher interest rates in the last ten years, you should have been asking me what the catalyst was. That is an acceptable question to ask: what will be the catalyst for the bond bull market coming to an end. It turns out to be a presidential election.

Where is the deflation? We heard so much about this endless deflation just six months ago. Deflation forever. Deflation as far as the eye can see.

Things can change just that quickly.

10y Yields

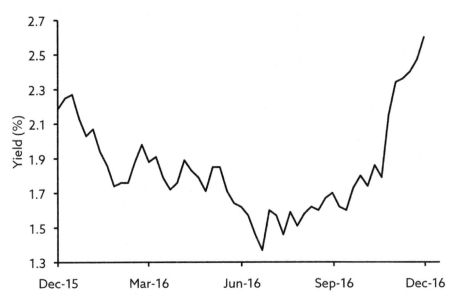

Source: Bloomberg

Interest rates are going up for three reasons (I repeat):

1. Supply
2. Real rates
3. Inflation

How long will they go up? If you think Volcker and Reagan set lower rates in motion for decades, Trump and Bernanke/Yellen might have set higher rates in motion for decades. Think about what the world looks like when those trillions in excess reserves get deployed, instead of being held at the Fed.

I suppose the Fed could raise IOER, but I doubt they will – at least not much.

* * *

It will be interesting to see how far Trump goes on trade. If he really goes far on trade, the price increases will be noticeable. It won't be 1 or 2%. It will be much higher than that.

Will consumers tolerate higher prices? Will they have a choice?

What if Trump is successful in reversing the psychology of inflation, where people come to expect price increases in things like TVs and such.

It will be impossible to slow down.

The Fed somehow thinks that all they have to do is raise Fed funds a couple of times, and voila, inflation is over. It doesn't work that way. Once it gets going, you can't stop it.

There are a number of ways to play the bond bear market.

The easiest thing to do is to short bonds.

I don't want to get into all the stupid inverse ETFs. Some are certainly better than others, but none of them are free.

Maybe there is a better way to play the bond bear market than bonds?

How about shorting the world's biggest bond manager?

Blackrock breaking out to new highs. Does that make any sense? That does not make any sense.

I don't short charts that don't make any sense. You only short stocks that are down.

But think about this. It doesn't matter if BLK's funds are in the 99th percentile. If they are down 8% in a year, assets are going to flee to another strategy. Plain and simple.

This is perhaps one of the best short ideas in the history of TDD. But no reason to execute on it yet – not until the chart shows signs of weakness. Right now, it is showing the opposite of weakness. Screaming to new highs.

Lucky for the BLK folks, I guess.

BLK

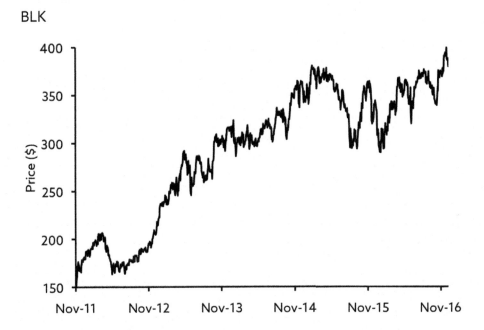

Source: Bloomnberg

ABOUT JARED DILLIAN

Jared Dillian is the editor of *The Daily Dirtnap*, a daily market newsletter for investment professionals, continuously published since 2008. He graduated from the United States Coast Guard Academy in 1996 with a B.S. in Mathematics and Computer Science, and from the University of San Francisco in 2001 with a Masters in Business Administration, concentration in Finance. Jared worked for a small floor market maker on the Pacific Options Exchange from 1999–2000, and was a trader for Lehman Brothers from 2001 to 2008, specializing in index arbitrage and ETF trading. He is also the author of *Street Freak: Money And Madness At Lehman Brothers*, which was named Businessweek's #1 general business book of 2011, and the novel *All The Evil Of This World*, published in 2016. Additionally, Jared is a teaching associate in the graduate business program at Coastal Carolina University. Jared is also a regular contributor at Forbes and Mauldin Economics. His media appearances include MSNBC, Bloomberg TV, BNN, *The New York Times*, *LA Times*, *Business Insider* and dozens of local and syndicated radio programs.

India

BY RAOUL PAL

I'm going to blow your mind with this following article. My mind is still reeling from my discovery and from writing this piece.

Let me enlighten you...

Companies that create massively outsized technological breakthroughs tend to capture the investing population's attention and thus their share prices trade at huge multiples, as future growth and future revenues are extrapolated into the future.

From time to time, entire countries re-model their economies and shift their growth trajectory. The most recent example was the liberalisation of China's economy and massive spending on infrastructure, which together created an incredibly powerful force for growth over the last two decades.

But it is very rare indeed that a country develops an outsized technological infrastructure breakthrough that leaves the rest of the world far behind.

But exactly this has just happened in India... and no one noticed.

India has, without question, made the largest technological breakthrough of any nation in living memory.

Its technological advancement has even left Silicon Valley standing. India has built the world's first national digital infrastructure, leaping at least two generations of financial technologies and has built something as important as the railroad was to the UK or the interstate highways were to the US.

India is now the most attractive major investment opportunity in the world.

It's all about something called Aadhaar and a breathtakingly ambitious plan with flawless execution.

What just blows my mind is how few people have even noticed it. To be honest, writing the article last month was the first time I learned about any of the developments. I think this is the biggest emerging market macro story in the world.

Phase 1 – The Aadhaar Act

India, pre-2009, had a massive problem for a developing economy: nearly half of its people did not have any form of identification. If you were born outside of a hospital or without any government services, which is common in India, you don't get a birth certificate. Without a birth certificate, you can't get the basic infrastructure of modern life: a bank account, driving license, insurance or a loan. You operate outside the official sector and the opportunities available to others are not available to you. It almost guarantees a perpetuation of poverty and it also guarantees a low tax take for India, thus it holds Indian growth back too.

Normally, a country such as India would solve this problem by making a large push to register more births or send bureaucrats into villages to issues official papers (and sadly accept bribes in return). It would have been costly, inefficient and messy. It probably would have only partially worked.

But in 2009, India did something that no one else in the world at the time had done before; they launched a project called Aadhaar which was a technological solution to the problem, creating a biometric database based on a 12-digit digital identity, authenticated by finger prints and retina scans.

Aadhaar became the largest and most successful IT project ever undertaken in the world and, as of 2016, 1.1 billion people (95% of the population) now has a digital proof of identity. To understand the scale of what India has achieved with Aadhaar you have to understand that India accounts for 17.2% of the entire world's population!

Figure 1: Indian Population as a % of Global Population

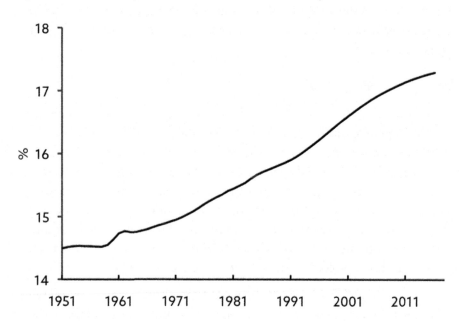

But this biometric database was just the first phase...

Phase 2 – Banking Adoption

Once huge swathes of the population began to register on the official system, the next phase was to get them into the banking system. The Government allowed the creation of 11 Payment Banks, which can hold money but don't do any lending. To motivate people to open accounts, it offered free life insurance with them and linked bank accounts to social welfare benefits. Within three years more than 270 million bank accounts were opened and $10bn in deposits flooded in.

People who registered under the Aadhaar Act could open a bank account just with their Aadhaar number.

Phase 3 – Building Out a Mobile Infrastructure

The Aadhaar card holds another important benefit – people can use it to instantly open a mobile phone account. I covered this in detail last month but the key takeaway is that mobile phone penetration exploded after Aadhaar and went from 40% of the population to 79% within a few years...

Figure 2: ITU India Mobile Phone Subscribers Per 100 Inhabitants

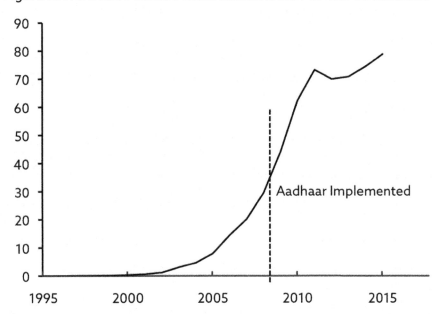

The next phase in the mobile phone story will be the rapid rise in smart phones, which will revolutionise everything. Currently only 28% of the population has a smart phone but growth rates are close to 70% per year.

In July 2016, the Unique Identification Authority of India (UIDAI), which administers Aadhaar, called a meeting with executives from Google, Microsoft, Samsung and Indian smartphone maker Micromax amongst others, to talk about developing Aadhaar compliant devices.

Qualcomm is working closely with government authorities to get more Aadhaar-enabled devices onto the market and working with customers – including the biggest Android manufacturers – to integrate required features, such as secure cameras and iris authentication partners.

Tim Cook, CEO of Apple, recently singled out India as a top priority for Apple.

Microsoft has also just launched a lite version of Skype designed to work on an unstable 2G connection and is integrated with the Aadhaar database, so video calling can be used for authenticated calls.

This rise in smart, Aadhaar compliant mobile phone penetration set the stage for the really clever stuff...

Phase 4 – UPI – A New Transaction System

But that is not all. In December 2016, India launched BHIM (Bharat Interface for Money) which is a digital payments platform using UPI (Unified Payments Interface). This is another giant leap that allows non-UPI linked bank accounts into the payments system. Now payments can be made from UPI accounts to non-UPI accounts and can use QR codes for instant payments and also allows users to check bank balances.

While the world is digesting all of this, assuming that it is going to lead to an explosion in mobile phone eWallets (which is happening already), the next step is materializing. This is where the really big breakthrough lies...

Payments can now be made without using mobile phones, just using fingerprints and an Aadhaar number.

Bloody hell. That is the biggest change to any financial system in history.

What is even more remarkable is that this system works on a 2G network so it reaches even the most remote parts of India!! It will revolutionise the agricultural economy, which employs 60% of the workforce and contributes 17% of GDP. Farmers will now have access to bank accounts and credit, along with crop insurance.

But again, that is not all... India has gone one step further...

Phase 5 – India Stack – A Digital Life

In 2016, India introduced another innovation called India Stack. This is a series of secured and connected systems that allows people to store and share personal data such as addresses, bank statements, medical records, employment records and tax filings and it enables the digital signing of documents. This is all accessed, and can be shared, via Aadhaar biometric authentication.

Essentially, it is a secure Dropbox for your entire official life and creates what is known as eKYC: Electronic Know Your Customer.

Using India Stack APIs, all that is required is a fingerprint or retina scan to open a bank account, mobile phone account, brokerage account, buy a mutual fund or share medical records at any hospital or clinic in India. It also creates the opportunity for instant loans and brings insurance to the masses, particularly life insurance. All of this data can also in turn be stored on India Stack to give, for example, proof of utility bill payment or life insurance coverage.

What is India Stack exactly?

India Stack is the framework that will make the new digital economy work seamlessly.

It's a set of APIs that allows governments, businesses, start-ups and developers to utilise a unique digital infrastructure to solve India's hard problems towards presence-less, paperless and cashless service delivery.

- **Presence-less**: Retina scan and finger prints will be used to participate in any service from anywhere in the country.

- **Cashless**: A single interface to all the country's bank accounts and wallets.

- **Paperless**: Digital records are available in the cloud, eliminating the need for massive amount of paper collection and storage.

- **Consent layer**: Give secured access on demand to documents.

India Stack provides the ability to operate in real time, transactions such as lending, bank or mobile account opening that usually can take few days to complete are now instant.

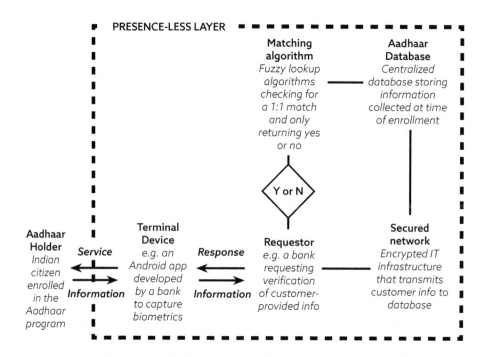

As you can see, smartphones will act as key to access the kingdom. This is fast, secure and reliable; this is the future...

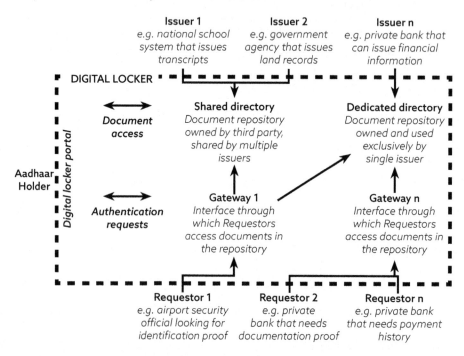

This revolutionary digital infrastructure will soon be able to process billions more transactions than bitcoin ever has. It may well be a bitcoin killer or at best provide the framework for how blockchain technology could be applied in the real world. It is too early to tell whether other countries or the private sector adopts blockchain versions of this infrastructure or abandons it altogether and follows India's centralised version.

India Stack is the largest open API in the world and will allow for massive fintech opportunities to be built around it. India is already the third largest fintech centre but it will jump into first place in a few years. India is already organizing hackathons to develop applications for the APIs.

It has left Silicon Valley in the dust.

Phase 6 – A Cash Ban

The final stroke of genius was the cash ban, which I have also discussed at length in the past. The cash ban is the final part of the story. It simply forces everyone into the new digital economy and has the hugely beneficial side-effect of reducing everyday corruption, recapitalising the banking sector and increasing government tax take, thus allowing India to rebuild its crumbling infrastructure...

Figure 3: Cash-Based Transactions as a % of Total Value

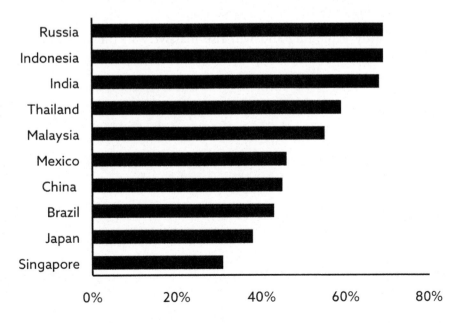

India was a cash society but once the dust settles, cash will account for less than 40% of total transactions in the next five years. It may eliminate cash altogether in the next ten years.

The cash ban digitizes India. No other economy in the world is even close to this.

Phase 7 – The Investment Opportunity

Everyone thinks they know about the Indian economy – crappy infrastructure, corruption, bureaucracy and antiquated institutions but with a massively growing middle class. Well, that is the narrative and has been for the last 15 years.

But that phase is over and no one noticed. So few people in the investment community or even Silicon Valley are even vaguely aware of what has happened in India and that has created an enormous investment opportunity.

The future for India is massive technological advancement, a higher trend rate of GDP and more tax revenues. Tax revenues will fund infrastructure – ports, roads, rail and healthcare. Technology will increase agricultural productivity, online services and manufacturing productivity.

Telecom, banking, insurance and online retailing will boom, as will the tech sector. Nothing in India will be the same again.

FDI is already exploding and will rise massively in the years ahead as technology giants and others pour into India to take advantage of the opportunity...

Figure 4: Indian FDI ($bn)

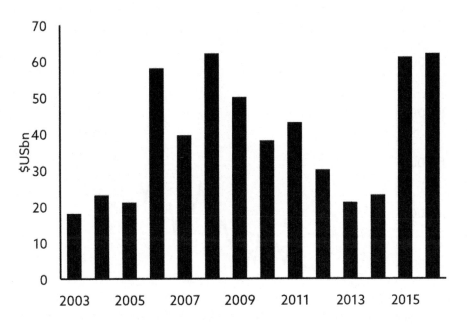

I am long the telco sector (Bharti)...

Figure 5: BHARTI Airtel

And I am long the Nifty Banks Index...

Figure 6: Nifty Banks Index

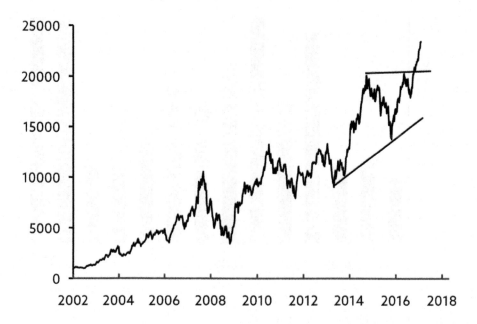

I think India is going to offer an entire world of opportunity going forwards.

If I can sum up, it's in this one chart: the SENSEX in US Dollars. It looks explosive for the next 10 years...

Figure 7: SENSEX Index ($US)

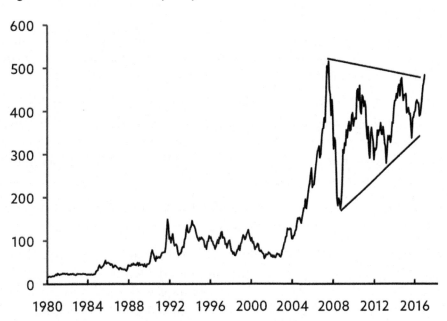

Incredible India indeed.

I decided to test the waters on Twitter to find out how many non-Indians were aware of India Stack/Aadhaar. I have 24,000 followers on Twitter, many of which are you guys, and hosts of others heavily engaged in financial markets, i.e. it's a decent data sample.

In the 12 hours since the survey began, around 900 people have responded. It appears that 90% of the investment world knows absolutely nothing about the biggest IT project ever accomplished and have never even heard of it.

Now, that is an informational edge.

ABOUT RAOUL PAL

Raoul Pal has been publishing *Global Macro Investor* since January 2005 to provide original, high quality, quantifiable and easily readable research for the global macro investment community hedge funds, family offices, pension funds and sovereign wealth funds. It draws on his considerable 26 years of experience in advising hedge funds and managing a global macro hedge fund.

Raoul Pal retired from managing client money at the age of 36 in 2004 and now lives in the tiny Caribbean island of Little Cayman in the Cayman Islands, population 150.

He is also the CEO and co-founder of Real Vision Group (www.realvision. com), a digital media company which features the world's first on-demand TV channel for finance – Real Vision Television, along with an online financial newsletter publishing business – Real Vision Publications and a podcast – Adventures in Finance.

Previously he co-managed the GLG Global Macro Fund in London for GLG Partners, one of the largest hedge fund groups in the world.

Raoul moved to GLG from Goldman Sachs where he co-managed the hedge fund sales business in Equities and Equity Derivatives in Europe. In this role, Raoul established strong relationships with many of the world's pre-eminent hedge funds, learning from their styles and experiences.

Other stop-off points on the way were NatWest Markets and HSBC, although he began his career by training traders in technical analysis.

Raoul makes frequent media appearances – along with hosting interviews on Real Vision TV, he is also a regular guest on CNBC and has been interviewed by the *New York Times*, *The Wall Street Journal*, *The Financial Times*, Bloomberg, Yahoo Finance and many others.

The Frightening Global Rise of Agnotology

BY BARRY RITHOLTZ

I spend much of my time shrugging off breathless news events. Ebola (now Zika), employment reports, Federal Reserve rate changes, government shutdowns, peak earnings and so on. Much of what passes for earth-shaking news turns out to be, with the benefit of hindsight, something in between idle gossip and fear-mongering. The genuine, not well-anticipated, actual market-moving news – such as the UK's vote to leave the European Union – is a relatively rare thing.

However, there is a disconcerting trend that has gained strength: agnotology. It's a term worth knowing, since it is going global. The word was coined by Stanford University professor Robert N. Proctor, who described it as "culturally constructed ignorance, created by special interest groups to create confusion and suppress the truth in a societally important issue." It is especially useful to sow seeds of doubt in complex scientific issues by publicizing inaccurate or misleading data.

Culturally constructed ignorance played a major role in the Brexit vote, as we shall see after a bit of explanation.

Perhaps the best-known example of agnotology is found in the tobacco industry's claims for many years that the evidence that smoking cigarettes causes cancer was "not yet in." The position of the industry and its executives was that the hazards of cigarette smoking were an open question. Of course, this was a huge lie, as the industry had scientific evidence that proved that smoking caused cancer, emphysema, heart and lung disease. As Proctor observed "The tobacco industry is famous for having seen itself as a manufacturer of two different products: tobacco and doubt."

That doubt, however, allowed cigarette sales to continue for decades before the inescapable truth came to light. And it forestalled broader regulatory oversight by the states and the federal government for years. But the truth can only be held back for so long, and eventually tobacco sales in the US fell off a cliff. But it was too late to save millions of people who became sick and died due to smoking.

Current agnotology campaigns seem to be having similarly desired effects. We see the results in a variety of public-policy issues where one side has manufactured enough doubt through false statements, inflammatory rhetoric and data from dubious sources that they can mislead public opinion in a significant way, at least for a time.

The backers of each of these public issues have used the technique of culturally constructed ignorance to affect public opinion, direct government policy and alter regulatory oversight. Here a just a few examples:

- Iraq has weapons of mass destruction
- Genetically modified crops are dangerous
- Global warming is a scientific hoax
- Vaccines cause autism
- Tax cuts pay for themselves
- Poor people caused the financial crisis

Each of these is, of course, wrong and lacking in any factual basis. Nevertheless, they have a following. Now, you can add Brexit to the list. Watching from across the Atlantic, it was a wonder to see the stream of claims that failed to stand up to even the slightest scrutiny.

Perhaps the biggest was the assertion by Nigel Farage, the loudest advocate for Brexit and leader of the UK Independence Party, that leaving would free up 350 million pounds ($460 million) a week that now goes to the EU for use by Britain's financially stretched National Health Service. Farage was forced to backtrack on this claim almost immediately. He was successful at frightening people with claims about immigration that he also was forced to "row back."

In the aftermath of the Brexit vote, there is evidence that people didn't fully understand what they were voting for. Some didn't think their protest vote would matter, or misunderstood what they were voting for, or what the EU actually was. There seems to be a rise in voters' remorse the days after. Many blamed the tabloids in the UK. The misstatements and myths which were being pressed by the leave campaign about the EU were so rampant and absurd that the European Commission had to put out repeated corrections and maintain a blog to rebut the nonsense.

Democracy is based on the concept of a marketplace of ideas. Supreme Court Justice Oliver Wendell Holmes described the "free trade in ideas" within "the competition of the market." By the time voters head to the polls, the participants will have chewed over the finer points, the details will be well known to all and, for the most part, everyone more or less understands what's at stake.

Or not.

The assumption underlying policy debates – their true purpose in a democracy – is to engage in a principled argument in order to reach a discernible truth. It isn't, as we have seen more and more often, to win a short-term victory at any and all costs.

Jonathan Swift once wrote, "Falsehood flies, and the Truth comes limping after it." That was never truer than today, when falsehoods and Facebook hoaxes can travel around the world at the click of a mouse.

Hyperbole and exaggeration is one thing, creating an alternative universe is something else entirely.

Originally published on BloombergView.com

Bloomberg View copyright © 2016 Bloomberg LP

www.bloomberg.com/view/articles/2016-06-27/culturally-constructed-ignorance-wins-the-day

---

ABOUT BARRY RITHOLTZ

Barry L. Ritholtz is the co-founder and chief investment officer of Ritholtz Wealth Management. Launched in 2013, RWM is a financial planning and asset management firm, with over $500 million in assets. The firm offers a variety of services to the investing public, including LiftOff – a low cost online-only investment site.

Ritholtz is a frequent commentator on many financial topics. He was named one of the '15 Most Important Economic Journalists' in the United States, and has been called one of The 25 Most Dangerous People in Financial Media. He writes a daily column for Bloomberg View and a twice monthly column on Personal Finance and Investing for *The Washington Post*. Ritholtz is the creator and host of *Masters in Business*, a popular podcast on Bloomberg Radio.

Beyond his commentary and published articles, Mr. Ritholtz also authors *The Big Picture* – a leading financial weblog, generating several million page views per month. In 2008–09, Ritholtz wrote the book *Bailout Nation*, published by Wiley in 2009; the updated paperback was released in 2010.

Mr. Ritholtz performed his graduate studies at Yeshiva University's Benjamin N. Cardozo School of Law in New York. His undergraduate work was at Stony Brook University, where on a Regents Scholarship, he focused on Mathematics and Physics, graduating with an Bachelor Arts & Sciences degree in Political Science.

Bull Market Charges on Regardless of a Growing Revolt

BY KEN FISHER

Why did so few foresee Brexit? And what does it mean for the rest of the world?

It's simple. The media, pundits, politicians and prediction markets were too London and urban-focused, underestimating rural voters everywhere. Outside Scotland, the vote was almost purely big cities for Remain versus tiny-town England for Leave. Tiny won.

Consider the US. Similar sources underrate Donald Trump's chances in the same way. They view politics as urban-based and top-down, tracking how states voted in past presidential elections. Twenty-one states and Washington DC voted Democratic in at least four of the last five, hence their label as "blue states". Twenty-four "red states" voted Republican, with five remaining swing states. Since blue states have 257 electoral votes – 13 short of what is needed – the media industry presumes Hillary Clinton has a huge edge.

Maybe. But viewed from the bottom up it's the reverse – and no one sees this. Republicans control most state governments bottom-to-top. Take Michigan, a so-called blue state in which Republicans now hold both legislative houses and all state officers. The same applies in other blue states: bottom-up they've evolved to be "red". Democrats control just 11 state legislatures, versus 31 for Republicans and eight split.

Republicans' dominance at the bottom is relatively recent and rural-based, hence overlooked. In 1978, Democrats held 31 state legislatures and 20 of the 33 poorest states. Now they hold just two of the 33 poorest. Republicans have now replaced them as the party of the poor in rural areas.

In the cities the poor are still heavily Democrat. If the US votes this time bottom up, as its legislatures are by state, Mr Trump would win 309 electoral college votes, 39 more than he needs – almost the reverse of the conventional top-down analysis. Will that happen? I don't have a clue. But he has better prospects than urbanites foresee – similar to the Brexit upset and surprise. It's a revolt of the invisible poor.

By my estimate, Mr Trump will win the presidency even if he loses the popular vote by several percent. How? He will be swamped in California, the biggest state with 12.2% of the population, likely by 20%-plus. He should win Republican Texas, the second-biggest, with 8.5% of the population, but by a much smaller margin.

That puts Mrs Clinton out ahead big time, assuming no unexpected electoral college outcomes. A similar tilt should come from getting swamped in Connecticut, Illinois, New York and Oregon versus slight Trump wins in traditionally Republican Georgia, Indiana, North Carolina and Tennessee. If he is then 2–3% behind in the popular vote nationally, he owns most of the remaining electoral college and becomes president.

I reiterate that I don't know what will happen. But the surprise potential is, as Mr Trump would say, "yuge". There is a similar, not-so-noticed phenomenon creeping across the continent. It's in Denmark with the rural based People's Party. In Italy the Five Star's strength stems primarily from small town and rural. Or France's National Front, which is mostly non-Parisian. Or Austria's support for presidential candidate Norbert Höfer, who just forced a revote.

To foresee the risk consider two tracking tools. First, regional economic indicators. They're less timely than national data, but trendy. The UK's showed big slowdowns in Wales, the Midlands, the north-west and the south in 2014 – all "Leave" strongholds. Identifying poorer, slower-growing areas helps gauge where voters feel abandoned and angst-prone.

Second, municipal elections, particularly the first round. The National Front won the most votes in round one of France's late-2015 local election – a bottom-up race – before top-down forces crushed them in round two.

What could all of this mean for investors in the long term, say over the next decade? Anything can happen in ten years. The UK could cease to exist. The world could end. Or we could have a golden age of peace and prosperity. If it's impossible to know, why sweat it?

Even if the next decade is below-average, that knowledge is largely useless now. There is nothing to act on. If stocks are great for some of it, you want to own them. People called the 2000s flat, but they weren't. They were hugely volatile with minimal net gain, but that isn't flat. There were big bear markets at the beginning and end, with a five-year bull in between. No long-term forecast, however "right" overall, could have told you markets' path. The path is what matters.

Then, too, if the ten-year outcome is right but the first five years are different, no one will care about the ten-year. They'll get carried away by the five-year, resetting expectations on recency bias. Our emotions simply can't live through a great or terrible five years and cling to an ancient forecast for the next five. We aren't wired that way. So just deal with the next 3–30 months. That's all the market pays attention to and all you can deal with now.

Finally, markets already told investors not to fret over Brexit. They shouldn't sweat about Mr Trump either. Buy stocks: it's still a bull market.

ABOUT KEN FISHER

Ken Fisher is the founder, Executive Chairman and Co-Chief Investment Officer of Fisher Investments, an $80+ billion money management firm serving large institutions and high net worth individuals throughout the world. With more than 2,200 employees, the firm has offices in Washington, California, the United Kingdom, Germany, Dubai, Australia, and Japan, with further global expansion under way.

Ken's prestigious 'Portfolio Strategy' column ran in *Forbes* from 1984 to 2017, making him the longest continuously running columnist in the magazine's history. He continues to write regular columns for the UK's *Financial Times* and Germany's *Focus Money*. Ken has also written 11 books, including four New York Times bestsellers.

Ken has been published, interviewed and written about in publications globally. In 2010, *Investment Advisor* recognized him on its 'Thirty for Thirty' list as among the industry's 30 most influential individuals of the last three decades. His 1970s theoretical work pioneered an investment tool called the Price-to-Sales Ratio, now a core element of modern financial curricula. A prize-winning researcher, his credits span a multitude of professional and scholarly journals in addition to his firm's output—both in traditional and behavioral finance.

PRICING

&

VALUATION: FROM MICRO TO MACRO

Price-to-Book's Growing Blind Spot

BY CHRIS MEREDITH

Value has broadly been accepted as an investing style and, historically, portfolios formed on cheap valuations have outperformed expensive portfolios. But value comes in many flavors, and the factor(s) you choose to measure cheapness can determine your long-term success. In particular, several operating metrics of value, such as earnings and EBITDA, have outperformed the more traditional price-to-book (P/B) factor. A possible reason for the limited efficacy of price-to-book is because of the increase in shareholder transactions, primarily through the increase in share repurchases.

Valuation factors have the benefit of being simple, but can also have flaws. Price-to-sales (P/S) has the benefit of measuring against *revenue*, which is difficult to manipulate, but it doesn't take margins into account. Price-to-earnings (P/E) measures against the estimated *economic output* of the company, but also contains estimated *expenses* that can be manipulated by managers. EBITDA-to-enterprise-value (EBITDA/EV) has the benefit of including *operating cost* structures, but it misses payments to bondholders and the government. Even with these flaws, the factors are effective in practice. Figure 1 shows the quintile spreads of two factors within a universe of US Large Stocks from 1964 through 2015.[*]

---

[*] Quintile portfolios are formed on the Large Stocks universe (stocks in Compustat with a market capitalization greater than average) and rebalanced every month with a one-year holding period.

Figure 1: Quintile Spreads – P/E and EBITDA/EV – Large Stocks (1964–2015)

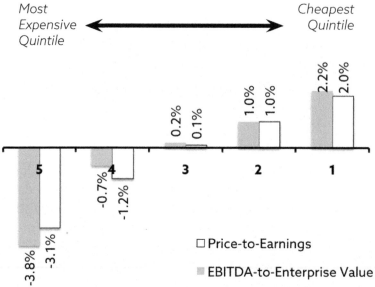

Source: OSAM calculations

Price-to-book is perhaps the most widely used valuation factor in the investing industry. Russell, the top provider of style indexes for the US market, uses the factor as its primary metric to separate stocks into Value and Growth categories. They use price-to-book in combination with forecasted two-year growth and historical five-year sales-per-share growth, but price-to-book is the chief determinant, comprising 50% of the methodology.

Russell's choice of price-to-book most likely comes from its long history in academic research. The seminal work on price-to-book is Fama-French's 1992 paper 'The Cross-Section of Expected Stock Returns', which established the three-factor model of Market, Size, and Price-to-Book.

But when you start looking closely at price-to-book, a few issues start to become apparent. First, the overall spread on the factor isn't as strong as it is with other operating metrics. The spread between price-to-book's highest and lowest quintiles (see Figure 2) is only 2.8% – versus price-to-earnings' 5.1% spread and EBITDA-to-enterprise value's 6.0% spread.

Second, when breaking down the efficacy of the factor based on market capitalization, price-to-book is least effective within the largest cap stocks. Table 1 shows the same quintile spreads of price-to-book in the US Large Stocks universe, but separates out the smallest and largest third based on market cap. Price-to-book degrades in efficacy as the market cap gets larger – the quintile spread within the largest third of stocks is only 1.2%. This is especially noteworthy because Russell market cap-weights their benchmark and about two-thirds of it is in that Largest Third (with the lowest price-to-book spread of the three Large Stocks groups).

Figure 2: Quintile Spreads – Price-to-Book

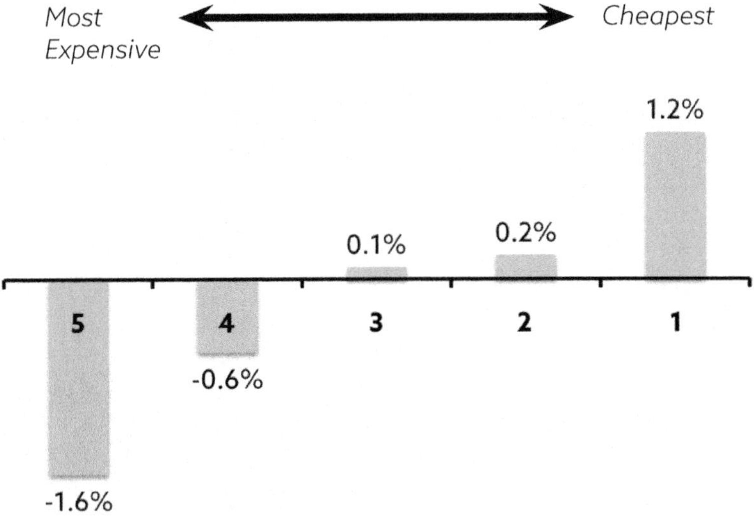

Source: OSAM calculations

Table 1: Excess Return of Price-to-Book in US Large Stocks by Market Cap Grouping

	Most Expensive				Cheapest	
Market Cap:	5	4	3	2	1	Spread
Largest Third	−1.5%	−0.9%	−0.8%	0.6%	−0.3%	1.2%
Middle Third	−2.3%	−1.1%	0.0%	0.4%	0.9%	3.1%
Smallest Third	−0.9%	−0.3%	0.7%	−0.5%	2.0%	2.9%

Source: OSAM calculations

Last, the efficacy of price-to-book has been waning, especially since the turn of the century. Figure 3 shows the rolling 20-year quintile spread (the difference between the portfolio of the cheapest 20% and the portfolio of most expensive 20%). Comparing price-to-book against EBITDA-to-enterprise value and price-to-earnings, it shows how all three metrics behaved very similarly before 2000. They had generated consistent outperformance until being inverted in the dot-com bubble of the late 1990s, when the most expensive stocks outperformed. But coming out of the dot-com bubble, price-to-book has started behaving differently than other valuation factors, degrading to the point where for the past 20 years it has had almost no discernible benefit on stock selection.

Figure 3: Rolling 20-Year Quintile Spread – Large Stocks

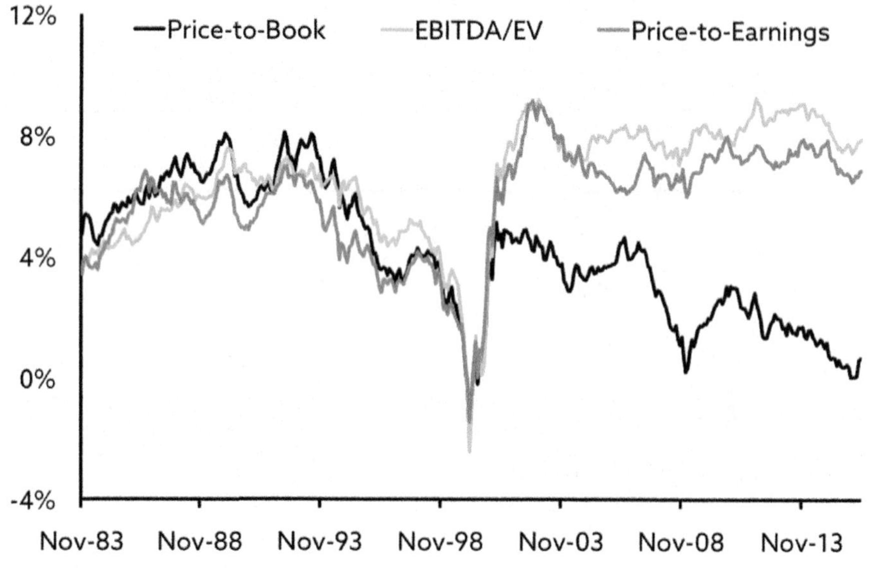

Source: OSAM calculations

On the surface, using book value in relation to price makes intuitive sense. The book value of equity is the total amount of common equity shareholders would receive in liquidation (the difference between the accounting value of the total assets and the total liabilities and preferred equity). The price-to-book factor is meant to be a quick measure for seeing how cheaply the company could be acquired. The factor will move around based on changes in either the market value or book value of equity. But the factor comes with assumptions. "Clean surplus accounting" is based on the assumption that equity only increases (or decreases) from the earnings (or losses) in *excess of dividends*. In practice, there is another influence on equity: transactions with shareholders.

When a company repurchases shares, the market effect is straightforward. The number of shares outstanding are reduced while the price remains the same, so the market capitalization goes down. When taking the share buybacks into account for financial reporting, the repurchase of shares does not create an asset as if the company had repurchased equity in another company. Instead, the equity value is decreased by *the amount spent in purchasing the shares*.

As a hypothetical example, take a company with a $200 million market cap, $100 million in book value of equity, and $10 million in earnings. The company has a price-to-earnings ratio of 20, and a price-to-book ratio of 2.

$$\frac{P}{E} = \frac{200}{10} = 20 \qquad \frac{P}{B} = \frac{200}{100} = 2$$

If that company becomes an aggressive Repurchaser and decides to acquire $50 million worth of its own equity, it will alter the results significantly. The earnings remain the same but the market cap goes down, adjusting the price-to-earnings down to 15. But the price-to-book ratio will be reduced on both the top and bottom *and* it will actually *increase* to three.

$$\frac{P}{E} = \frac{200 - 50}{10} = \frac{150}{10} = 15 \qquad \frac{P}{B} = \frac{200 - 50}{100 - 50} = \frac{150}{50} = 3$$

As a practical example, Viacom has been aggressively repurchasing its own shares after separating from CBS in 2006, spending almost $20 billion over the past ten years. In 2015 alone, it repurchased about $1.4 billion in shares. So even though the company has been seeing retained earnings of about $1.5 billion per year, its common equity has reduced from $8 billion to $4 billion over that same time frame.[*]

---

[*] Compustat used as source for the Viacom data.

Figure 4: Historical Financial Metrics – VIACOM

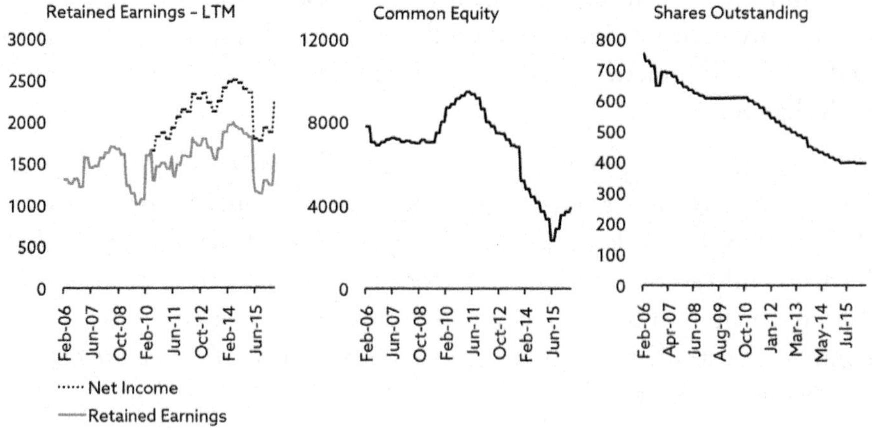

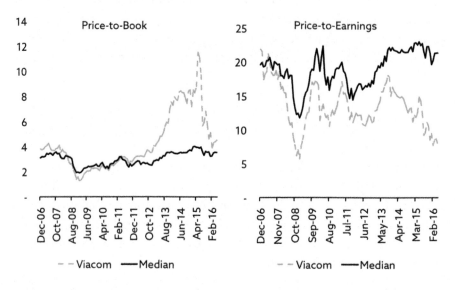

Source: Compustat, OSAM calculations

You can see how this distorts valuation factors. Viacom trades at a significant discount on earnings versus the median price-to-earnings for other large stocks, while at the same time looking as though it trades at a significant premium on the book value of equity.

Figure 5: Historical Valuation Factors – VIACOM

Source: Compustat, OSAM calculations

A company issuing shares will have the reverse effect. The company will actually *increase* its book value, even though the earnings and cash flows are diluted across more investors. Any transaction for a company, through the issuance or reduction of equity, flows through the book value of the equity.

Table 2 compares median valuation factors for companies with a market capitalization greater than average. Two groups are compared with the median large stock: those companies that have repurchased the most shares over the past five years (Repurchasers) and those that have issued the most shares (Diluters). The top 25 Repurchasers have better operating valuation metrics (e.g., sales, earnings, EBITDA, free cash flow) than the median, and the top 25 Diluters have worse results – with the standout exception of price-to-book. Repurchasers have an average price-to-book of 4.5, almost 20% higher than the median 3.8, while Diluters look cheap with a price-to-book of only 2.7 – an apparent discount of almost 30%.[*]

Table 2: Valuation Factors for Large Stocks by Share Activity

	Top 25 Repurchasers	US Stocks Larger than Average	Top 25 Diluters
Price-to-Sales	1.4	2.3	5.2
*Percentile**	30	50	84
Price-to-Earnings	16.8	22.5	286.3
*Percentile**	29	50	88
EBITDA-to-Enterprise Value (%)	4.0	2.8	2.0
*Percentile**	32	50	64
Free Cash Flow-to-Enterprise Value (%)	26.9	15.7	6.2
*Percentile**	37	50	84

[*]   Compustat source used for R1000V constituents (as of 5/31/16).

	Top 25 Repurchasers	US Stocks Larger than Average	Top 25 Diluters
Price-to-Book	4.5	3.8	2.7
Percentile*	58	50	34
Percentage of Names in R1000V	44.0%	57.8%	56.0%

Source: Compustat, OSAM calculations * The lower the number, the better the score.

This distortion suggests that using price-to-book could lead to misclassifications of stocks as a Value investment. Stocks that are cheap on operating metrics like sales, EBITDA, or earnings could end up classified as Growth. Conversely, that universe could include a company that has issued a lot of stock and has inflated its book value of equity. This is something to keep in mind, as a number of quantitative managers start with the *benchmark* as their universe. Starting with the Russell 1000® Value could bias you towards a number of companies that look cheap on price-to-book but are not cheap on other important valuation metrics.

Over the past 50 years, there has been a gradual increase in the amount of company equity transactions. In particular, larger companies have been increasing their share repurchase activity. In classifying companies based on a trailing five-year change in shares outstanding, we can see which companies have consolidated shares by more than 5%, issued shares more than 5%, or have been relatively inactive. In 1982, the US loosened regulation around a company's restrictions for repurchasing shares and there has been a significant increase in activity. This has led to a change in the overall market, where the percentage of companies inactive has been reduced – from almost 60% in the 1960s down to around 28% – with the activity mainly being driven from companies consolidating shares.[*]

Figure 6: Large Stocks by Rolling Five-Year Share Activity

---

[*] Large Stocks universe, with Compustat as source for share repurchases. Price-to-earnings (earnings yield) generates a spread of 5.1% between the highest and lowest quintile, and EBITDA-to-enterprise value generates a 6.0% spread.

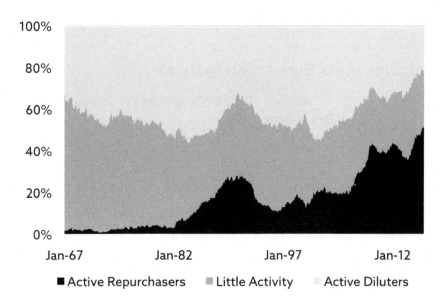

Source: OSAM calculations

This begs the question: Does a moderate increase in shareholder transactions result in price-to-book gradually becoming ineffectual as a valuation factor? The first rule in analysis is not to confuse *correlation* with *causation*. However, the rolling 20-years when price-to-book has been less effective coincides quite well with the increase in shareholder transaction activity. Price-to-book is also the least effective in the largest cap stocks, which have the greatest volume of dollars affecting book value of equity. Perhaps the most interesting analysis is looking at the efficacy of price-to-book within those large stocks that have been relatively *inactive* with shareholders over a trailing five-year period versus those that have been *active*, either on issuance or repurchase. From the 1982 legislation change to the present, there is a different level of valuation metrics' efficacy for companies that are active or inactive with shareholders. If your investments are focused on companies with share issuance or repurchase activity, there has been no relative benefit to buying companies that look cheap on price-to-book and there's almost no difference between high and low valuations. But, when limited to companies that are relatively inactive, you can get a spread of 6.4% between the highest and lowest 20% based on the price-to-book factor. Using a different valuation metric, such as EBITDA-to-enterprise value, works well – regardless of a company's activity in issuing or repurchasing shares.

Table 3: Large Stocks Share Activity by Decade

Year	Active Repurchasers	Little Activity	Active Issuers
1967–69	2.1%	59.6%	38.3%
1970s	2.6%	52.4%	45.0%
1980s	12.3%	37.8%	49.9%
1990s	17.9%	38.3%	43.7%
2000s	24.5%	31.2%	44.3%
2010s	41.7%	27.8%	30.5%

Source: OSAM calculations

Even with the long-term degradation of returns from price-to-book, it is possible that it may revert to an effective investment factor. Price-to-book has been off to a strong start in 2016 and is outperforming other valuation factors, particularly in small cap stocks. But there are structural challenges to the factor and, before using it, investors need to be made aware of the embedded noise from repurchases that could be misleading.

Figure 7: Factor Quintiles by Share Activity (1983–2015)

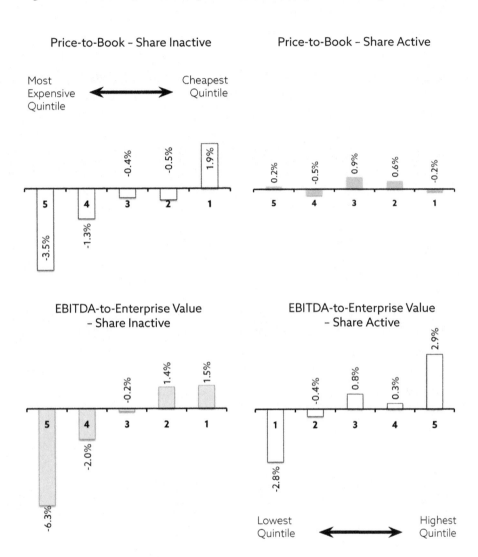

ABOUT CHRIS MEREDITH

Chris Meredith is the Director of Research and a Senior Portfolio Manager at O'Shaughnessy Asset Management (OSAM). He is responsible for managing investment related activities at the firm: investment strategy research, portfolio management, and the firm's trading efforts. He directs the Director of Portfolio Management and the Director of Trading on managing daily investment decisions. Chris has authored several whitepapers including 'Price-to-Book's Growing Blind Spot' and 'Microcap as an Alternative to Private Equity'. He is also the author of the *Cutting Through Noise* blog (www.cuttingthroughnoise.com). Chris is also a Visiting Lecturer of Finance at the Johnson School of Business at Cornell University, where he co-teaches Applied Portfolio Management and co-manages the student-run Cayuga Fund.

Prior to joining OSAM, Chris was a Senior Research Analyst on the Systematic Equity team at BSAM. He was a Director at Oracle Corporation and spent eight years as a technology professional before attending the Johnson School at Cornell University. Chris holds a B.A. in English from Colgate University, an M.B.A. from Cornell University, and an M.A. of Financial Mathematics from Columbia University. He is a Chartered Financial Analyst.

Superman and Stocks: It's not the Cape (CAPE), it's the Kryptonite (Cash flow)!

BY ASWATH DAMODARAN

Just about a week ago, I was on a 13-hour plane trip from Tokyo to New York. I know that this will sound strange but I like long flights for two reasons. The first is that they give me extended stretches of time when I can work without interruption, no knocks on the door or email or phone calls. I readied my lecture notes for next semester and reviewed and edited a manuscript for one of my books in the first half of the trip. The second is that I can go on movie binges with my remaining time, watching movies that I would have neither the time nor the patience to watch otherwise. On this trip, however, I made the bad decision of watching *Batman versus Superman, Dawn of Justice*, a movie so bad that the only way that I was able to get through it was by letting my mind wander, a practice that I indulge in frequently and without apologies or guilt. I pondered whether Superman needed his suit or more importantly, his cape, to fly. After all, his powers come from his origins (that he was born in Krypton) and not from his outfit and the cape seems to be more of an aerodynamic drag than an augmentation. These deep thoughts about Superman's cape then led me to thinking about CAPE, the variant on PE ratios that Robert Shiller developed, and how many articles I have read over the last decade that have used this measure as the basis for warning me that stocks are headed for a fall. Finally, I started thinking about Kryptonite, the substance that renders Superman helpless, and what would be analogous to it in the stock market. I did tell you that I have a wandering mind and so, if you don't like Superman or stocks, consider yourself forewarned!

The Stock Market's CAPE

As stocks hit one high after another, the stock market looks like Superman, soaring to new highs and possessed of super powers.

S&P 500: it's a bird, it's a plane, it's Superman, it's Stocks!!!!

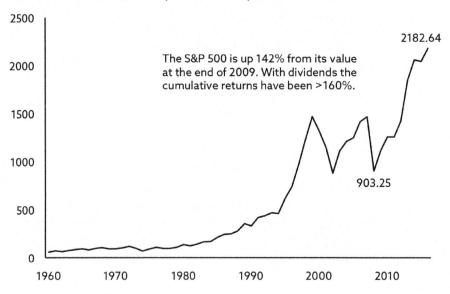

There are many who warn us that stocks are overheating and that a fall is imminent. Some of this worrying is natural, given the market's rise over the last few years, but there are a few who seem to have surrendered entirely to the notion that stocks are in a bubble and that there is no rational explanation for why investors would invest in them. In a post from a couple of years ago, I titled these people as bubblers and classified them into doomsday, knee jerk, conspiratorial, righteous and rational bubblers. The last group (rational bubblers) are generally sensible people, who having fallen in love with a market metric, are unable to distance themselves from it.

One of the primary weapons that rational bubblers use to back up their case is the Cyclically Adjusted Price Earnings (CAPE), a measure developed and popularized by Robert Shiller, Nobel prize winner whose soothsaying credentials were amplified by his calls on the dot-com and housing bubbles. For those who don't quite grasp what the CAPE is, it is the conventional PE ratio for stocks, with two adjustments to the earnings. First, instead of using the most recent year's earnings, it is computed as the average earnings over the prior ten years. Second, to allow for the effects of inflation, the earnings in prior years is adjusted for inflation. The CAPE case against stocks is a simple one to make and it is best seen by graphing Shiller's version of it over time.

Shiller CAPE; 1881–2016

	Average	25th percentile	Median	75th percentile
1881–2016	16.69	11.75	16.06	20.32
1916–2016	16.80	11.01	15.87	21.27
1966–2016	19.77	13.50	19.87	24.89
1996–2016	26.98	22.92	25.82	28.18
2006–2016	23.10	20.98	23.47	25.92

Shiller CAPE data (from www.econ.yale.edu/~shiller/data.htm)

The current CAPE of 27.27 is well above the historic average of 16.06 and if you buy into the notion of mean reversion, the case makes itself, right? Not quite! As you can see, even within the CAPE story, there are holes, largely depending upon what time period you use for your averaging. Relative to the full history, the CAPE looks high today, but relative to the last 20 years, the story is much weaker. Contrary to popular view, mean reversion is very much in the eyes of the beholder.

The CAPE's Weakest Links

Robert Shiller has been a force in finance, forcing us to look at the consequences of investor behavior and chronicling the consequences of "irrational exuberance". His work with Karl Case in developing a real estate index that is now widely followed has introduced discipline and accountability into real estate investing and his historical data series on stocks, which he so generously shares with us, is invaluable. You can almost see the "but" coming and I will not disappoint you. Of all of his creations, I find CAPE to be not only the least compelling but also potentially the most dangerous, in terms of how often it can lead investors astray. So, at the risk of angering those of you who are CAPE followers, here is my case against putting too much faith in this measure, with much of it representing updates of my post from two years ago.

1. The CAPE is not that informative

The notion that CAPE is a significant improvement on conventional PE is based on the two adjustments that it makes, first by replacing earnings in the most recent period with average earnings over ten years and the second by adjusting past earnings for inflation to make them comparable to current earnings. Both adjustments make intuitive sense but at least in the context of the overall market, I am not sure that either adjustment makes much of a difference. In the graph below, I show the trailing PE, normalized PE (using the average earnings over the last ten years) and CAPE for the S&P 500 from 1969 to 2016 (last 12 months). I also show Shiller's CAPE, which is based on a broader group of US stocks in the same graph.

First, it is true that especially after boom periods (where earnings peak) or economic crises (where trailing earnings collapse), the CAPEs (both mine and Shiller's) yield different numbers than PE. Second, and more important, the four measures move together most of the time, with the correlation matrix shown in the figure. Note that the correlation is close to one between the normalized PE and the CAPE, suggesting that the inflation adjustment does little or nothing in markets like the US and even the normalization makes only a marginal difference with a correlation of 0.86 between the unadjusted PE and the Shiller PE.

PE Ratios for S&P 500 & Shiller PE: 1969 to 2016

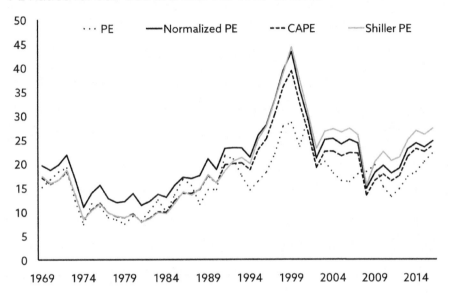

Correlations across PE ratios

Variable	PE	Normalized PE	CAPE	Shiiller PE
PE	1.0000			
Normalized PE	0.8746	1.0000		
CAPE	0.8871	0.9939	1.0000	
Shiller PE	0.8642	0.9677	0.9860	1.0000

2. The CAPE is not that predictive

The question then becomes whether using the CAPE as a valuation metric yields judgments about stocks that are superior to those based upon just PE or normalized PE. To test this proposition, I looked at the correlation between the values of different metrics, including trailing PE, CAPE, the inverse of the dividend yield, earnings yield and the ratio of Shiller PE to the Bond PE today and stock returns in the following year and the following five years:

	PE	Shiller PE	Shiller PE/ T.Bond PE	Price/ Dividends	Earnings Yield	Stock return next year	Stock return next 5 years
PE	1.0000						
Shiller PE	0.8545	1.0000					
Shiller PE/ T.Bond PE		0.5093	1.0000				
Price/ Dividends	0.7829	0.9327	0.4522	1.0000			
Earnings Yield	−0.9182	−0.7814	−0.2877	−0.6802	1.0000		
Stock return next year	−0.3185	−0.2711	−0.1759	−0.2751	0.2946	1.0000	
Stock return next 5 years	−0.4884	−0.5539	−0.3387	−0.5544	0.4480	0.4955	1.0000

There is both good news and bad news for those who use the Shiller CAPE as their stock valuation metric. The good news is that the fundamental proposition that stocks are more likely to go down in future periods, if the Shiller CAPE is high today, seems to be backed up. The bad news is two fold. First, the relationship is noisy or in investment parlance, the predictive power is low, especially with one-year returns. Second, the trailing PE actually does a better job of predicting one-year returns than the CAPE and while CAPE becomes the better predictor than trailing PE over a five-year period, it is barely better than using a dividend yield indicator. While I have not included these in the table, I will wager that any multiple (such as EV to EBITDA) would do as good (or as bad, depending on your perspective) a job as market timing.

As a follow-up, I ran a simple test of the payoff to market timing, using the Shiller CAPE and actual stock returns from 1927 to 2016. At the start of every year, I first computed the median value of the Shiller CAPE over the previous 50 years and assumed an overpriced threshold at 25% above the median (which you can change). If the actual CAPE was higher than the threshold, I assumed that you put all your money in treasury bills for the following year and that if the CAPE was lower than the threshold, that you invested all your money in equities. (You can alter these values as well.) I computed how much $100 invested in the market in 1927 would have been worth in August of 2016, with and without the market timing based on the CAPE:

End value of $100 invested in 1927 in August 2016

CAPE overvalued cut off	% invested in equities			
	0%	25%	50%	75%
10%	$21,371	$49,125	$101,448	$189,332
25%	$59,992	$101,656	$160,083	$234,694
50%	$137,943	$179,065	$224,536	$272,432

With no market timing, you invest all your money in equities each year. A $100 investment in 1927 would have been worth $320,173 in August 2016.

Note that as you trust CAPE more and more (using lower thresholds and adjusting your equity allocation more), you do more and more damage to the end-value of your portfolio. The bottom line is that it is tough to get a payoff from market timing, even when the pricing metric that you are using comes with impeccable credentials.

3. Investing is relative, not absolute

Notwithstanding its weak spots, let's take the CAPE as your measure of stock market valuation. Is a CAPE of 27.27 too high, especially when the historic norm is closer to 16? The answer to you may sound obvious, but before you do answer, you have to consider where you would put your money instead. If you choose not to buy stocks, your immediate option is to put your money in bonds and the base rate that drives the bond market is the yield on a riskless (or close to riskless) investment. Using the US treasury bond as a proxy for this riskless rate in the United States, I construct a bond PE ratio using that rate:

Bond PE = 1/ Treasury Bond Rate

Thus, if you invest in a treasury bond on August 22, 2016, with a yield of 1.54%, you are effectively paying 64.94 (1/.0154) times your earnings. In the graph below, I graph Shiller's measures of the CAPE against this T.Bond PE from 1960 to 2016:

Shiller PE versus T.Bond PE

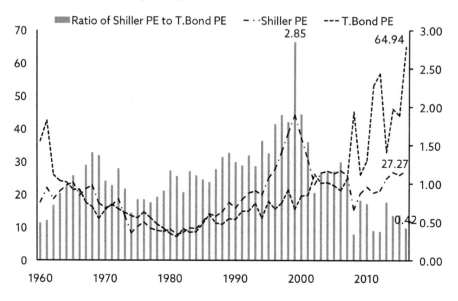

	Shiller PE	T.Bond PE	Shiller PE/T.Bond PE
1969–2016	19.79	20.69	1.10
1986–2016	24.31	25.50	1.17
1996–2016	27.28	31.02	1.11
2006–2016	23.45	40.53	0.66
2009–2016	23.15	41.35	0.60

I also compute a ratio of stock PE to T.Bond PE that will use as a measure of relative stock market pricing, with a low value indicating that stocks are cheap (relative to T.Bonds) and a high value suggesting the opposite. As you can see, bringing in the low treasury bond rates of the last decade into the analysis dramatically shifts the storyline from stocks being overvalued to stocks being undervalued. The ratio is at 0.42 right now, well below the historical average over any of the time periods listed, and nowhere near the 1.91 that you saw in 2000, just before the dot-com bust or even the 1.04 just before the 2008 crisis.

4. It's cash flow, not earnings that drives stocks

The old adage that it is cash flows, not earnings, that drives stocks is clearly being ignored when you look at any variant of PE ratios. To provide a sense of what stock prices look like, relative to cash flows, I computed a multiple of total cash returned to stockholders by companies (including buybacks) and compared these multiples to Shiller's CAPE in the graph below.

Here again, there seems to be a disconnect. While the CAPE has risen for the market, from 20.52 in 2009 to 27.27 in 2016, as stocks soared during that period, the Price to CF ratio has remained stable over that period (at about 20), reflecting the rise in cash returned by US companies, primarily in buybacks over the period.

Am I making the case that stocks are undervalued? If I did, I would be just as guilty as those who use CAPE to make the opposite case. I am not a market timer, by nature, and any single pricing metric, no matter how well reasoned it may be, is too weak to capture the complexity of the market. Absolutism in market timing is a sign of either hubris or ignorance.

Shiller PE versus Price/Cash Return for S&P 500

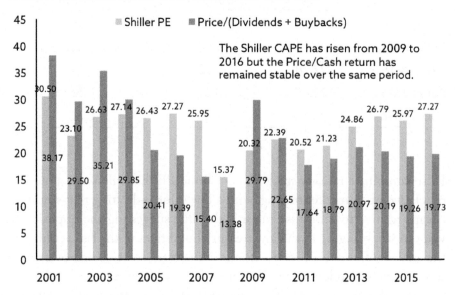

S&P 500 earnings and cash payout

The Market's Kryptonite

At this point, if you think that I am sanguine about stocks, you would be wrong, since the essence of investing in equities is that worry goes with it. If it's not the high CAPE that is worrying me, what is? Here are my biggest concerns, the kryptonite that could drain the market of its strength and vitality.

1. *The Treasury Alternative (or how much are you afraid of your central bank?)*: If the reason that you are in stocks is because the payoff for being in bonds is low, that equation could change if the bond payoff improves. If you are Fed-watcher, convinced that central banks are all-powerful arbiters of interest rates, your nightmares almost always will be related to a meeting of the Federal Open Market Committee (FOMC), and in those nightmares, the Fed will raise rates from 1.50% to 4% on a whim, destroying your entire basis for investing in stocks. As I have noted in earlier posts, where I have characterized the Fed as the Wizard of Oz ('The Fed and Interest Rates: Lessons from Oz') and argued that low rates are more a reflection of low inflation and anemic growth than the result of quantitative easing ('The Fed, Interest Rates and Stock

Prices: Fighting the Fear Factor'), I believe that any substantial rate rises will have to come from shifts in fundamentals, either an increase in inflation or a surge in real growth. Both of these fundamentals will play out in earnings as well, pushing up earnings growth and making the stock market effect ambiguous. In fact, I can see a scenario where strong economic growth pushes T.Bond rates up to 3% or higher and stock markets actually increase as rates go up.

2. *The Earnings Hangover*: It is true that we saw a long stint of earnings improvement after the 2008 crisis and that the stronger dollar and a weaker global economy are starting to crimp earnings levels and growth. Earnings on the S&P 500 dropped in 2015 by 11.08% and are on a pathway to decline again in 2016 and if the rate of decline accelerates, this could put stocks at risk. That said, you could make the case that the earnings decline has been surprisingly muted, given multiple crises, and that there is no reason to fear a fall off the cliff. No matter what your views, though, this will be more likely to be a slow-motion correction, offering chances for investors to get off the stock market ride, if they so desire.

3. *Cash flow Sustainability*: My biggest concern, which I voiced at the start of the year, and continue to worry about is the sustainability of cash flows. Put bluntly, US companies cannot keep returning cash at the rate at which they are today and the table below provides the reason why:

Year	Earnings	Dividends	Dividends + Buybacks	Dividend Payout	Cash Payout
2001	38.85	15.74	30.08	40.52%	77.43%
2002	46.04	16.08	29.83	34.93%	64.78%
2003	54.69	17.88	31.58	32.69%	57.74%
2004	67.68	19.407	40.60	28.67%	59.99%
2005	76.45	22.38	61.17	29.27%	80.01%
2006	87.72	25.05	73.16	28.56%	83.40%
2007	82.54	27.73	95.36	33.60%	115.53%
2008	49.51	28.05	67.52	56.66%	136.37%
2009	56.86	22.31	37.43	39.24%	65.82%

Year	Earnings	Dividends	Dividends + Buybacks	Dividend Payout	Cash Payout
2010	83.77	23.12	55.53	27.60%	66.28%
2011	96.44	26.02	71.28	26.98%	73.91%
2012	96.82	30.44	75.90	31.44%	78.39%
2013	107.3	36.28	88.13	33.81%	82.13%
2014	113.01	39.44	101.98	34.90%	90.24%
2015	100.48	43.16	106.10	42.95%	105.59%
2016 (LTM)	98.61	43.88	110.62	44.50%	112.18%

In 2015, companies in the S&P 500 collectively returned 105.59% of their earnings as cash flows. While this would not be surprising in a recession year, where earnings are depressed, it is strikingly high in a good earnings year. Through the first two quarters of 2016, companies have continued the torrid pace of buybacks, with the percent of cash returned rising to 112.18%. The debate about whether these buybacks make sense or not will have to be reserved for another post, but what is not debatable is this. Unless earnings show a dramatic growth (and there is no reason to believe that they will), companies will start revving down (or be forced to) their buyback engines and that will put the market under pressure. (For those of you who track my implied equity risk premium estimates, it was this concern about cash flow sustainability that led me to add the option of allowing cash flow payouts to adjust to sustainable levels in the long term.)

So, how do these worries play out in my portfolio? They don't explicitly but they do implicitly affect my investment choices. I cannot do much about interest rates, other than react, and I will stay ready, especially if inflation pressures push up rates and the fixed income market offers me a better payoff. With earnings and cash flows, there may be concerns at the market level, but I bet on individual companies, not markets. With those companies, I can do my due diligence to make sure that they have the operating cash flows (not just dividends or buybacks) to justify their valuations. If that sounds like a pitch for intrinsic valuation, are you surprised?

The Market Timing Mirage

Will there be a market correction? Of course! When it does happen, don't be surprised to see a wave of "I told you so" coming from the bubblers. A clock that is stuck at 12 o'clock will be right twice every day and I would urge you to judge these market timers, not on their correction calls, which will look prescient, but on their overall record. Many of them, after all, have been suggesting that you stay out of stocks for the last five years or longer and it would have to be a large correction for you to make back what you lost from staying on the sidelines. Some of these pundits will be crowned as great market timers by the financial press and they will acquire followers. I hope that I don't sound like a Cassandra but this much I know, from studying past history. Most of these great market timers usually get it right once, let that success get to their heads and proceed to let their hubris drive them to more and more extreme predictions in the next cycle. As an investor, my suggestion is that you save your money and your sanity by staying far away from market prognosticators.

ABOUT ASWATH DAMODARAN

Aswath Damodaran is a Professor of Finance at the Stern School of Business at New York University. He teaches the corporate finance and valuation courses in the MBA program as well as occasional short-term classes around the world on both topics. He received his MBA and Ph.D degrees from the University of California at Los Angeles. His research interests lie in valuation, portfolio management and applied corporate finance. His papers have been published in the *Journal of Financial and Quantitative Analysis*, the *Journal of Finance*, the *Journal of Financial Economics* and the *Review of Financial Studies*.

Professor Damodaran has written four books on equity valuation (*Damodaran on Valuation, Investment Valuation, The Dark Side of Valuation, The Little Book of Valuation*) and two on corporate finance (*Corporate Finance: Theory and Practice, Applied Corporate Finance: A User's Manual*). He also co-edited a book on investment management with Peter Bernstein (*Investment Management*) and he has two books on portfolio management – one on investment philosophies (*Investment Philosophies*) and one titled *Investment Fables*. His newest book, *Narrative and Numbers*, was published in January 2017.

The Greatest Bubble of All-Time?

BY BEN CARLSON

Thinking and acting long term for the long term is one of the few edges remaining in the markets. Bring up this idea and there will almost always be someone waiting to take the other side with the 'what about Japan?' argument.

Japan's two-and-half decade economic and market struggles make for some important lessons but most investors seem to have the wrong takeaways.

One of my favorite market history books is *Devil Take the Hindmost* by Edward Chancellor. The book provides one of the best historical accounts of financial speculation that I've read. Some of my favorite anecdotes and stats came from the section on the Japan real estate and stock market bubble from the 1980s:

- From 1956 to 1986 land prices increased 5000% even though consumer prices only doubled in that time.

- In the 1980s share prices increased 3x faster than corporate profits for Japanese corporations.

- By 1990 the total Japanese property market was valued at over 2,000 trillion yen or roughly 4x the real estate value of the entire United States.

- The grounds on the Imperial Palace were estimated to be worth more than the entire real estate value of California or Canada at the market peak.

- There were over 20 golf clubs that cost more than $1 million to join.

- In 1989 the P/E ratio on the Nikkei was 60x trailing 12 month earnings.

Over the next decade the Japanese stock market lost roughly 80% of its value (which is still far below that peak today):

Meb Faber also has a great chart on how truly massive the Japanese bubble was in terms of its CAPE valuation relative the US tech bubble:

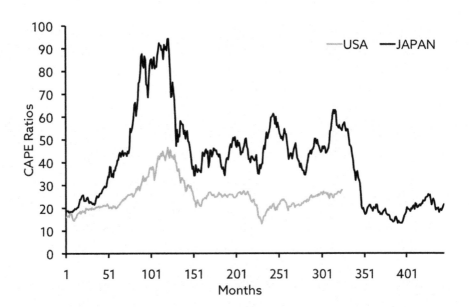

As crazy as things got in the tech bubble, those peak valuations were still a little less than half the peak valuations in Japan.

This was a bubble of massive scale in both stocks and real estate.

The returns also tell the story when you break them down by different periods from 1970 through 2015:

	Japan Large Caps	Japan Small Caps	EAFE	EAFE ex-Japan
Totals	8.96%	12.97%	9.45%	9.73%
1970–1989	22.43%	29.74%	16.26%	12.78%
1990–2015	−0.39%	1.56%	4.49%	7.44%

Indexes: MSCI Nomura, DFA Japan Small Caps, MSCI EAFE, MSCI EAFE ex-Japan

A $100,000 investment in Japanese large cap stocks in 1970 would have turned into $5.7 million by 1989. In small cap Japanese stocks that $100,000 would have grown to $18.3 million! Yet from 1990–2015 the same $100,000 would have turned into $90,400 and $149,000, respectively.

You can also see the affect Japanese stocks had on the foreign developed stock market performance by looking at the difference in returns between the EAFE and EAFE ex-Japan. Avoid Japan in the '70s and '80s and you would have been kicking yourself. Include it since then and you would be kicking yourself.

Japan has surely been a cautionary tale since 1990 but you have to take into account how truly insane the markets went to get to that point.

Here are some of the wrong lessons investors have taken away from Japan's bubble deflating:

- Buy and hold doesn't work. The truth is buy and hold doesn't always work over every single period. There almost have to be periods where buy and hold doesn't work, otherwise everyone would do it. If something worked all the time, eventually it wouldn't work because too many people would join in. This extreme example shows that buy and hold worked mighty well in one time frame but terribly in another. Still, in the overall period it looks like it still "worked." It really matters how you define your time frame. Both sides could claim victory on this one.

- The US is the next Japan. We have quite a ways to go to ever reach the speculative excesses that had to be worked off in Japan. Not to mention there are enormous differences in demographics, the diversity of the US economy and the immigration policy differences between the two countries.

And the right lessons:

- Never underestimate how far people can take the markets to the extremes. This works in both directions. The pendulum swings back and forth but always seems to go further than most would assume is possible. Japan offers what I would consider the largest bubble in history, but people have a habit of forgetting about these things and assuming they can't happen again.

- Valuations matter. Valuations don't work as a timing tool. If you tried to use them in Japan you probably would have gotten out of the market a decade before the peak. It's easy to say this in hindsight, but there were few scenarios where the late-1980s real estate and stock market valuations could have been validated going forward.

- Certainty rarely helps make good decisions. People were certain that Japan was going to zoom by the US and overtake it as the largest economy in the world. And who could blame them? Very few people predicted the other side of that one.

- Avoid home country bias. If you live in Japan and had all of your investments in Japanese stocks you've not only lived through a few decades of poor investment returns but also a slow growing economy.

- Avoid investing all of your money in a single asset class. Japanese government bonds returned over 6.1% per year from 1990–2015, far outpacing the stock market in that time.

- Diversification, as always, is the key to avoiding a blow-up. The entire point of diversification is to avoid having your entire portfolio in a Japan situation. The global stock market has done just fine since 1990 even when you include Japan in the results.

Source: *Devil Take the Hindmost: A History of Financial Speculation*

ABOUT BEN CARLSON

Ben Carlson is the Director of Institutional Asset Management at Ritholtz Wealth Management. He has spent his entire career managing institutional portfolios. He started out with an institutional investment consulting firm developing portfolio strategies and creating investment plans for various foundations, endowments, pensions, hospitals, insurance companies and high net worth individuals. More recently, he was part of the portfolio management team for an investment office that managed a large endowment fund for a charitable organization.

Ben is the author of the books *A Wealth of Common Sense: Why Simplicity Trumps Complexity in Any Investment Plan* and *Organizational Alpha: How to Add Value in Institutional Asset Management*.

Ben is the creator of the blog *A Wealth of Common Sense* and he is also a columnist for Bloomberg.

How Illiquid are Bond ETFs, Really?

BY DAVE NADIG

"Transcendent liquidity" is a somewhat silly-sounding phrase coined by the equally silly Matt Hougan, former CEO of ETF.com, to discuss the odd situation in fixed-income ETFs – specifically, fixed-income ETFs tracking narrow corners of the market like high-yield bonds.

But it's increasingly the focus of regulators and skeptical investors like Carl Icahn. Simply put: Flagship funds like the iShares iBoxx High Yield Corporate Bond ETF (HYG) trade like water, while their underlying holdings don't. Is this a real problem, or a unicorn?

Defining Liquidity

The problem with even analyzing this question starts with definitions. When most people talk about ETF liquidity, they're actually conflating two different things: tradability and fairness.

Tradability is actually a pretty simple concept: How well will the market let me get in or out of an ETF? And for narrow fixed-income ETFs (I'm limiting myself to corporates, in this analysis), most investors should be paying attention to the fairly obvious metrics, e.g., things like median daily dollar volume and time-weighted average spreads. By these metrics, a fund like HYG looks like the easiest thing to trade ever:

HYG Spread

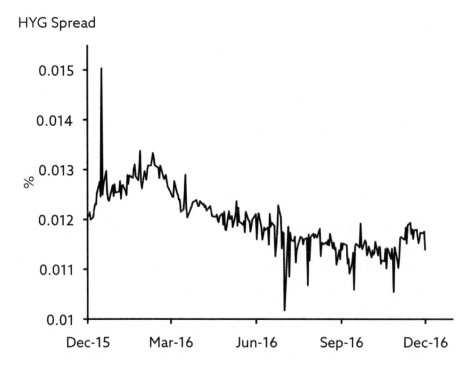

On a value basis, the average spread for HYG on a bad day of the past year is under 2 basis points. It's consistently a penny wide on a handle around $80, with nearly $1 billion changing hands on most days. That puts it among the most liquid securities in the world. And that easy liquidity is precisely what has the SEC – and some investors – concerned.

Fairness

But that's tradability, not fairness. Fairness is a unique concept to ETF trading. We don't talk about whether the execution you got in Apple was "fair." You might get a poor execution, or you might sell on a dip, but there's no question that your properly settled trade in Apple is "fair."

That's because Apple stock is always worth precisely what you pay for it. That's the entire function of the market – to determine the fair price for Apple based on the collective wisdom of buyers and sellers.

Of course, even Apple can get a bad print, and there are rules for breaking really erroneous trades, but for the most part, if Apple's down 10%, nobody considers it anything other than a bad day for Apple.

In an ETF, however, there is an inherent "fair" price – the net asset value of the ETF at the time you trade it – intraday NAV or iNAV. If the ETF only holds Apple and Microsoft, that fair price is easy to calculate, and is in fact disseminated every 15 seconds by the exchange.

But when the underlying securities are illiquid for some reason (hard to value, time-zone disconnects or just obscure), assessing the "fair" price becomes difficult, if not impossible.

If the securities in the ETF are all listed in Tokyo, then your execution at noon in New York will necessarily not be exactly the NAV of the ETF, because none of those holdings is currently trading.

Premiums & Discounts

In the case of something like corporate bonds, the issue isn't one of time zone, it's one of market structure. Corporate bonds are an over-the-counter, dealer-based market. That means the iNAV of a fund like HYG is based not on the last trade for each bond it holds (which could literally be days old), but on a pricing services estimate of how much each bond is worth. That leads to the appearance of premiums or discounts that swing to +/- 1%.

HYG Premium/Discount

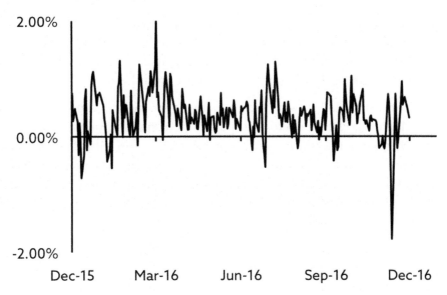

Compare that with the handful of basis points typical in the SPDR S&P 500 ETF (SPY | A-98).

SPY Premium/Discount

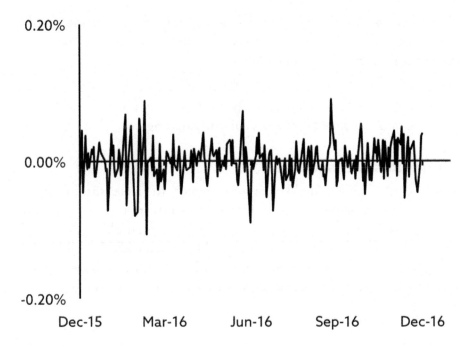

Importantly, this is over the last year, which has been a pretty calm market for HYG. During crisis periods, HYG can spike a premium or discount of more than 10%. The reason is pretty simple: profit motive.

ETFs only trade in line with their underlying securities because authorized participants (APs) can make or dispose of new shares through the creation and redemption process. If there is a premium, they can sell at that premium and make new shares by delivering the underlying. They can do the opposite if the ETF is at a discount: buying the cheap ETF shares and returning them to the issuer for a basket of underlying securities. In each case, they're buying low and selling high.

But if the underlying market can't actually handle the volume implied in making or redeeming shares, the APs will let the price drift until the gap is so wide they're positive they can make money. And because there are multiple APs all trying to book a profit, when the gap widens and stays wide, it points to costs and risks that may not be obvious just looking at the numbers.

In the case of corporate bonds, the reality is that the underlying markets simply can't absorb large amounts of creation and redemption activity, so the flow of money into or out of the ETFs will almost always force a premium or discount. Take a look at 2012 in HYG – a period where we had a nice clean opinion shift on junk bonds to analyze:

HYG: Premiums vs. Flows

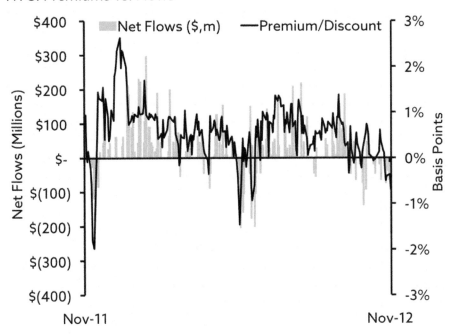

You can see in the fall of 2011, everyone wanted out, and the fund traded to a 2% discount. Then everyone wanted back in for months, and it consistently traded at premiums as high as 2.5%. Then in mid-2012, again, people wanted out, and boom, right back to a 1.5% discount.

It's critical to note that all of these premiums and discounts happened while HYG continued to trade a penny wide. So there was enormous liquidity – it was just centered around a price that was "too high" or "too low."

This connect can have two explanations: Either the ETF is in fact "right" and is serving as the price discovery vehicle, or the NAV is "right" and the ETF is overpriced. It's not possible to prove without question which is going on, but I tend to side with the market. If billions of dollars are going to change hands at a price that's "too high," I think the billions of dollars are the market, and this is price discovery on an illiquid market.

The Underlying Problem

So just how illiquid are corporate bonds? Very. Consider the dollar value traded in HYG, and the dollar value traded in all of the underlying bonds it owns, combined, in a two-month window in fall 2015:

HYG $ Value Traded vs. Underlying

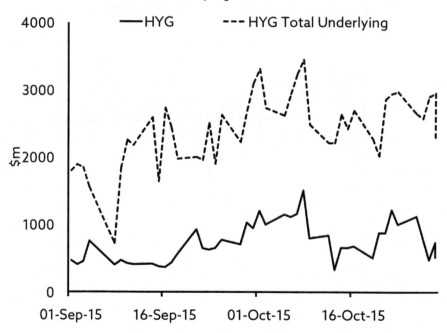

While it's not the case that HYG trades more than the overall portfolio consistently, it's definitely the case that HYG provides much more accessible liquidity than the underlying bonds – and that's what makes the SEC and skeptics nervous, because that on-screen liquidity can dry up. Looking under the hood, the average daily dollar volume in the underlying bonds is just $3.4 million:

HYG Holdings: Avg. Daily $ Volume

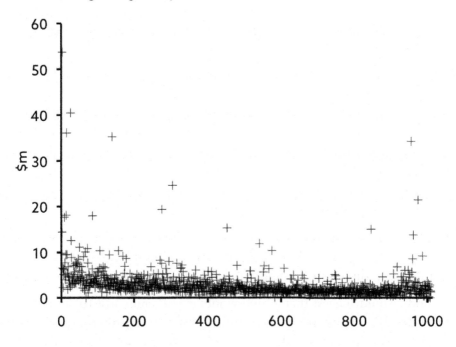

In fact, if you look at the largest corporate bond ETFs, the picture doesn't get much better when you go into the investment-grade or short-duration space. The most liquid ETF, the iShares iBoxx $ Investment Grade Corporate Bond ETF (LQD), has underlying bonds that on average only trade $4.7 million per day, and short-term bonds, represented by the Vanguard Short-Term Corporate Bond ETF (VCSH), fare worst of all.

Ticker	Weighted Avg. Underlying Daily $ Vol.	Weighted Avg. Day-to-Trade	AUM	AD$V
HYG	$3,445,647	9.7	$15.3 B	$750 M
JNK	$3,638,273	9.3	$11.3 B	$406 M
CORP	$3,025,376	3.2	$250 M	$4.3 M
LQD	$4,737,805	10	$24.8 B	$385 M
VCSH	$2,471,173	16.3	$10.7 B	$53 M
IWM	$20,974,893	4.7	$26.5 B	$4.2 B

By comparison, the ETF on the equity side you'd expect to be truly illiquid – the iShares Russell 2000 ETF (IWM) – has underlying holdings that are an order of magnitude more traded on a daily basis than the most liquid bonds issued by the largest companies in the world.

Days-to-Trade

I've tossed an additional stat in the table above – days-to-trade. The SEC has proposed that mutual funds and ETFs manage the liquidity of their portfolios such that 85% of a fund consists of positions that could be liquidated within seven days without market impact. (An interesting test, especially for bond funds. After all, the whole point of bonds is to collect interest until maturity and get your capital back.)

Larger funds with big positions will obviously be more impacted than small funds, so when you combine the huge size of a fund like VCSH with the relative illiquidity of its holdings, it's hard to see how they pass the test.

Nobody would suggest that a fund would ever literally just try and dump an entire day's worth of volume into the market, day after day, and not impact prices. Instead, a trade impact model would map out a much longer time window to unwind a position. So the true time to unwind the average VCSH position might actually be more like 40 or 60 days (and on top of that, VCSH is just a share class of a larger mutual fund).

Does that mean every corporate bond fund closes? Probably not – I expect the SEC to revise their proposal several times before anything becomes the law of the land. However, it will likely highlight the real problem here – the broken nature of the bond market (and possibly make it worse, if significant assets must be liquidated to comply with the rules).

Already only about one-third of corporate bonds actually trade more than once every few months, and just 11% of the listed corporate ponds represent almost 60% of the actual dollars trading in corporate bonds, according to Tabb group.

The dealer market has collapsed, and all that's left are investors trading the same few bonds back and forth, leaving pricing services guessing with bigger and bigger margins of error on the real value of illiquid debt.

That's the real problem. And it's not one the SEC can fix by targeting "transcendent liquidity" in ETFs.

ABOUT DAVE NADIG

Dave Nadig is CEO of ETF.com. Previously, he was Director of Exchange-Traded Funds at FactSet Research Systems, a position he took when ETF.com divested itself of its ETF data business. Prior to that sale, Dave was ETF.com's Chief Investment Officer, and has served in the company since 2008. He returned to ETF.com as CEO in November 2016.

Dave has been involved in researching, reporting and analyzing the investment management industry for more than 20 years, and recently co-authored a definitive book on ETFs, *A Comprehensive Guide To Exchange-Traded Funds* for the CFA Institute.

As a managing director at Barclays Global Investors, Dave helped design and market some of the first ETFs. With partner Don Luskin, he went on to found MetaMarkets.com, a revolutionary transparent mutual fund company that pushed fund disclosure to the top of the SEC agenda. As co-founder at Cerulli Associates in the early '90s, he conducted some of the first research on fee-only financial advisors and the rise of indexing. Dave is widely quoted in the financial press, a regular speaker at finance conferences, and publishes a widely read blog at ETF.com. He has an MBA in finance from Boston University.

Everyone is a Closet Technician

BY JOSH BROWN

This will be a fairly controversial post, but I'm going to say it anyway.

Everyone is a closet technician. *Everyone*. And in a panic or a market correction, this truism is even more, um, *truistic*.

First, what is a technician? Here's my own handy definition, I think you'll like it: A technician is someone who cuts right to the chase and studies *actual* prices and behavior instead of puzzling over *the causes* of prices and behavior like everyone else.

Discussing causes is a much more interesting conversation and it gets you on all the talk shows. Discussing price – the sum total of all investor fear and greed, both historical and real-time – tells you the truth about what's actually going on, it does not offer an opinion.

Besides, price dictates what the news is, not the other way around. Consider:

If the price of Yahoo common stock was higher today than it was when Marissa Mayer first joined, she'd be hailed as the second coming of Lou Gerstner or Steve Jobs, not a punching bag whose business initiatives and party-throwing receipts are dissected in the tech press each week.

If the S&P had rallied throughout 2015 instead of flatlined, we'd be throwing a parade for the plunging oil price, not freaking out over it.

When Apple shares trade higher over the course of a given quarter, it is the highest quality stock in the world with a vast opportunity ahead to take on automobiles, TV, virtual reality and the Internet Of Things. When Apple falls over the course of a quarter, Apple is a Too Big To Sail rotting old galleon, with a caretaker captain who can't turn it and a crew who can't innovate in time to save the ship from capsizing.

When a social media startup prices a financing round at a higher level than the previous one, it is heralded as The Next Big Thing, a disruptor on its way to riches and glory. If that same startup does a down-round, it's already dead; all that's left to happen is the exodus of the talent and the selling off of the servers.

Price creates the reality for investors, because investors take their behavioral cues from price and the media fashions its headlines from it.

Technicians believe that there is wisdom in price. That *price has memory*. That people who were inclined to buy at a certain price are somewhat likely to buy there again. Unless something's changed, in which case their failure to re-buy (or buy more) at that formerly significant price level can be interpreted in an entirely new way – what was once an area of *support* on a chart becomes an area of *resistance*.

Technicians believe that trends persist, in both directions, because market participants act on "news" at different speeds and act more boldly (or fearfully) the longer a particular movement in the markets goes on. This is why bull markets often end with a buying crescendo in the riskiest securities. Risk appetites grow as an uptrend persists, the desperation to participate gets stronger, it does not fade gently.

This is also why selling becomes more fierce when the market is at a 20% discount to its previous high than when it is at a 10% discount. *"How could it be even more urgent to sell down 20% than it is down 10%?"* someone would ask. Going by fundamentals, it isn't. But investors only pay lip service to fundamentals. What they are more concerned with is owning less of the thing that looks stupid to own – and the lower it goes, the stupider it looks.

Unless you buy into the idea that rational behavior rules the investment markets. In which case, you're reading the wrong writer.

Technicians find truth in price, rather than attempting to parse the impossibly conflicted and intentionally obscured opinions of the commentariat. Technicians find meaning in the actual buying and selling activity happening today, not in the dusty old 10Q's of 90 days ago or in the projected estimates being bandied about among the discounted cash-flow analysis crowd on the sell-side.

But above all, technicians respect the power of sentiment more than their fundamentalist counterparts. And sentiment, after all, is how valuations actually come to be – the P in the PE Ratio or the PEG Ratio or the P/B calculation. In the real equation, the only one that counts, the P is what pays, not the E, not the EG and certainly not the B. Buffett would tell you the B (book value) is what pays over time (the market going from a voting machine to a weighing machine). But Buffett can afford to ride it out, having permanent capital under management and an ocean of insurance premiums sloshing in over the transom every hour of the day. Most market players do not.

What I am not saying is that *price is truth*.

Price lies all the time. Facebook can be valued at $40 billion and then $20 billion and then $200 billion inside of a four-year period of time. Which of these prices is the truth? None of them. But all of them were momentarily true, until they were rendered a lie, and a new truth was forged in the fires of the marketplace. Sunrise, sunset. Prices change and, with them, the truth itself.

Everyone knows this, but many have not come to terms with it yet. Or it would hurt their career to admit that buyers and sellers will pretty much lead the way and our opinions will closely follow behind.

This is how you get a chief investment strategist whose year-end price target is raised and lowered throughout the course of the year as the stock market rises and falls. The strategist starts out with a view, and then tailors her view to match the reality being generated by price. Or fails to do so and is eventually fired.

Have a look at the commentary surrounding oil. It falls from 80 to 70, and Wall Street's seers say 65 is possible. It falls to 60 and then the downside target is lowered to 40. Over the last 30 days, we've seen Goldman Sachs and Morgan Stanley take their oil price targets down to 30 and 20 respectively, just as its price was slicing through the 30's on its way to the 20's.

If it continues to fall, you will hear calls for oil priced in the teens! If it stabilizes and trades higher, you will see targets lifted. I ask you – which is the truth, then? Price itself or the commentary around why price should be at this level or that?

When analysts and strategists adjust their views, they couch their targets in the language of fundamental developments, potential events and the news of the moment. But in truth, what they are really doing is extrapolating what's happening today into the fog of tomorrow. Another way of saying extrapolation is to say that they are betting on a continuation or a reversal of *trend*. Trend is a technical concept, hence, they are dressing up technical calls in the wardrobe of fundamentals, and speaking in the language of the high priests of finance: profits, revenues, cash flows, capacity, demand, market share.

In the midst of the October 2014 correction, I said that the fundamentally inclined start looking at charts and "levels" when uncertainty strikes.

> **Fundamentalists will believe in technical analysis.** But only temporarily. You'll hear people who analyze balance sheets and income statements start to use the term "oversold" not understanding that they're accidentally referring to RSI data, something you couldn't pay them to pay attention to during a market uptrend. There are no atheists in a foxhole and there are no pure fundamentals guys in a correction. Believe me, they're all looking at the charts. Even Bruce Berkowitz.

It happens each time and it is always hilarious. They'll deny it: "The market is wrong" or "these are mispriced securities."

The technician is one step ahead: "The market is not wrong, it has a current set of collective beliefs that are subject to change. Price will tell us when there is a likelihood that this change is at hand."

Let's get back to the "Why?" question and the fact that technicians don't waste their time with it.

There's a cognitive foible common to human beings known as the Hindsight Bias. As investors, there's nothing we like to do more than looking back at an event that's just taken place and reciting the reasons for what caused it as though they were obvious to us in advance. "I knew it all along! It was China, Greece, the Fed, that magazine cover, Obama, the rate hike."

The hindsight bias is a strong tendency in humans because it helped our ancestors survive on the Savannah – telling stories of cause and effect to the next generation so no one gets themselves killed trying to harvest a wasps' nest full of honey or having intercourse with a saber-toothed tiger. Early humans who did not carry the trait to tell these stories did not pass their genes on, they were stung to death or had their genitals ripped off.

We, on the other hand, *did* have ancestors who concerned themselves with explaining recent events. They survived and passed these tendencies down to us. And after a million years of bee stings and foiled tiger rape, we carry on the same tradition.

But it's all made up.

No one knows why a million market participants thought one thing on a Monday and something completely different on the following Thursday. The fundamentalists will share their explanations and guesses with anyone willing to listen. The technicians will take these reasons in stride and focus on what is happening, not why. The why will always be much more apparent after the fact, after it no longer matters. We still don't have the agreed-upon why nailed down for the Crash of '29, the Crash of '87 or even the Great Financial Crisis of a decade ago. We have theories and arguments and half-truths and politically-charged polemics.

But price did its thing regardless.

It always will.

Your favorite fundamentalist is adjusting his insights accordingly.

ABOUT JOSH BROWN

Josh Brown is a New York City-based financial advisor and the CEO of Ritholtz Wealth Management.

He is also the author of the books *Backstage Wall Street* and *Clash of the Financial Pundits* from publisher McGraw-Hill. In addition, he serves on the advisory board of financial technology firm Riskalyze as well as CNBC's Financial Advisor Council.

In 2015, he was named to the *Investment News* "40 Under 40" list of top financial advisors.

THE BEHAVIORAL
SIDE OF
INVESTING

Even God Would Get Fired
as an Active Investor

BY WESLEY R. GRAY

Empirical asset pricing research can sometimes get monotonous because you end up circling back relentlessly to the same conclusions: value, momentum, trend-following are all interesting, and yet, markets are remarkably competitive (perhaps not efficient). But, *sometimes*, research uncovers absolutely stunning and counter-intuitive results – and this is where things get truly exciting. The study below is what we consider "exciting" research because the results are so profound (at least to us).

Our bottom line result is that perfect foresight has great returns, but gut-wrenching drawdowns. In other words, an active manager who was clairvoyant (i.e. "God"),* and knew ahead of time exactly which stocks were going to be long-term winners and long-term losers, would likely get fired many times over if they were managing other people's money.

Question: If God is omnipotent, could he create a long-term active investment strategy fund that was so good that he could never get fired?

The answer is striking: *God would get fired.*

Let that settle in a bit.

The Design of Our "God" Study

Starting on 1/1/1927 we compute the five-year "look ahead" return for all common stocks for the 500 largest NYSE/NASDAQ/AMEX firms. For

---

* We mean no offense by the use of the term and this could be construed as a single deity, multiple deity, or whatever fulfills your definition of an entity or concept that is all powerful and all knowing.

simplicity, we eliminate any firms that do not have returns for a full 60 months.* We look at gross returns and all returns are total returns including dividends. Next we create decile portfolios based on the *forward* five-year compound annual growth rate (CAGR).

We rebalance the names in the portfolio on January 1st of every fifth year. The first portfolio formation is January 1, 1927 and is held until December 31, 1931. The second portfolio is formed on January 1, 1932 and held until December 31, 1936. This pattern repeats every fifth year. To be clear, this is a non-investable portfolio that would require one to know with 100% certainty the performance of the top 500 stocks over the next five years.

We are explicitly engaging in look-ahead bias.

Returns are analyzed from 1/1/1927 to 12/31/2016. Portfolios are value-weighted returns for month t are weighted using the market capitalization at the end of month t-1. All returns are gross of transaction costs, taxes, and fees.

Performance of the Decile Portfolios

We first look at the decile portfolios rebalanced every five years. These portfolios highlight what perfect foresight can achieve. The Decile 10 portfolios represent value-weighted portfolios sorted on future top five-year performers and the Decile 1 represent value-weighted portfolios sorted on future bottom five-year performers. The compound annual growth rates for the ten decile look-ahead portfolios are mapped in the chart below.

As expected, a portfolio formed on the names that have the best five-year performance, have the best five-year performance. Duh. God would compound at nearly 29% a year, in theory. In practice he would run into capacity constraints and own the entire market (see my piece 'Mission Impossible: Beating the Market Forever' for details).

We know God would knock it out of the park, but the details are interesting...

---

*   Results are similar with or without this assumption.

CAGR by Ranking Decile (1927–2016)

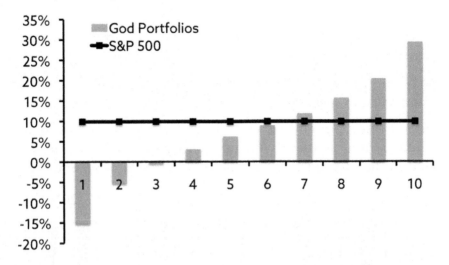

The results in all charts and tables in this chapter are hypothetical results and are NOT an indicator of future results and do NOT represent returns that any investor actually attained. In fact, these returns are EXPLICITLY IMPOSSIBLE TO ACHIEVE. Indexes are unmanaged, do not reflect management or trading fees, and one cannot invest directly in an index. Additional information regarding the construction of these results is available upon request. Note: these results were updated on 6/14/2017.

Summary Statistics

Here we investigate some statistics and charts on the performance of the five-year look ahead portfolio.

- God_Best = Top decile five-year winner portfolio

- God_Worst = Bottom decile five-year loser portfolio

- SP500 = S&P 500 Total Return Index

First, the raw summary statistics:

Summary Statistics	God_Best	God_worst	SP500
CAGR	29.37%	−15.32%	9.87%
Standard Deviation	22.41%	29.13%	18.96%
Sharpe Ratio (RF=T-Bills)	1.12	-0.53	0.42
Worst Drawdown	−75.94%	−99.99	−84.59%

The 29% CAGR is obviously awesome for the look-ahead portfolio. Expected.

The volatility is high on the God_Best portfolio – higher than the market. Interesting.

The Sharpe Ratio is above 1, but not by much. A far cry from the 2+ Sharpe Ratios touted by some hedge funds. Interesting.

But how about them drawdowns! The perfect foresight portfolio eats a devastating 76% drawdown (Aug 1929 to May 1932). But the pain doesn't end there, here is chart of the drawdowns on the portfolio over time:

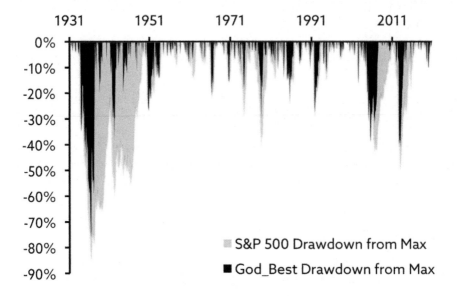

And here are some details on the drawdowns:

Drawdown Rank	Drawdown	Date of Prior Peak	Date of Low	Date of Recovery	Peak to Low (days)	Low to Recovery (days)	Peak to Peak (days)
1	−75.94%	8/30/1929	5/31/1932	6/30/1933	1005	395	1400
2	−40.75%	5/31/2008	2/28/2009	3/31/2010	273	396	669
3	−39.51%	8/31/2000	9/30/2001	9/30/2003	395	730	1125
4	−38.54%	2/27/1937	3/31/1938	12/31/1938	397	275	672
5	−30.81%	12/31/1973	9/30/1974	4/30/1975	273	212	485
6	−27.69%	8/31/1987	11/30/1987	1/31/1989	91	428	519

Drawdown Rank	Drawdown	Date of Prior Peak	Date of Low	Date of Recovery	Peak to Low (days)	Low to Recovery (days)	Peak to Peak (days)
7	−26.94%	5/31/1946	11/30/1946	4/30/1948	183	517	700
8	−24.61%	11/30/1980	9/30/1981	8/31/1982	304	335	639
9	−21.53%	2/28/1962	6/30/1962	1/31/1963	122	215	337
10	−20.13%	3/31/1934	7/31/1934	4/30/1935	122	273	395

Clearly, even a "perfect" long portfolio can bring a long-only investor a ton of pain.

How About We Create A Hedge Fund Managed by God?

In the analysis above we highlight that God's long portfolio can endure enormous drawdowns and enhanced volatility. But perhaps we can leverage God's perfect foresight and go long the known winners and short the known losers. Slam dunk, right?

Let's investigate…

• God's long/short portfolio is constructed as follows:

Long God_Best and short God_Worst, rebalanced monthly.

The following portfolios are examined:

• God L/S = Long five-year decile winners; short five-year decile losers

• SP500 = S&P 500 Total Return index

Summary Statistics

Here are the high-level stats:

Summary Statistics*	God L/S	SP500
CAGR	46.23%	9.87%
Standard Deviation	20.08%	18.96%
Sharpe Ratio	1.86	0.42
Worst Drawdown	−47.28%	−84.59%

Yowza!

Clearly, the ultimate hedge fund does amazingly well – 46% CAGRs would have you owning the world's stock market in short order. Obviously, this sort of return is not possible over a long period – even if someone had perfect "Biff-like" foresight.

Yet, check out the worst drawdown on the PERFECT hedge fund – 47%+. Incredible. And it gets better…

The next chart shows the time series of drawdowns over time for the God L/S portfolio. Certainly not a cake walk!

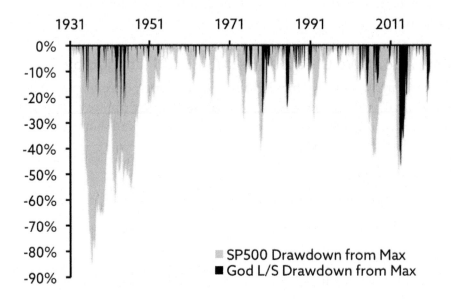

Let that chart sink in a bit. Multiple opportunities to lose 20%+ over time. Clearly not riskless. But it gets even better…

As many investment pros painfully recognize, managing money is often not about absolute performance, but relative short-term performance. Another truism is that the S&P 500 ends up *being everyone's benchmark*, regardless of the strategy – especially during a long-term bull market!

Let's look at the one-year relative CAGR over time between God L/S and the S&P 500, on the next page.

What the chart highlights is that even GOD HIMSELF would get fired multiple times over. The relative performance on God's hedge fund is often abysmal and he'd surely make the cover of Barron's or the WSJ on multiple occasions throughout his career. The passive index would eat his lunch on multiple occasions — often getting beaten by 50 percentage points — or more — on multiple occasions!

These results highlight the fickle nature of assessing relative performance over short horizons. We've shown this quantitatively, but Ben Carlson talks about the challenge of short horizon thinking in his piece 'Short-Term Thinking With Long-Term Capital', and Meb Faber highlighted that investors are terrible at timing active investments in his article 'Institutional Investors, They're Just Like Us!'.

1-Year Rolling CAGR Relative to S&P 500

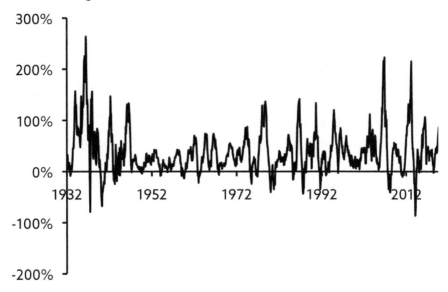

What the chart highlights is that even GOD HIMSELF would get fired multiple times over. The relative performance on God's hedge fund is often abysmal and he'd surely make the cover of Barron's or the WSJ on multiple occasions throughout his career. The passive index would eat his lunch on multiple occasions — often getting beaten by 50 percentage points — or more — on multiple occasions!

These results highlight the fickle nature of assessing relative performance over short horizons. We've shown this quantitatively, but Ben Carlson talks about the challenge of short horizon thinking here, and Meb Faber recently highlighted that investors are terrible at timing active investments.

Conclusions

The famous quote attributed (wrongly) to Keynes is spot-on: **Markets can remain irrational longer than you can remain solvent!**

This study also highlights a truism for all active investors: **Active investors MUST have a long-horizon!**

Good luck out there…[*]

ABOUT WESLEY R. GRAY

After serving as a Captain in the United States Marine Corps, Dr. Gray earned a PhD, and worked as a finance professor at Drexel University. Dr. Gray's interest in bridging the research gap between academia and industry led him to found Alpha Architect, an asset management that delivers affordable active exposures for tax-sensitive investors. Dr. Gray has published four books and a number of academic articles. Wes is a regular contributor to multiple industry outlets, to include the following: Wall Street Journal, Forbes, ETF.com, and the CFA Institute. Dr. Gray earned an MBA and a PhD in finance from the University of Chicago and graduated magna cum laude with a BS from The Wharton School of the University of Pennsylvania.

---

[*] Huge thanks to Arturo B., an old Chicago PhD (1980) we met at the Nantucket Project, who suggested we explore this research question…

Outperforming by Underperforming

BY COREY HOFFSTEIN & JUSTIN SIBEARS

In our opinion, the *Alpha Architect* post titled 'Even God Would Get Fired as an Active Investor', should be required reading for those looking to better understand active investing. Quoting from the post:

> "Our bottom line result is that perfect foresight has great returns, but gut-wrenching drawdowns. In other words, an active manager who was clairvoyant, and knew ahead of time exactly which stocks were going to be long-term winners and long-term losers, would likely get fired many times over if they were managing other people's money.
>
> Question: If God is omnipotent, could he create a hedge fund that was so good that he could never get fired? No. It turns out even God would most likely get fired as an active investor."

We covered this post and extended the analysis in the piece, 'God, Buffett, and the Three Oenophiles'.*

For us, the clear takeaway is that there is no holy grail to investing. Asset classes and strategies will always ebb and flow through periods of out and underperformance. No strategy will beat the market year in and year out. It just won't happen.

If we want to outperform standard benchmarks over the long-run, we must hold positions that are different from the benchmark. Holding different securities creates tracking error. And tracking error inevitably means that short-term underperformance will occur.

Even Warren Buffett, by many measures the best investor in US history, is not immune from this truth.

---

* blog.thinknewfound.com/2016/02/god-buffett-three-oenophiles

From March 1980 to October 2016, Berkshire Hathaway A Shares delivered an annualized total return of 20.2%, 9.7% more per year than the Vanguard S&P 500 Index Fund (ticker: VFINX) over the same period. Berkshire's risk-adjusted returns are more than 60% better than the Vanguard benchmark (Sharpe ratio of 0.74 vs. 0.46) and the stock's alpha is an astonishing 1.0% per month.

While there are many traits that likely contribute to his success, the one that we find most awe-inspiring is his discipline. The graph below plots Buffett's one-year rolling relative performance vs. VFINX. Positive (negative) numbers indicate that Berkshire beat (trailed) the index fund over the prior 12 months.

One Year Rolling Relative Performance – BRK-A vs. VFINX

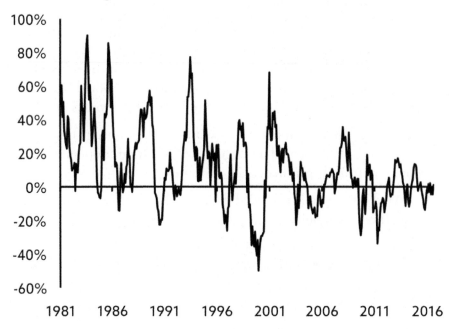

Data Source: Yahoo Finance. Calculations by Newfound Research. Past performance does not guarantee future results.

Even the great Warren Buffett has lagged the market one out of every three years. And in many cases this underperformance was significant. There have been ten separate episodes where Berkshire underperformed the index fund by more than 10% over a one-year period and many periods of underperformance lasted significantly longer.

Peak	Trough	Recovery	Peak-to-Trough Underpeformance	Time to Breakeven
Oct-85	Jan-86	Sep-87	18.1%	1.9 Years
Oct-89	Sep-90	Feb-93	25.6%	3.3 Years
Feb-96	Nov-96	Mar-98	22.1%	2.1 Years
Jun-98	Feb-00	Jul-02	54.4%	4.1 Years
Sep-02	Sep-05	Feb-08	29.9%	5.4 Years
Oct-08	Apr-12	Ongoing	32.7%	8.1 Years

Data Source: Yahoo Finance. Calculations by Newfound Research. Past performance does not guarantee future results.

Through these difficult times, Buffett and Berkshire have remained committed to their investment process.

However, a manager committed to his or her investment process is only one ingredient for client success. Investing is a team sport where managers must be committed to their process and investors must be committed to their managers. This is precisely why we believe setting appropriate expectations is so critical. The Buffett case study points to a number of key lessons for expectations management.

1. Underperformance is not bad.

In isolation, underperformance, while it may be frustrating, is not necessarily evidence that a strategy is broken or should be abandoned. One way we can think of Berkshire is as a portfolio of two different assets. The first asset is simply the S&P 500. The second asset is a long/short stock picking strategy driven by Buffett.

When the long/short stock picking strategy delivers a positive return, Berkshire will beat the market and vice versa.

Would most investors abandon the first part of the portfolio (the S&P 500) just because it loses money over a given period of time? Probably not. Firing Buffett just because the long/short strategy loses money (i.e. Berkshire underperforms the market) would be no different.

2. In fact, occasional underperformance is to be expected.

For a manager to beat the market, they must be different than the market. Being different means taking on tracking error. Buffett could reduce the risk of significantly lagging the market by allocating less to his "long/short" portfolio.

However, doing so would come at the cost of less outperformance (assuming that Buffett isn't able to further increase his investment skill). As an example, for Buffett to cut the probability of lagging the market by 10%+ in half, he would have to sacrifice about half of his annualized outperformance.

Furthermore, risk-free outperformance is impossible over the long-run. To the extent that such opportunities actually exist, they would most likely be arbitraged away very quickly. Even low-risk outperformance would require unrealistic degrees of investing skill. As an example, assume that Buffett was able to improve the performance of his "long/short" portfolio to such as a degree that the probability of underperformance in any given year was just one in ten (instead of the one in three that we see in the actual data). This would imply such massive long-term outperformance that Berkshire's market-cap would currently exceed the rest of the S&P 500 combined.

3. Placing "stop-losses" on managers is counterproductive.

While formal stop-losses on active strategies/managers may be rare, many investors operate with them in the form of annual or semi-annual performance reviews, eliminating managers when they underperform by too wide a margin.

These stop-losses are counterproductive because they are almost guaranteed to be tripped, even by strategies exhibiting statistically significant alpha. Going back to the early 1980s, the "long/short" component of Buffett's portfolio has had an annual return of 9.8% with volatility of 20.5%. Using this data, we can compute the probability of hitting certain informal stop-loss triggers over various holding periods.

How to read the table: The highlighted row (10% Loss Trigger) and column (Five-Year Holding Period) means that the probability of seeing at least one year of 10%+ underperformance during a five-year holding period is 60%. If an investor would fire a manager for this degree of underperformance, they would more likely than not fire Buffett within the next five years.

Loss Trigger	Holding Period (Years) 1	2	3	4	5	6	7	8	9	10
2.5	24.7	47.0	61.8	72.0	79.8	85.4	89.5	92.3	94.4	95.9
5.0	23.4	41.7	55.2	66.0	73.8	79.9	84.6	88.2	90.9	93.1
7.5	19.9	35.7	48.5	59.1	67.2	73.8	78.9	83.1	96.2	89.1
10.0	16.7	30.7	42.1	51.9	60.0	66.5	72.2	76.8	80.5	83.8
12.5	13.8	25.8	36.0	44.7	52.5	58.9	64.6	69.6	73.8	77.4
15.0	11.4	21.5	30.1	37.8	45.2	51.2	56.8	61.9	66.2	70.0
17.5	9.2	17.6	24.9	31.7	38.0	43.7	48.8	53.7	57.8	62.0
20.0	7.3	14.2	20.3	26.2	31.5	36.4	41.4	45.6	49.5	53.2

Data Source: Yahoo Finance. Calculations by Newfound Research. Past performance does not guarantee future results. All figures %.

We see that the probability of hitting certain pain points is quite high, especially when the tolerance for relative underperformance is low and holding periods are long. And remember, this data is calibrated to reflect perhaps the best equity investor in history.

4. Tracking error can be managed in the portfolio construction process.

Of course, none of this is meant to imply that investors have to just accept tracking error to the market. Different investors will have different tolerances for tracking error. In all likelihood, these tolerances will also change over time.

These preferences are best addressed in the portfolio construction process where asset classes and strategies are blended together. In fact, we explicitly account for the pain of tracking error to popular benchmarks when we construct our own strategic portfolios.

5. Understanding when a strategy may excel and when it may struggle should be a core part of the diligence process.

We believe that by better understanding the potential magnitude and duration of underperformance, as well as the types of markets in which it is most likely to occur, investors can start to exhibit Buffett-like discipline.

To illustrate the initial steps of this type of analysis, let's turn to an example that is near and dear to our hearts: momentum-based tactical equity.

We built a simple momentum strategy with a methodology similar to that used in AQR's article 'Back in the Hunt.' Using data from Fama and French, we measure the trailing one-year return for large-cap US equities. The allocation to equities ranges from 0% to 200% (i.e. no exposure to a 2x levered position) depending on how the most recent one-year return compares to past one-year returns. When the current return is above the historical median, the strategy will have more than 1x exposure to the equity market. When the current return is below the historical median, the strategy will have less than 1x exposure to the market. At each point in time, we only use data that would have been available to investors at that time (i.e. the median is computed on a rolling bias). This methodology is used to avoid hindsight bias.

Note: We use a 0% to 200% range for equity exposure as this allows us to both under and overweight equities. This mirrors the recommendation that clients use our tactical equity strategies – which can shift equity exposure between 0% and 100% – as a pivot between their stock and bond allocations. This pivot usage also allows for both the under and overweighting of equities.

This simple, hypothetical strategy beats the market by 86bps per year with a 20% reduction in the duration and magnitude of drawdowns. *(All returns are backtested and hypothetical and this hypothetical strategy was created and performance was calculated in connection with the writing of this analysis. Index returns include the reinvestment of dividends and are gross of all fees and expenses. Past performance does not guarantee future results.)*

Like with Buffett, we see that the long-term, risk-adjusted outperformance of the strategy does not eliminate the possibility of significant short-term underperformance.

One Year Rolling Relative Performance – BRK-A vs. VFINX and Tactical Momentum Timing vs. Market

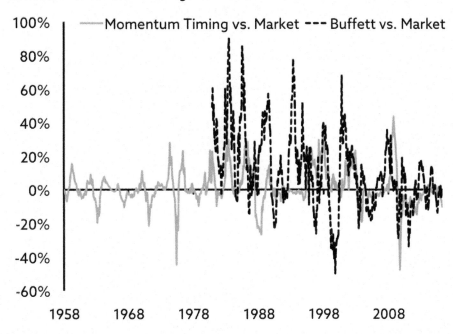

Data Source: Yahoo Finance, Fama/French data website. Calculations by Newfound Research. Past performance does not guarantee future results. The momentum timing strategy is hypothetical and backtested. It reflects the reinvestment of dividends and does not include the payment of any fees or expenses. The index is not representative of any Newfound strategy or index.

The recent underperformance of the momentum strategy (+1.8% YTD through 9/30 compared to +7.5% for the market) is well within historical bounds.

Digging into the data a little deeper, we see that the tactical momentum strategy tends to outperform when the market is down and when the market is up big (30% or more). In more mild up markets, the strategy tends to underperform.

1-Year Returns: Market vs. Momentum Timing

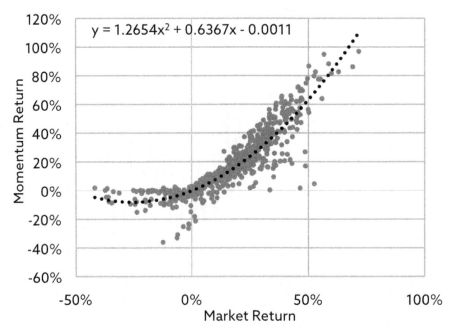

$$y = 1.2654x^2 + 0.6367x - 0.0011$$

Data Source: Yahoo Finance, Fama/French data website. Calculations by Newfound Research. Past performance does not guarantee future results. The momentum timing strategy is hypothetical and backtested. It reflects the reinvestment of dividends and does not include the payment of any fees or expenses. The index is not representative of any Newfound strategy or index.

We can also use the data to set expectations around the risk-mitigating properties of momentum-driven tactical equity. We see below that the hypothetical strategy generally does a solid job protecting against large losses. In most cases, downside protection tends to kick in when the market is down between –10% and –20%.

That being said, we also see that momentum is not a perfect risk management tool. In 1987, the strategy actually would have been down more than the market. This makes sense since momentum is by definition backward, not forward, looking, and the strategy could be up to 2x levered. As a result, it is not equipped to deal with unexpected rapid sell-offs like what was seen in 1987. This is exactly why we advocate for a holistic approach to risk management, incorporating complementary tools like high quality fixed income, tactical asset allocation, and alternative strategies (e.g. managed futures).

Drawdown

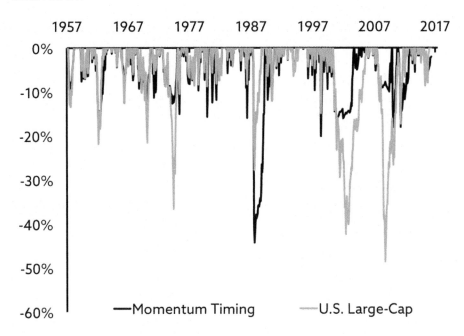

Data Source: Yahoo Finance, Fama/French data website. Calculations by Newfound Research. Past performance does not guarantee future results. The momentum timing strategy is hypothetical and backtested. It reflects the reinvestment of dividends and does not include the payment of any fees or expenses. The index is not representative of any Newfound strategy or index.

Conclusion

No investor, not even the great Warren Buffett, is immune from bouts of short-term underperformance. Short-term underperformance is a necessary, if annoying, reality for investors seeking to outperform the market on a risk-adjusted basis.

Rather than engage in the fruitless pursuit of constant outperformance, investors should seek to fully understand how their asset classes, strategies, and managers may perform in different market regimes. This analysis can help users distinguish between benign underperformance and underperformance that may be a symptom of a serious problem (i.e. a manager deviating from his stated investment process).

Underperformance that occurs in environments where a strategy is expected to struggle may be good evidence of a manager staying true to his process.

ABOUT COREY HOFFSTEIN & JUSTIN SIBEARS

Corey Hoffstein is a frequent speaker on industry panels and contributes to ETF.com, ETF Trends, and Forbes.com's Great Speculations blog. He was named a 2014 ETF All Star by ETF.com.

Corey holds a Master of Science in Computational Finance from Carnegie Mellon University and a Bachelor of Science in Computer Science, cum laude, from Cornell University.

Justin Sibears is a frequent speaker on industry panels and contributes to ETF Trends.

Justin holds a Master of Science in Computational Finance and a Master of Business Administration from Carnegie Mellon University as a well as a BBA in Mathematics and Finance from the University of Notre Dame.

The Confounding Bias for Investment Complexity

BY JASON HSU & JOHN WEST

Key Points

- A preference for complexity is almost hardwired into investors, their agents, and asset managers because the intuition is that a complicated investment landscape requires a complex solution; a complex strategy also supports a higher fee from both agents and managers.

- Research shows that simple, low-turnover and complex, high-turnover strategies perform similarly on a before-fee basis, suggesting the former may have the advantage after tax.

- Simplicity leads to better investor outcomes not because simplicity in and of itself produces better investment returns, but because a simple strategy encourages investors to own their decisions and to less frequently overreact to short-term noise.

> *Simplicity is a great virtue but it requires hard work to achieve it and education to appreciate it. And to make matters worse: complexity sells better.*
>
> — Edsger W. Dijkstra[*]

Our tenure in the investment business has made us keenly aware of a profound investor bias toward complexity. In this article, we examine the reasons for the bias, which we believe are behavioral in nature. One

[*]   Edsger W. Dijkstra was a Dutch computer scientist and winner of the Turing Prize in 1972 for fundamental contributions to developing programming languages.

reason is the rationalization by asset managers that to charge higher fees requires offering more complex strategies. A similar line of reasoning may also influence those who recommend managers: consultants and advisors. A second reason for the bias is the rationalization by investors that a complicated strategy is necessary to beat the market. Each explanation has implications – biased toward the negative – for an investor's long-term performance.

Complexity Can Confound Performance

In contrast to the overwhelming pressure from all sides in advancing complexity, our experience, as well as our research and that of others, supports the virtues of a simple approach. For example, in 2009, DeMiguel, Garlappi, and Uppal demonstrated that numerically optimized portfolios using various expected return models generally perform no better than a simple equal-weighted approach.

An example of our research in this area, the article 'A Survey of Alternative Equity Index Strategies' by Chow et al. (2011), is an analysis of the most popular smart beta strategies. We found that simple, low-turnover and complex, high-turnover strategies all work roughly the same on a gross-of-fee basis, suggesting on a net-of-fee basis the simple, low-turnover strategies might have an advantage.

Looking beyond the story telling that characterizes various investment philosophies, the long-term return drivers of many complex smart beta strategies are tilts toward well-known factor/style exposures, such as value, size, and low volatility. Each exposure is a natural outcome of breaking the link between portfolio weighting and price, and of the requisite rebalancing. Indeed, little data or research supports one "best" way to construct an exposure (e.g., value or low volatility) that maximizes the factor premium capture. Complex constructions in the historical backtest appear to mostly guarantee higher turnover, higher management fees, and potentially worse out-of-sample returns.

So, if complexity doesn't naturally lead to outperformance, why do asset managers persist in offering increasingly complicated strategies to investors, and why do investors persist on investing in them? Allow John to tell an illustrative parable.

John's Fish Tale

The oceans in which fish hide from fisherman are amazingly complex ecosystems. The circumstances leading to a successful day (or not) on the water are almost innumerable. The fish obviously have to be at the fishing spot. But that's probably less than half the battle. A veritable mosaic of tides, currents, sunlight, moonlight the night before, available prey, time of day, tackle, and so on, influence the catch. With such myriad factors, it's no small wonder that tens of thousands of fishing products jam their way into even the smallest of tackle shops.

But, as an avid deep sea angler, I can attest to catching twice as many tuna with the simplest of lures than all of the rest combined. The lure? The innocuous-looking cedar plug pictured in **Exhibit A**. Simple? Yes! For crying out loud, it's a piece of lead attached to an unpainted piece of wood with one lousy hook! It looks like an industrial part. Sexy and complex? Most certainly not.

Exhibit A. The Remarkably Simple Cedar Plug Lure

Imagine you get the itch to catch some tuna. Perhaps it's your first foray into tuna fishing so you decide to delegate the task to an expert charter boat captain. But which one? You stroll along the dock and ask each captain how they catch tuna. The first presents a cedar plug, just like the one in Exhibit A, and tells you, "I go out to where I see signs of fish and then I drag four of these lures behind the boat at a steady speed until I catch some. Then I keep doing it until it's time to head in." The second captain displays a dozen tackle drawers filled with lures resembling those shown in **Exhibit B** and proclaims, "Tuna are very elusive. I have perfected a system over many years that optimizes my lure selection among 60 lures, five sunlight conditions, seven moon phases, and six different tidal stages. I troll, adjusting my speed in five-minute intervals, based again on very extensive testing." You hate long boat rides, but are starving for fresh sashimi. Which captain would you choose?

Exhibit B. The Psychedelically Hued Synthetic Lure

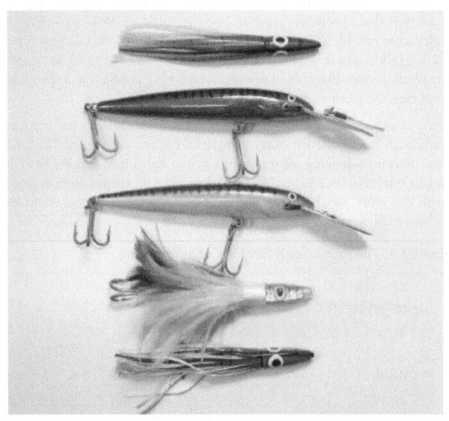

Most sashimi lovers would pick the second captain. The ocean is big, and multiple factors influence the tuna catch. It seems like the higher-calibrated approach would be the way to go. But I can tell you (admittedly anecdotally, as I'm still waiting for Research Affiliates to approve my request for a more exhaustive scientific survey!) that it would probably yield a lower catch.

Investors' Preference for Complexity

Complexity likewise appeals to investors because the markets that drive securities prices, like the teeming and mysterious ocean, are deep and complex. It only stands to reason (right?) that a sophisticated strategy is a requirement for mastering and benefiting from the intricate web of financial markets and asset classes. The globally integrated investment markets and economies are anything but simple, so it would not at first appear that a simple strategy could carry the day. The belief that simple relationships exist is absolutely counterintuitive to most casual – and sometimes, not so casual – market observers.

Persuading an investor that a complicated strategy – often derived through data mining (i.e., back testing historical data until it produces what can be viewed as a signal) – is unlikely to perform as expected, can be a real challenge. The air of scientific authority exuded by PhDs who scribble differential calculus equations as fast as Charles Schultz drew *Peanuts* comic strips gives just that much more "credibility" to black box approaches.

And agents compound the issue. Advisors or consultants hired to help investors make sense of the noise in the market and to find the skilled managers are also incented by the complex. Charging a respectable fee for a manager selection process that puts the client into a simple, straightforward strategy is not so easily justified to the client. The very natural, economic, and rational response to this conundrum is to recommend (in the case of advisors) or to offer (in the case of managers) the more complex strategies. Asset managers certainly find it easier to charge a higher fee for a complex strategy (i.e., flashier lures with molded plastic and psychedelic paints) than for a simple strategy (i.e., unpainted cedar plugs).

Simplicity vs. Complexity: Why Does It Matter?

The point we wish to make is not that simple strategies always perform on par or better than the complex ones. Our point is that complexity creates a problem for investors, which is unfortunately largely self-induced: complexity encourages performance chasing. We can better understand why this is true if we apply Daniel Kahneman's construct of System 1 and System 2 thinking, as described in his book *Thinking, Fast and Slow* (2011). System 1 thinking is described as automatic, emotional, and passive, whereas System 2 thinking is effortful, deliberate, and active.

When presented with a complicated investment strategy, an investor engages first in System 1 thinking, which triggers an immediate response such as "I don't understand the strategy. Clearly I'm not as smart as this asset manager." System 2 thinking then takes over, and the investor's response transitions to "Because this asset manager is so smart, her strategy must outperform. I think I'd like to invest with this asset manager." The investor then feels safe and comfortable in making a rational delegation decision. At the end of the day, the acceptance of complexity is related to calming the investor's ego – at least, temporarily.

This thinking works in reverse, however, if the asset manager fails to perform as expected. Neuroscientists, such as Knutson and Peterson (2004), have demonstrated that the anticipation of receiving money triggers a dopamine reward in the brain. Conversely, the anticipation of losing money removes that pleasurable experience. When this happens, the System 1 response is "Yikes! I need to fire this manager so I can stop feeling so bad." Then the System 2 response kicks in with the rationalization, "I didn't make the decisions that created the underperformance, so I'm not to blame." Because the investor doesn't "own" making the "bad" decisions, it is easier to end the relationship.

Following this line of thinking, investors are liable to sell a complicated, poorly understood strategy with little provocation as soon as performance takes a nose dive. The long-term result is apt to be especially disappointing performance if the investor becomes ensnared in a whipsaw pattern of buying and selling at all the wrong times. Our research (Hsu, Myers, and Whitby [2015]) shows that the frequent hiring and firing of managers based on short-term performance is the primary cause of investor underperformance. Our findings are valid even when investors hire skilled managers. Although never a good idea for investors to make buy and sell decisions based on short-term performance, a poorly understood strategy can compound the harm.

An example of how Kahneman's System 1 and 2 thinking supports an investor's choice of a simple behavioral factor strategy, let's consider the following scenario. Upon first encountering the strategy, the investor's System 1 thinking blurts, "This strategy is intuitive to me. I am a smart investment professional. This will work." But soon his System 2 thinking chimes in, "I don't need to pay a high fee for this. I just need a low-cost implementer of systematic strategies to execute on my chosen factor." When the strategy fails to perform as expected, the investor's System 1 reaction is, "I am not wrong. The market is wrong." Then his System 2 thinking kicks in, reasoning, "I vetted the research behind this factor carefully. Short-term performance is noisy. This exposure will work well in the long run." The investor chooses to hold his strategy.

Investors in simple strategies generally trade in and out of their managers infrequently. Our research finds that these investors tend to achieve meaningfully better results versus their counterparts who actively turn over managers due to recent performance. Simplicity leads to better investor outcomes not because simplicity in and of itself produces better investment returns, but because a simple strategy forces investors to own their decisions and to be less likely to overreact to short-term noise.

A Simple Choice

We believe that making investors aware of the benefits of selecting a simple approach, strategy, or model is important. Unnecessary complexity is costly, not only directly (i.e., fees), but indirectly. Complexity can dampen investor understanding, which can lead to poor investment decision making so that an investor's long-term financial goals are not achieved. As Steve Jobs said, "Some people think design means how it looks. But of course, if you dig deeper, it's really how it works" (Wolf, 1996). If a simple design works, ample evidence suggests that the investor benefits by choosing simplicity.

References

Chow, Tzee Mann, Jason Hsu, Vitali Kalesnik, and Bryce Little. 2011. 'A Survey of Alternative Equity Index Strategies.'" *Financial Analysts Journal*, vol. 67, no. 5 (September/October): 37–57.

DeMiguel, Victor, Lorenzo Garlappi, and Raman Uppal. 2009. 'Optimal Versus Naïve Diversification: How Inefficient Is the 1/N Portfolio Strategy?' *Review of Financial Studies*, vol. 22, no. 5 (May): 1915–1953.

Hsu, Jason, Brett Myers, and Brian Whitby. 2016. 'Timing Poorly: A Guide to Generating Poor Returns While Investing in Successful Strategies.' *Journal of Portfolio Management*, vol. 42, no. 2 (Winter): 90–98.

Kahneman, Daniel. 2011. *Thinking, Fast and Slow*. New York: Farrar, Straus and Giroux.

Knutson, Brian, and Richard Peterson. 2005. 'Neurally Reconstructing Expected Utility.' *Games and Economic Behavior*, vol. 52, no. 2 (August): 305–315.

Wolf, Gary. 1996. 'Steve Jobs: The Next Insanely Great Thing.' *Wired Magazine* (February)

ABOUT JASON HSU & JOHN WEST

Jason is chairman and CIO of Rayliant Global Advisors and vice chairman of Research Affiliates. He is at the forefront of the smart beta revolution and is a recognized innovator and thought leader in the space. Building on his pioneering work on the RAFI™ Fundamental Index™ approach to investing with Rob Arnott in 2005, he has published numerous articles on the topic, notably including 'A Survey of Alternative Equity Index Strategies', which won a 2011 Graham and Dodd Scroll and the Readers' Choice Award from CFA Institute, and 'The Surprising Alpha from Malkiel's Monkey and Upside-Down Strategies', which won the 2013 Bernstein Fabozzi/Jacobs Levy Award for Outstanding Paper in the *Journal of Portfolio Management*. In 2005 and 2013, he received the William F. Sharpe Award for Best New Index Research, which is awarded by Institutional Investor Journals, for his research on smart beta.

Jason has authored more than 40 peer-reviewed articles. He is an associate editor of the *Journal of Investment Management* and serves on the editorial board of the *Financial Analysts Journal, Journal of Index Investing, Journal of Investment Consulting,* and *Journal of Investment Management.*

Jason graduated with a BS *summa cum laude* in physics from the California Institute of Technology, was awarded an MS in finance from Stanford University, and earned his PhD in finance from UCLA.

John West is Managing Director and Head of Client Strategies at Research Affiliates, where he is responsible for maximizing the investor impact of Research Affiliates' insights and products. Previously, John was vice president of research and senior consultant at Wurts & Associates (now called Verus), a consulting firm on the West Coast for institutional investors.

John holds the Chartered Financial Analyst® designation and is a member of CFA Institute and CFA Society Los Angeles. He is also a co-author of *The Fundamental Index: A Better Way to Invest* (Wiley 2008). He graduated from the University of Arizona with a BS in finance.

Would You Bail on Warren Buffett? Investors Make that Mistake all the Time

BY JOHN REESE

Even the best ideas flounder some of the time.

The overwhelming majority of top mutual fund managers – those who had the best record over a decade – spent at least three years lagging well behind others during that time, according to Joel Greenblatt, a hedge fund manager and author of *The Little Book That Still Beats the Market*.

More than three-fourths of these star managers spent three years at the very bottom of the performance ladder, something short-term-minded investors tend to flee. But too bad for them. These managers all outperformed over the longer run – the decade-long period through the end of 2009.

That is a lesson for all of us. Sometimes success means sticking to your plan even if things are not working out so well at the moment. Given the constant ups and downs of the market, strategies that outperform all the time should be looked at with skepticism. Investing is a long-term commitment that involves risk as well as reward. This is relevant today because active managers have had a few very difficult years in beating their benchmarks; and the flow into passive investing continues to be a trend.

Ups and downs

Take a look at the top-performing US diversified stock fund of the 1980s, Ken Heebner's $3.7 billion CGM Focus Fund. It was up 18% annually, but the average investor lost 11% a year because impatient people kept leaving and coming back based on the ebbs and flows of short-term returns. When performance is up, investors pour their money into a fund. And when it is down, they sell.

CGM was up a stunning 80% in 2007, focusing on a super-concentrated basket of 25 stocks. Investors put $2.6 billion into it in 2008 – the year the financial crisis sent global stock markets into a tailspin. CGM fell 48% that year, and predictably, investors pulled $750 million from the fund in 2009. But 2009 would prove to be a rebound both for the markets and the fund's performance. Over the past one, three, five and even ten-year periods, CGM Focus Fund has trailed the S&P 500 Index, but over the past 15 years it is still outperforming the S&P 500 by two percentage points and is ranked fourth overall in its fund category by Morningstar.

Wise investors would resist the impulse to flee. A portfolio of hand-selected stocks or managers is supposed to deliver something the benchmark index does not. When the benchmark does well, the portfolio might trail it. When the benchmark does poorly, the portfolio might outperform. Reaching for returns that beat the benchmark requires the emotional discipline to stick with an investment manager through thick and thin, knowing that no strategy can beat the market all the time.

Even Warren Buffett, the billionaire head of Berkshire Hathaway who is followed by millions of investor devotees, has bad years. Newfound Research analyzed Buffett's track record and found he underperforms the broad index about once every three years and he's had ten periods when he missed the benchmark by 10% or more over a significant period of time.

But those who stuck with Buffett through the years have benefited from being patient. From March 1980 to October 2016, Berkshire Hathaway's A shares delivered annual return of 20.2%, nearly 10% more annually than the S&P 500, according to Newfound Research. On Tuesday 13 December 2016, A shares of Berkshire Hathaway briefly passed $250,000 for the first time, a landmark eclipsed 54 years and a day after Buffett bought his first shares of then-textiles company Berkshire in 1962.

This dispels the notion that short-term underperformance is bad. After all, would you fire Buffett from managing your portfolio just because one of his current investments has taken a hit lately? Buffett famously says investors should take advantage of downturns to buy what others are selling.

Risk-free outperformance isn't possible. A manager with an expected annual outperformance of 3% has a four-in-five chance of lagging the benchmark by 10% or more at least once in a five-year period, according to Newfound Research's analysis. Shifting in and out of that manager's fund just because he underperforms would be costly. As hedge fund manager Greenblatt notes, there isn't a correlation between a manager's three-, five- and ten-year records in the past and how they will do in the future. What's more important is understanding the strategy and having the confidence to follow it long term.

But truth be told, many investors, including professionals, can find it difficult to grasp the facets of an investment strategy and tend to overweight recent returns. (For the record, Berkshire Hathaway is up 25% in 2016 – 15% since November – with the Trump election boom in bank stocks a big part of that move up.)

Even if investors do understand what goes into the investment approach, it can be hard to distinguish between luck and skill. This is why indexing can be a good option for many investors, assuming they can stick with an index through the market's good and bad times. However, for those investors who seek outperformance over the market and are willing to tolerate relative underperformance over periods of time, the key ingredient to success is staying committed to an active strategy or manager when it underperforms.

In the end, investors should understand and accept how much risk they are willing to take and build a portfolio that tries to match it and stick to it for the long term. An investor who understands there is a certain element of risk to investing is more likely not to panic when markets go awry.

ABOUT JOHN REESE

John Reese is the co-founder and CEO of Validea Capital Management manager of an ETF that utilizes the stock-picking strategies of Wall Street Legends. He is a frequent speaker on quantitative investing and holds two US patents for automated stock analysis.

John is also the founder of Validea.com and the author of *The Guru Investor: How to Beat the Market Using History's Best Investment Strategies*. He holds his Master's in Business Administration from Harvard Business School and a computer science degree from the Massachusetts Institute of Technology. John co-founded Validea Capital in 2004.

Thinking Can Hurt Your Investments

BY LARRY SWEDROE

One of the most common arguments I hear against passive investing (which we can define as the use of a systematic approach to gain exposure to a factor or factors) goes like this: How can good management that is "thinking" not be superior to "nonthinking" management? I have found most investors harbor a strong opinion on this question.

Fortunately, we have evidence to help settle this matter. We'll begin with a study by Lewis Goldberg, a psychology professor, who in 1968 analyzed the Minnesota Multiphasic Personality Inventory (MMPI) test responses of more than 1,000 patients and their final diagnoses as neurotic or psychotic.

Goldberg used this data to develop a simple model to predict the final diagnosis based on the MMPI test results. He found that, out-of-sample, his model had a 70% accuracy rate. He then gave the MMPI scores to experienced as well as inexperienced clinical psychologists and asked them to diagnose the patient. Goldberg found that his simple model outperformed even the most experienced psychologists.

Taking it one step further, Goldberg reran the test, this time providing the clinical psychologists with the model's predictions. Goldberg was shocked that, while their performance did improve, they still underperformed the model, even armed with the benefit of its predictions.

The conclusion one might draw is that the results of quantitative models may be a performance ceiling from which humans are more likely to subtract (due to our behavioral biases, such as overconfidence) than exceed.

But, does the field of investing produce the same results in the contest of man versus machine?

Man Vs. Machine: Hedge Funds

Campbell Harvey, Sandy Rattray, Andrew Sinclair and Otto Van Hemert provide evidence on the subject with their December 2016 paper, 'Man vs. Machine: Comparing Discretionary and Systematic Hedge Fund Performance'.

They analyzed and contrasted the performance of systematic hedge funds, which use rules-based strategies involving little or no daily intervention by humans, with the performance of discretionary hedge funds, which rely on human skills to interpret new information and make the day-to-day investment decisions.

The study covered the period 1996 through 2014, and included data on more than 9,000 macro and equity hedge funds. To adjust returns for exposure to common factors, they used stock factors (beta, size, value and momentum) and bond factors (term and credit), as well as FX carry and volatility.

Investors have a clear preference for discretionary funds, given they make up about 70% of the hedge fund universe and control approximately 75% of the assets under management. However, the authors found no evidence to support such a preference.

For equity hedge funds, they found both that, after adjusting for exposure to well-known risk factors, risk-adjusted performances were similar, and that for discretionary funds (in aggregate), more of the average return and volatility of returns can be explained by risk factors.

In addition, when looking at what they called the "appraisal ratio" (the ratio of the average risk-adjusted return to its volatility), the authors found that systematic funds outperformed 0.35 to 0.25. For macro funds, they found systematic funds outperformed discretionary funds both on an unadjusted and on a risk-adjusted basis. The appraisal ratios were 0.44 for systematic funds and just 0.31 for discretionary funds. They concluded "the lack of confidence in systematic funds is not justified."

Systematic Strategies Protect Investors (From Themselves)

In their excellent book, *Quantitative Value*, Wesley Gray and Tobias Carlisle provide further support for the power found in systematic, quantitative investing. They write that the objectiveness of the approach acts as a shield, protecting us against our own biases, while also acting as a sword, allowing us to exploit the cognitive biases of others.

To make this point, they presented the following example from Joel Greenblatt. Greenblatt's firm, Gotham Capital, had compounded at a phenomenal rate of 40% annually, before fees, for the ten years from Gotham's formation in 1985 to its return of outside capital to investors in 1995.

In his own book, *The Little Book That Beats the Market*, Greenblatt describes an experiment he conducted in 2002. He wanted to know if Warren Buffett's investment strategy could be quantified. He studied Buffett's annual shareholder letters and developed his "magic formula," which he published.

Gray and Carlisle show that study after study has found "the model is the ceiling of performance from which the expert detracts, rather than the floor to which the expert adds. Even Greenblatt has said the he cannot outperform the Magic Formula."

We can perform another test in the ongoing battle of "machine (systematic) versus man (discretionary)" by examining the relative performances of two leading providers of passively managed funds, Dimensional Fund Advisors (DFA) and Vanguard. (Full disclosure: My firm, Buckingham, recommends DFA funds in constructing client portfolios.)

The following table shows the percentile rankings compiled by Morningstar for the 15-year period ending Dec. 7, 2016. Note that Morningstar's data contains survivorship bias, as it compares only returns of the funds that have survived the full period.

What's more, that bias is significant, because about 7% of actively managed funds disappear every year, with their returns being buried in the mutual fund graveyard. Thus, the longer the period, the worse the survivorship bias becomes. At 15 years, it's quite large.

Fund	15-Year Morningstar Percentile Ranking
Domestic	
Vanguard 500 Index (VFIAX)	28
DFA US Large (DFUSX)	29
Vanguard Value Index (VVIAX)	31
DFA US Large Value III (DFUVX)	4
Vanguard Small Cap Index (VSMAX)	28
DFA US Small (DFSTX)	20
DFA US Micro Cap (DFSCX)	13
Vanguard Small Cap Value Index (VISVX)	55
DFA US Small Value (DFSVX)	6
Vanguard REIT Index (VGSLX)	38
DFA Real Estate (DFREX)	43
International	
Vanguard Developed Markets Index (VTMGX)	31
DFA International Large (DFALX)	38
DFA International Value III (DFVIX)	8
DFA International Small (DFISX)	18
DFA International Small Value (DISVX)	1
Vanguard Emerging Markets Index (VEIEX)	43
DFA Emerging Markets II (DFEMX)	24
DFA Emerging Markets Value (DFEVX)	2
DFA Emerging Markets Small (DEMSX)	1
Average Vanguard Ranking	36
Average DFA Ranking	16

Ranking Results

The average 15-year ranking of the seven Vanguard index funds put them in the 36th percentile. The average 15-year ranking of the 13 passively managed

DFA funds put them in the 16th percentile, meaning they outperformed 84% of surviving funds. If Morningstar were to account for survivorship bias, these rankings would almost certainly be considerably higher.

It's also important to note the rankings are based on pretax returns. In most cases, index and other passively managed funds will be more tax efficient, due to their typically lower turnover. And ETF versions would further enhance the tax efficiency of index funds.

Another important observation is that the highest rankings earned by the DFA funds were in the very asset classes that proponents of active management say are the most inefficient (and thus where discretion can add the most value): international small and small value stocks, and emerging market equities.

In fact, both DFA's international small value fund (DISVX) and their emerging market small-cap fund (DEMSX) achieved a first-percentile ranking. This comparison provides strong evidence against the argument that actively managed funds are more likely to outperform in "inefficient" markets. In reality, that is just another myth the mutual fund industry tries to perpetuate, as is the superiority of the discretionary (man) over the systematic (machine) approach.

ABOUT LARRY SWEDROE

Larry Swedroe is a principal and the director of research for Buckingham Strategic Wealth, an independent member of the BAM Alliance. Previously, he was vice chairman of Prudential Home Mortgage.

Larry was among the first authors to publish a book that explained the science of investing in layman's terms, *The Only Guide to a Winning Investment Strategy You'll Ever Need*. He has since authored seven more books: *What Wall Street Doesn't Want You to Know* (2001), *Rational Investing in Irrational Times* (2002), *The Successful Investor Today* (2003), *Wise Investing Made Simple* (2007), *Wise Investing Made Simpler* (2010), *The Quest for Alpha* (2011) and *Think, Act, and Invest Like Warren Buffett* (2012).

He has also co-authored seven books about investing. His latest work, *Your Complete Guide to Factor-Based Investing*, was co-authored with Andrew Berkin and published in October 2016.

He has also had articles published in the *Journal of Accountancy*, *Journal of Investing*, *AAII Journal*, *Personal Financial Planning Monthly* and *Journal of Indexing*. Larry has made appearances on national television shows airing on NBC, CNBC, CNN and Bloomberg Personal Finance.

Larry holds an MBA in finance and investment from New York University, and a bachelor's degree in finance from Baruch College in New York.

How to Avoid the Problem of Short-Termism

BY CULLEN ROCHE

If I had to pinpoint the biggest problem for most asset allocators I would probably say short-termism. Short-termism is the tendency to judge financial markets in periods that are so short that it results in higher fees, higher taxes and lower average performance. We've become accustomed to judging the financial markets in quarterly or annual periods which contributes to this short-termism, but some context will show that this makes very little sense.

This has become an increasingly problematic reality for the modern asset allocator as we are bombarded with investment options, the 24-hour financial news cycle and are regularly told that we're stupid if we can't "beat the market" (even though 80%+ of the pros consistently fail to beat the market also). The result has been a dramatic decline in the average holding period of stocks. In 1940 the average stock was held for seven years, whereas today the average stock is held for one month! As I've noted before, I suspect all of this information and "news" is actually making us worse investors as it's feeding on our behavioural biases.

The arithmetic of global asset allocation clearly shows that more activity leads to higher taxes, higher fees and lower average returns, however, asset allocators are constantly falling victim to the myth that more activity leads to more control or better results. In fairness, this short-termism is understandable. No one likes to work for years earning their savings only to see it decline in value as the markets shift daily, monthly and annually. **So, how can we be better prepared to overcome the problem of short-termism? You just have to arm yourself with a bit of knowledge regarding the process of asset allocation so you put the problem of time in the proper context.**

Average Stock Holding Period (Months)

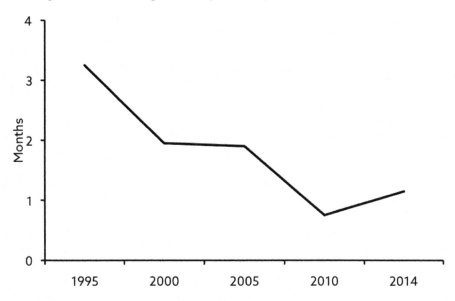

Source: Orcam Financial Group

As I noted in my new paper on portfolio construction, the allocation of savings is ultimately about asset and liability mismatch.* Cash lets us protect perfectly against permanent loss risk and maintain certainty over being able to meet our short-term spending liabilities, however, because it loses purchasing power it leaves us exposed to this risk in the long term. Cash feels safe in the short term, but in the long term it is the riskiest asset because it is guaranteed to decline in value relative to inflation. We can extend the duration of our financial assets to better protect against the risk of purchasing power loss, however, this increases the odds of permanent loss risk (the risk of being forced to take a loss at an inopportune time) and not having the funds when you need them.

Thinking of your savings in terms of a specific duration can be extremely helpful for overcoming the problem of short-termism. For instance, we know that cash is essentially a zero duration asset that will lose purchasing power over the long term so if you have no temporal flexibility allocating

---

* 'Understanding Modern Portfolio Construction' (papers.ssrn.com/sol3/papers.cfm?abstract_id=2740027)

your savings then your duration is zero and you should remain in cash. On the other hand, if you wanted to reduce your risk of purchasing power loss you could buy a bond aggregate fund which pays about 2% every year and has a duration of about 5.5 years. You might not beat the rate of inflation, but you'll do better than cash thanks to your temporal flexibility. Of course, you need to be able to put the funds away for 5.5 years to ensure high odds that you'll get your principal back at that time.

The stock market is what makes all of this tricky since the stock market doesn't have a specific duration like a bond does. In the paper I used a rough heuristic technique calculating the break-even point on a range of stock market declines in an attempt to calculate the stock market's sensitivity to price changes. I arrived at a duration of 25 years which I think is both quantitatively satisfactory and intuitively correct since the global stock market tends to have a very low probability of multi-decade bear markets.[*]

This puts things in a nice perspective for us because it allows us to allocate our assets in a way that properly contextualizes our asset and liability mismatch problem. For instance, we can now run a simple calculation using an aggregate bond index with duration of 5.5 years and the total stock market with duration of 25 years:

$$PD = (S \times 25) + (B \times 5.5)$$

Where PD = Portfolio Duration, S = % stock allocation and B = % bond allocation.

Here's a basic cheat sheet for thinking about this across different time periods:

Portfolio Allocations to Stocks and Bonds

	Portfolio Duration (Years)				
	5	10	15	20	25
Stocks	0%	25%	50%	75%	100%
Bonds	100%	75%	50%	25%	0%

---

[*] This is clearly an imperfect, but sufficient approach for understanding duration in a diversified portfolio.

By quantifying the concept of time within our portfolios we're able to become more comfortable with the way we allocate the assets. We're able to increase the certainty in the way we balance that asset and liability mismatch. And importantly, what this exposes is a crucial reality – when we're dealing with stocks and bonds we're dealing with inherently medium-term and long-term instruments which means that this rat race of short-termism is completely inconsistent with the actual structure of these instruments. After all, you'd never judge the performance of a two-year CD inside of a one-month period, but that's the equivalent of what someone is doing when they judge stock market performance based on a one-year period.

By putting the concept of duration in the proper context you can improve the odds that you won't fall victim to the problem of short-termism. And most importantly, by being armed with this knowledge going into the asset allocation process you'll reduce the odds of falling victim to the many behavioural biases that plague modern asset allocators. As a result, you'll reduce your fees, reduce your tax bill and increase your average performance. But most importantly, you'll sleep better at night.

ABOUT CULLEN ROCHE

Mr. Cullen Roche is the Founder of Orcam Financial Group, LLC a financial services firm offering fee only financial advisory services. He has over a decade of experience in the financial services industry working with some of the biggest firms in finance as well as founding his own firms.

Prior to establishing Orcam, Mr. Roche founded his own investment partnership in 2005 after working at Merrill Lynch Global Wealth Management where he worked on a team overseeing $500MM+ in assets under management. Over the next seven years he guided the partnership to average annual returns of 14.5% with a Sharpe Ratio of 1.21 and no negative full year returns during one of the most turbulent periods in stock market history.

He is the author of the popular book *Pragmatic Capitalism: What Every Investor Needs to Know About Money and Finance* as well as *Understanding the Modern Monetary System*, one of the top 10 all-time most downloaded research papers on the SSRN network. He is the long-time #1 economics writer on the popular financial website Seeking Alpha, was named one of the 'Top Wall Street Economists, Experts and Opinion Leaders' of 2011 by Wall

Street Economists and was named one of the '101 Best Finance People' and "one of the most influential economic thinkers today" by *Business Insider*. In 2015 Mr. Roche was named one of the '40 Under 40' most influential people in finance by *InvestmentNews*. He is regularly cited in the *Wall Street Journal*, on CNBC and in the *Financial Times*.

Mr. Roche is an alumnus of Georgetown University.

PERSONAL FINANCE

FINANCE

&

WEALTH-
BUILDING

Reflect, Pause and Focus

BY JONATHAN CLEMENTS

Want to get more out of your money? Whether you're spending or investing, try this three-pronged strategy:

1. Reflect

There's ample evidence that most of us aren't good at investing or figuring out what will make us happy. Looking to improve? Spend a little time pondering the past.

When during your life were you happiest – and what were you doing? This may help you figure out whether you should change careers and what you might do with your spare time or with your retirement. Also think about the money you've spent in recent years. Which expenditures delivered plenty of happiness – and which do you recall with a shrug of the shoulders and maybe even a touch of regret?

Research suggests that spending on experiences delivers more happiness than spending on possessions. One reason: We tend to forget the incidental annoyances of vacations, dinner parties and other experiences, and instead recall the overall good time. By contrast, it's hard to forget the annoyances that accompany possessions, because they stick around and we have to watch them deteriorate.

Recalling past investments is a little more perilous because our recollection may be sanitized, as we remember our successes and conveniently forget our mistakes. In fact, we may not simply forget our mistakes, but recall doing the exact opposite.

We might have two contradictory thoughts. One says, "I believe I'm smart about money." The other says, "I sold stocks at the March 2009 market bottom." To ease our psychological distress, we might conveniently forget our panic selling– and perhaps even decide that we were buyers of stocks in early 2009.

A possible cure: Dive into the filing cabinet and pull out your old account statements. That could be a sobering reminder of all the bum investments you've bought over the years– and all the ill-timed purchases and sales you have made.

2. Pause

I have become increasingly convinced that there's great value in pausing between an initial thought and acting upon it. There are two reasons.

First, it gives us a cooling-off period, during which we can ponder whether we have settled on the right course of action. We've all had snap reactions – for example, to an email from a colleague or family member – that we later regret and which, with a few hours delay, we would have handled differently.

The same holds true for spending and investing decisions. We fall in love with an expensive pair of shoes or a new electronic toy, make the impulse purchase and later wonder whether it was money well spent. The market surges or sinks, we make a change to our portfolio and later wish we hadn't been so hasty.

Moving slowly doesn't just help us avoid mistakes. It can also boost happiness. That brings us to the second reason to pause. It turns out that delaying spending, whether on experiences or possessions, can bring with it a pleasurable period of anticipation. The implication: If you plan to buy a new car or take a special vacation, start thinking about it far in advance, so you have a long time to savor the eventual prize. You may even discover the months of anticipation prove more pleasurable than the car or vacation itself.

3. Focus

When one of my favorite sports teams loses, I don't bother to read the account in the newspaper. Why upset myself further? But when they win, I go hunting for the newspaper recap – even if I had watched the game. In terms of our happiness, what matters is what we focus on.

For instance, research suggests that high-income earners don't enjoy their daily lives any more than the rest of us and yet, when surveyed, they're more likely to say they are happy. Why? When asked about their level of happiness, those with high incomes ponder their fat paychecks – and that prompts them to say they're happy.

This mindset creates a conundrum, even for those with plenty: Unless you're the world's richest individual, there will always be somebody who has more money than you. Don't want to feel relatively deprived? Don't put yourself in a position where you feel poor. That means avoiding high-end stores and restaurants that you can barely afford, and resisting the temptation to move to a town where others are much wealthier.

Even as you avoid thinking about those who have more, you should spend time considering your own good fortune. Remember the expensive kitchen renovation you undertook two years ago – and which today you barely notice? Spend some time admiring your fine kitchen and you'll squeeze a little more happiness out of the dollars spent.

This notion of focus can also help with investing. If an investment is volatile and hence likely to fall hard during declining markets, experts will often describe it as risky. But this risk is much reduced if we don't need to sell during the market decline – and the sense of risk is diminished even further if we don't pay attention.

Indeed, I've heard many folks say they look at their brokerage and mutual fund accounts less often when the markets are falling. That strikes me as entirely sensible. If you are well diversified, there's no need to torture yourself with frequent reminders that you're now poorer. As a money manager once told me, "If you own growth stocks, you should only look at the price every 12 months. That way, you'll only suffer one sleepless night a year."

ABOUT JONATHAN CLEMENTS

Jonathan Clements is the founder and editor of HumbleDollar.com. He's also the author of a fistful of personal finance books, including *How to Think About Money*, and he sits on the advisory board and investment committee of Creative Planning, one of America's largest independent financial advisors.

Jonathan spent almost 20 years at *The Wall Street Journal*, where he was the newspaper's personal finance columnist. Between October 1994 and April 2008, he wrote 1,009 columns for the *Journal* and for *The Wall Street Journal Sunday*. He then worked for six years at Citigroup, where he was Director of Financial Education for Citi Personal Wealth Management, before returning to the *Journal* for an additional 15-month stint as a columnist.

The Four Phases of Saving and Investing for Retirement

BY MICHAEL KITCES

Executive Summary

The traditional approach to saving for retirement is all about starting early, saving consistently, and letting compounding growth do most of the heavy lifting over time.

Yet the reality is that for those who are still early in their careers, there really may not be enough income coming in to save in the first place. It's only as income rises that savings behaviors really start to matter. And for those who have saved long enough, eventually the impact of savings is muted by the sheer size of the portfolio, as compounding growth becomes the driving factor in reaching retirement success. Until the retirement date actually looms close, and then preserving the portfolio for the retirement transition is more important than just trying to maximize growth.

In fact, this framework of Earn, Save, Grow, and Preserve can be a helpful way to think about the progression of accumulating for retirement. Each phase has its own unique issues to be navigated, and success in one phase leads to the challenges of the next.

Most importantly, though, considering the four phases of saving and investing for retirement is crucial to ensuring that the retirement advice being delivered is relevant in the first place. After all, focusing on strategies to maximize portfolio growth are irrelevant for those who can't afford to save yet, and for those with a large retirement portfolio, ongoing contributions become irrelevant and the focus must be on growing and preserving the nest egg instead!

Conventional View Of Saving And Investing For Retirement

The conventional view of saving and investing for retirement holds a consistent series of core tenets:

- Spend less than you make

- Automate your savings strategy ("pay yourself first")

- Maintain a healthy exposure to equities for long-term growth

- Maintain a diversified portfolio to manage your risk

In turn, this leads to a relatively straightforward retirement savings strategy of "start early, save consistently, and let compounding growth work for you over time." After all, it takes just $300/month of savings from age 25 to 65 to accumulate a $1,000,000 nest egg (assuming an 8% growth rate over time).

Portfolio Value After Saving $300/Month for 40 Years, Earning 8%

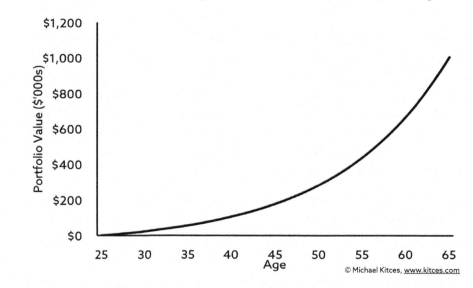

© Michael Kitces, www.kitces.com

The Four Phases Of Saving And Investing For Retirement

The caveat to the traditional view on accumulating for retirement is that in reality, an individual's income, spending, and ability to save vary greatly throughout life. From the impact of raises and promotions (especially significant in the early years of a career), to starting a family (and then moving on to the empty nest phase later), steady saving for retirement is not necessarily as feasible as the conventional view would suggest.

Similarly, the reality is that the importance of investment returns and risk management vary over time as well. Those still in the early years of accumulation have such a long time horizon, they still have the capacity to take significant risk in the portfolio, while in the later years an adverse market event could drastically derail a retirement plan and the planned retirement date. And the simple truth is that in the early years, the actual dollar amount of growth is so small, it's often dwarfed by ongoing contributions; it's only in the later years that growth becomes the real engine driving the portfolio to the retirement finish line.

In other words, accumulators progressing towards retirement will actually go through phases that have distinct challenges. After all, focusing on whether you Save isn't relevant until you're Earning enough to save. And success in the Saving behavior itself eventually creates a portfolio large enough that the Growth is what matters the most. And years of compounding Growth is what closes the gap on retirement, bringing the retirement date closer but also accentuating the need to Preserve the portfolio and manage the retirement date risk.

Thus, over time an accumulator will need to navigate each of these four distinct phases in turn: Earn, Save, Grow, and Preserve.

THE FOUR PHASES OF SAVING AND INVESTMENT FOR RETIREMENT

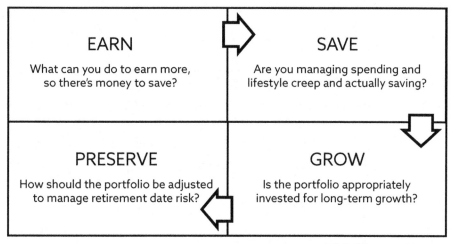

EARN	SAVE
What can you do to earn more, so there's money to save?	Are you managing spending and lifestyle creep and actually saving?
PRESERVE	GROW
How should the portfolio be adjusted to manage retirement date risk?	Is the portfolio appropriately invested for long-term growth?

© Michael Kitces, www.kitces.com

Earn: CAN YOU Save For Retirement?

In the first stage of saving for retirement, the driving issue is simply whether you earn enough that you *can* afford to save or not. In other words, does your income exceed your expenses, such that there is something left over to save in the first place?

Of course, the reality is that at virtually any income level, there will be a group of people who spend more than they make, and can't seem to find any available dollars to save. But for prospective savers in their early working years, who may still only be earning minimum wage, they really may not be earning enough yet to have any material dollars left over to save, after covering just the basic household essentials (food, shelter, and clothing). Or perhaps they are earning slightly more than minimum wage, but are burdened by student loan or other debt payments that leave little cash flow available for saving.

For people facing this situation, the 'traditional' advice to spend less and save more isn't very effective, because there really isn't much of any spending to cut in order to spend less. Instead, the real path to financial success from here is not to spend less and save more, but to *earn more to save more*.

In other words, the key issue for those in Earn stage of saving for retirement is to figure out how to increase their income earnings so they can save in the first place. That could be figuring out a side hustle for some extra income, or reinvesting any available dollars (if there are any!?) into a course or training to improve the career trajectory, or even just coaching on how to ask for a raise.

But again, the fundamental point is that early on, the best advice to save more for retirement is to *earn more* so you *can* save in the first place!

Save: ARE YOU Saving For Retirement?

As income begins to rise during the early working career, suddenly a prospective saver may reach the point where there's enough income to cover the bills (and outstanding debts) with something left over. So what do you do with the extra income? At this stage, it's no longer a question of the sheer capacity to save, but instead about taking action to save, or whether that extra income is spent instead.

Certainly, one of the great 'joys' of generating additional income is the opportunity to spend it on the pleasures of life, but allowing the lifestyle to creep higher every time there's a raise means no saving will ever actually get done. At some point, it's necessary to actually commit that not all of the next raise will be consumed, and instead that some of it will be saved, instead.

Of course, the temptation to spend more is ever present, and lifestyle creep is called that precisely because it tends to "creep up" slowly and steadily without realizing it… until the realization comes that income has significantly risen and there's *still* no money left over to save at the end of the month!

Accordingly, success in this stage of retirement savings is all about managing spending and saving behavior to actually facilitate saving. Whether it's automating savings behaviors, or finding other ways to "pay yourself first", or committing to "Save More Tomorrow", or trying to actually cut spending to free up more money to save, the outcomes will be driven not by the financial capacity to save, but the behavioral ability to reign in lifestyle choices and direct free cash flow to savings instead.

Grow: How Much Is Your Retirement Nest Egg GROWING?

As savings behaviors are cemented into place, and fuel a rising balance for the retirement nest egg, eventually the portfolio becomes so large that each incremental contribution no longer has a significant impact.

For instance, saving $300/month allows an account balance to grow to $3,600 by the end of the first year. In the second year, the account may grow slightly, but the increase in the account balance will again be driven primarily by the contributions (as a year's worth of growth may still be less than a single month's worth of contributions). After ten years of the same behavior, though, suddenly only half of the annual increase in the account balance is driven by new contributions, while the remainder is driven by growth on the existing balance. After 20 years, growth will drive 75% of the annual increases in the account balance. After 30 years, it's almost 90%.

Contributions To Annual Increases In Account Value: Investment Growth Vs New Cash Flow Contributions

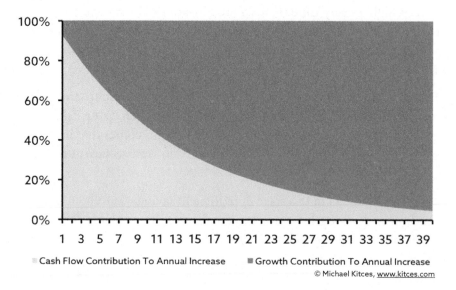

■ Cash Flow Contribution To Annual Increase ■ Growth Contribution To Annual Increase

© Michael Kitces, www.kitces.com

This shifting dynamic means that after a decade or two of ongoing contributions, the greatest driver of the outcome isn't the spending behavior and ongoing contributions anymore; now it's the ability to grow the portfolio, and the returns being generated.

In turn, this means that as the portfolio grows, paying attention to *how* it's invested begins to matter, a lot. In the early years, improving returns by 1%/year still has a trivial impact compared to saving another $100/month. In the later years, adding 1%/year to returns is highly material.

Accordingly, in the Grow phase, it becomes necessary to really look at the portfolio itself. Is it properly invested for growth? Is there a reasonable asset allocation? If investment/fund managers are being used, are they really providing value for their cost? And are the portfolio costs being managed overall, given the dramatic impact they have on long-term returns?

The bottom line: in the Grow phase, paying attention to the finer point details of how the portfolio is invested can really begin to pay off (for the first time).

Preserve: Are You MANAGING THE RISK As Retirement Approaches?

As the planned date of retirement draws near, the dynamics shift once again, as the shortening time horizon becomes highly relevant. Suddenly, as the portfolio reaches its largest value, contributions are dwarfed by the portfolio volatility, and the risk of a severe bear market in the final years (and the time it would take to recover) can substantially derail the planned retirement date. In other words, Preserving the portfolio and managing the risk becomes the dominating factor for success.

Of course, the reality is that retirement itself can entail a multi-decade time horizon, so it's not feasible to eliminate all portfolio risk. Nonetheless, as the retirement date approaches, preserving the portfolio and managing "retirement date risk" is increasingly relevant, as if a market decline occurs, savings alone can no longer make up the difference.

In point of fact, target date funds already engage in this strategy, with an "equity glidepath" that decreases in the final years to preserve the portfolio as retirement approaches. And many variable annuities with "living benefit" riders (e.g., GMWB or GMIB riders) are used for a similar purpose in the final accumulation years. In theory, even a simple strategy of buying out-of-the-money puts to preserve the portfolio by hedging the magnitude of any downside risk in the final years could be effective (akin to how many structured notes are put together).

Nonetheless, by whatever means, the key issue for a prospective retiree in the final years leading up to retirement is less about generating growth, or making ongoing contributions, and is more about sustaining moderate growth while also Preserving the portfolio to manage the looming retirement date risk exposure.

Progressing Through The Four Phases Of Retirement Accumulation

A successful accumulator who is "on track" for retirement from their early 20s through their mid-60s might spend most of their 20s just trying to improve their earnings enough to save, would focus on sustaining their savings (and avoiding lifestyle creep) in their 30s and early 40s, allow compounding growth to work for them through the rest of their 40s and 50s, and start considering the risk management issues as they approach their

60s and the retirement transition looms. In other words, the Earn, Save, Grow, and Preserve phases will come sequentially over time, as success in each leads to the next.

How An Accumulator Progresses Through The Four Phases Of Retirement Saving

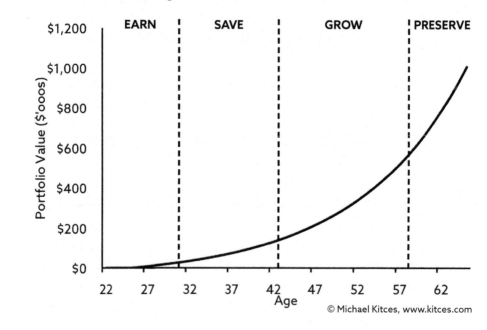

© Michael Kitces, www.kitces.com

Of course, for an accumulator who is not on track for retirement, their progression through the phases may not align with the ages noted above. Nonetheless, from the perspective of achieving retirement success, the fundamental point is that the "right" advice for an accumulator depends on which phase they're in. Giving advice focused on the later stages of growth and preservation is largely irrelevant to someone still in the Earn or Save phases, just as focusing on earning more or saving more is not very relevant for someone in the preserve stage leading up to the retirement transition (where the portfolio is so large that incremental earnings and savings won't have much impact anyway).

Ultimately, though, the point is simply that effective advice for retirement accumulators will vary over time. In the Earn phase, it's all about increasing your income so that you *can* save. The Save phase focuses on savings (and spending) behavior. The Grow phase is where the portfolio's investment strategies matter. And the Preserve phase is about managing the upcoming retirement transition. For retirement advice to be effective, it must be paired to the appropriate phase.

ABOUT MICHAEL KITCES

Michael E. Kitces, MSFS, MTAX, CFP®, CLU, ChFC, RHU, REBC, CASL, is a partner and the Director of Research for Pinnacle Advisory Group, a private wealth management firm located in Columbia, Maryland that oversees approximately $1.4 billion of client assets. He is the former practitioner editor of the *Journal of Financial Planning*, and the publisher of the e-newsletter The Kitces Report and the popular financial planning industry blog Nerd's Eye View through his website www.Kitces.com.

Beyond his website, Michael is an active writer and editor across the industry and has been featured in numerous print, radio, and television appearances. In addition, Michael has co-authored several books, including *The Annuity Advisor* with John Olsen (now in 3rd edition), the first balanced and objective book on annuities written for attorneys, accountants, and financial planners, and *Tools & Techniques of Retirement Income Planning* with Steve Leimberg and others.

Michael is one of the 2010 recipients of the Financial Planning Association's 'Heart of Financial Planning' awards for his dedication to advancing the financial planning profession. In addition, he has variously been recognized as financial planning's 'Deep Thinker', a 'Legacy Builder', an 'Influencer', a 'Mover & Shaker', part of the 'Power 20', and a 'Rising Star in Wealth Management' by industry publications.

Michael is also a co-founder of NexGen, a community of the next generation of financial planners that aims to ensure the transference of wisdom, tradition, and integrity, from the pioneers of financial planning to the next generation of the profession.

The Passive Investor Test

BY CHARLIE BILELLO

Passive investing is all the rage. Active has become a four-letter word.

Are you a passive investor? Let's find out…

1. Do you own a higher percentage of stocks in your portfolio than bonds?

2. Does your house make up the largest component of your net worth?

3. Do you ever rebalance or sell/change the holdings in your portfolio?

4. Do you dollar-cost average, reinvest interest/dividends, or engage in tax loss harvesting?

5. Do you own any individual stocks/bonds/real estate?

6. Do you own only bonds issued and stocks domiciled in your home country?

7. Do you invest in lifecycle or target date funds that change the mix of stocks/bonds over time?

8. Do you own anything other than cap-weighted index products?

9. Do you hold a large amount of cash for emergencies, for when the market "finally" pulls back, or to "sleep at night?"

10. Do you exclude private equity, preferred stock, MLPs, commodities, collectibles, and other more esoteric asset classes from your portfolio?

If you answered *YES* to **any** one of these questions, you have failed the test. You are not a passive investor. Do not be dismayed. Everyone will have answered yes to at least one of these questions which is why, in practice, there are no truly passive investors. There are only varying degrees of active.

Let's go through each of the above questions to make this point clearer.

1) 60/40: An Active Bet

A 60/40 portfolio of US stock and bond index funds is often referenced as the passive standard. In reality, though, it's far from passive because it's not close to the "market portfolio."

Public equities accounted for only 36% of investable assets at the end of 2012 (see Doeswijk, Lam, and Seinkels). Of this, US equities represented roughly half. So instead of holding 60% in US equities, a passive exposure would be closer to 18%.

Figure 1: Estimated Market Values (US$ trillions) and Weights in the Global Market Portfolio at the End of 2012

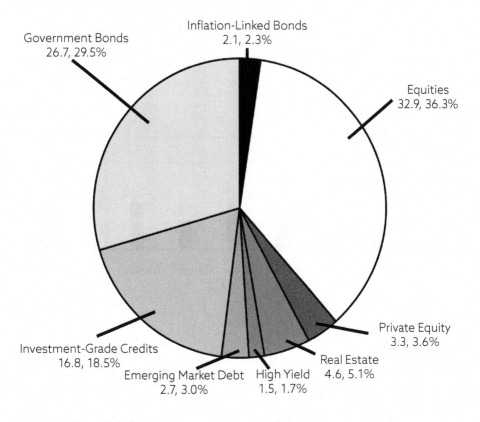

Source: 'The Global Multi-Asset Market Portfolio', *Financial Analysts Journal* (2014)

On the bond side, the active bet most U.S. investors are making is even greater. According to Vanguard, non-US bonds are the world's largest asset class (at 32% as of 2013), while most US investors have very little international bond exposure.

2) Your Home is Your Castle ... and an Active Bet

If you're like most Americans, the vast majority of your net worth is tied up in your house. The median 65–69 year old American has $194,226 in net worth but only $43,921 if you exclude home equity.

Figure 2: Americans' Median Net Worth ($)

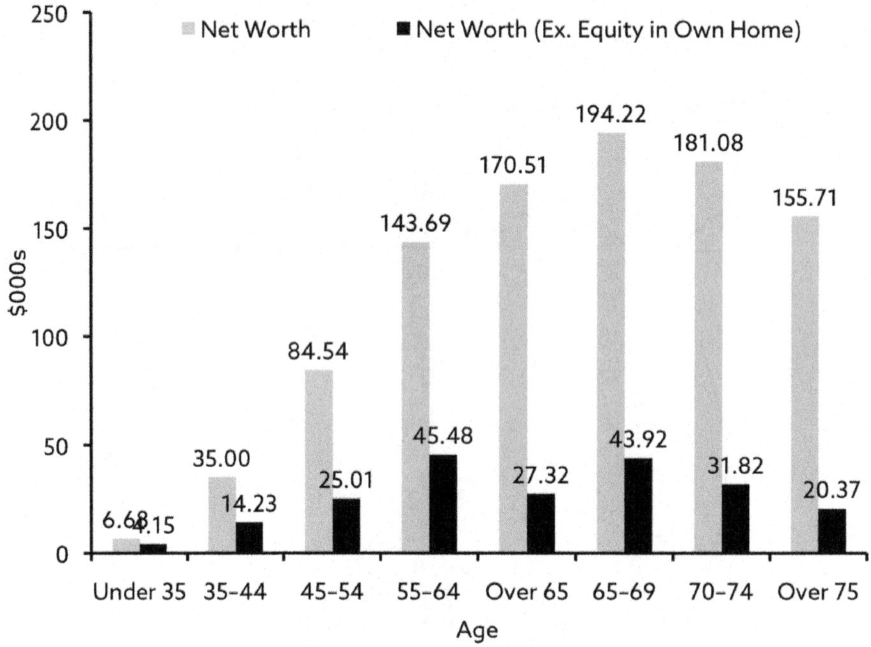

Source: Motley Fool via US Census Bureau

Leaving the question of whether a house is a good investment aside, putting most your money into your primary residence is an extremely active, concentrated bet. The truly passive investor would never buy a home. They would instead be a renter and invest all savings into the global market portfolio.

3) Rebalancing is Not a Passive Activity

Rebalancing a portfolio back to "target" asset allocation weights is said to help investors control risk and maintain their desired risk-profile over time. There are a number of rebalancing strategies in existence. They are all active.

Why? Because a true passive investor would buy the market portfolio and let the weights float over time to wherever the market goes. If that meant owning a much higher percentage of equities and tech stocks in 2000 because of the dot-com bubble, then you'd have to live with that.

Rebalancing in 2000 (selling stocks and adding to bonds) may have been a prudent decision to control risk, but it was very much an active bet.

4) The Lump Sum Fallacy

In its purest form, passive requires a lump sum investment into the market portfolio on the day you are born and only sold on the day you die.

But that's not how investing works for anyone. For in between, life happens. And a life worth living is not a passive event.

Most don't start investing until their twenties and when they do it's not a lump sum but **dollar-cost averaging** small amounts into a 401k or IRA. The amounts are not static over time but hopefully growing as you advance in your career. Those dollar-cost average returns can look very different from buy-and-hold returns and since you're not dollar-cost averaging into the true market portfolio, you are by definition making an active bet.

Even if you did buy the "market" on the day you were born the question of **reinvestment** of dividends and interest payments comes into play. Do you reinvest, which greatly enhances long-term returns, or do you take the money and spend it? If you spend it, that's an active decision. If you reinvest but not into the true market portfolio, that's also an active decision.

Do you engage in tax loss harvesting to offset taxable gains and potentially reduce ordinary income up to $3,000 per year? That sounds like an active decision to me.

5) The Stock Pickers' Dream

Indexing is becoming more and more popular but the temptation to pick individual stocks is still strong. Anyone who dreams of being the next Warren Buffett won't get there by buying an index fund. If you own any individual stocks, bonds, or real estate investments you are deviating from the market portfolio and making an active bet.

This is true regardless of whether you ever sell that stock or not. Buying and holding Apple is an active bet.

6) Jack Bogle is Home Biased and So Are You

The father of indexing and founder of Vanguard, Jack Bogle, does not diversify abroad, holding only a portfolio of US stocks and bonds (he also believes in 60/40 and rebalancing, which as we established above are both active bets). His rationale: "I like the US. We still have plenty of problems, but we're much better than France, Britain, and Germany. And we don't even want to talk about Italy and Greece. And importantly – people forget this too quickly – we have the most established government and legal institutions."

Bogle is not alone. Equity market home country bias is pervasive in not only the US but globally.

Figure 3: Equity Market Home Bias By Country

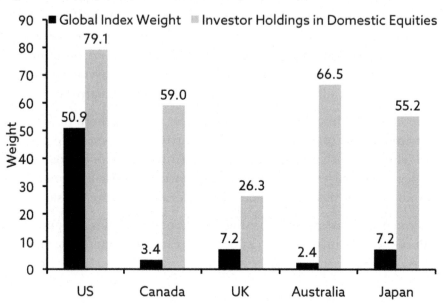

Source: The global case for strategic asset allocation and an examination of home bias, Vanguard (2017)

7) Targeting a Date is an Active Decision

Target Date or Lifecycle funds have become increasingly popular in recent years. Just pick a retirement date (2035, 2040, etc.) and the funds will automatically shift the mix of stocks/bonds to a more conservative allocation over time. This automation is said to make the shift passive, but it is nothing of the sort. The starting and ending allocations are hardly representative of the global market portfolio, and managing risk as you approach retirement, while often prudent, is an active decision.

8) Value Investors = Active Investors

Just because you turn something into an index doesn't mean it is passive. If you are deviating from the market portfolio by owning only what you deem to be "cheap" stocks, even if done in a systematic (rules-based) fashion, you are making an active bet. The same is true for any "smart beta" product, momentum strategy, trend following strategy, etc. If you don't own the entire market you are actively avoiding what you don't own.

9) Cash is the Active King

Cash may be king but it does not mesh with passive investing. If you are holding a large cash balance for emergencies, because you are waiting to buy a house, or because you are waiting for better investing opportunities, you are making an active decision. It may be a wise decision, but it is still active.

10) The "Market" is Not Just Stocks/Bonds

Thus far we've been largely focused on "investable" asset classes. Richard Roll (Roll's critique) argued back in 1977 that the true market portfolio is "unobservable" as it would need to include every "single possible available asset, including real estate, precious metals, stamp collections, jewelry, and anything with any worth." This would include your own business if you are self-employed, one of the most concentrated active bets one can make.

Needless to say, it is impossible to gain exposure to such a portfolio. As such, it is impossible to be a true passive investor.

* * *

Moving On, Elevating the Discourse

Once we can acknowledge that there is no such thing as a true passive investor we can move on to a more intellectual conversation than the juvenile "active is bad, passive is swell" discussion that has dominated in recent years.

A more interesting debate to me would include the following questions:

1. Should one ever deviate from the investable market portfolio (as anyone with a 60/40 allocation is already doing)? If yes, when/why?

2. Is the significant concentration of wealth that Americans have in their primary residence a good thing for the economy? Is such an active bet warranted? Do other developed nations have the same concentration?

3. Is rebalancing a form of market timing with a more palatable name?

4. Did the exponential increase in ETF assets in recent years, even passive index ETFs, encourage more/less activity from investors? Do investors in ETFs reinvest dividends/interest at the same rate as mutual fund investors?

5. Starting your own company is one of the most active decisions you can make. Most startups fail ("half of the businesses started in the US live five years or less"). Does portfolio theory suggest one should not make such a bet and instead assume a more passive role within an established multi-national company?

6. Has Jack Bogle's decision to invest only in the US hurt him or helped him from a risk and return standpoint? Should that matter for your own portfolio going forward?

7. Are lifecycle funds and robo advisors really an effective replacement for an investment advisor? How closely do they track the true market portfolio?

8. Are stocks/bonds good enough? How much additional benefit do investors get by including more esoteric asset classes? Should commodities be a part of the market portfolio?

9. How many ETFs would it take to replicate the investable global market portfolio? What single fund/ETF most closely approximates this portfolio currently?

10. Does strategy diversification (managed futures, value, momentum, merger arbitrage, etc.), while a deviation from the market portfolio, provide any benefit to investors over time?

ABOUT CHARLIE BILELLO

Charlie Bilello is the Director of Research at Pension Partners, LLC, an investment advisor that manages mutual funds and separate accounts. He is the co-author of four award-winning research papers on market anomalies and investing. Mr. Bilello is responsible for strategy development, investment research and communicating the firm's investment themes and portfolio positioning to clients. Prior to joining Pension Partners, he was the Managing Member of Momentum Global Advisors and held positions as a Credit, Equity and Hedge Fund Analyst at billion dollar alternative investment firms.

Mr. Bilello holds a J.D. and M.B.A. in Finance and Accounting from Fordham University and a B.A. in Economics from Binghamton University. He is a Chartered Market Technician (CMT) and a Member of the Market Technicians Association. Mr. Bilello also holds the Certified Public Accountant (CPA) certificate.

Mr. Bilello is a contributor to Yahoo Finance and has been interviewed on CNBC, Bloomberg, and Fox Business.

20 Rules of Personal Finance

BY BEN CARLSON

Meb Faber asked a bunch of us bloggers to give him our top 3–5 most read blog posts of the year. I looked back at my trusty Google Analytics for the first time in a while and discovered that two of my top three in terms of readership were personal finance-related posts. I've always said that personal finances are more important than portfolio management, but I still think there's probably not enough people writing or providing education on the topic.

So I'm going to make a concerted effort to write more about personal finance in the coming year.

Here's my list of 20 personal finance rules:

1. **Salary is not the same as savings**. Your net worth is more important than how much money you make. It's amazing how many people don't realize this simple truth. Having a high salary does not automatically make you rich; having a low salary does not automatically make you poor. All that matters is how much you save out of your salary.

2. **Saving is more important than investing**. Pay yourself first is such simple advice, but so few people do this. The best investment decision you can make is setting a high savings rate because it gives you a huge margin of safety in life.

3. **Avoid credit card debt like the plague**. Carrying credit card debt is a great way to negatively compound your net worth.

4. **Live below your means, not within your means**. The only way to get ahead financially is to stay behind your own earnings power.

5. **But credit itself is important**. Likely the biggest expense over your lifetime will be interest costs on your mortgage, car loans, student loans,

etc. Having a solid credit score can save you tens of thousands of dollars by lowering your borrowing costs. So use credit cards, but always pay off the balance each month.

6. **If you want to understand your priorities look at where you spend money each month**. You have to understand your spending habits if you ever wish to gain control of your finances. The goal is to spend money on things that are important to you but cut back everywhere else. And if you pay yourself first you don't have to worry about budgeting, you just spend whatever's left over.

7. **Automate everything**. The best way to save more, avoid late fees, make your life easier and get out of your own way is to automate as much of your financial life as possible. It probably takes me one hour a month to keep track of everything because it's all on autopilot.

8. **Get the big purchases right**. I know I shouldn't be so judgmental but whenever I see $50–$70k SUVs on the road or enormous McMansions the first thing that pops into my head is, "I wonder how much they have saved for retirement?" Personal finance experts love to debate the minutia of brown bag lunches and lattes but the most important purchases in terms of keeping your finances in order will be the big ones — housing and transportation. Overextending yourself on these can be a killer.

9. **Build up that savings account**. I don't even like calling it an emergency savings account anymore because most of the time these "emergencies" are things you should plan on happening periodically. You have to have liquid assets to take care of things when life inevitably gets in the way.

10. **Cover your insurable needs**. This is another huge personal finance margin of safety item. Just remember that insurance is about protecting wealth, not building it.

11. **Always get the match**. I can't tell you how many times I've talked to people who aren't saving enough in their 401(k) plan to get the employer match. That's like turning down a tax-deferred portion of your salary each year. I'd like to see more people max out their retirement contributions, but at a minimum you should *always* save enough to get the match.

12. **Save a little more each year**. The trick is to increase your savings rates every time you get a raise so you'll never even notice that you had more

money to begin with. Avoiding lifestyle creep can be difficult, but that's how you build wealth.

13. **Choose your friends and neighborhood wisely**. Robert Cialdini has written extensively on the concept of social proof and how we mirror the actions of others to gain acceptance. Trying to keep up with spendthrift friends or neighbors is a never-ending game with no true winners.

14. **Talk about money**. It takes all of five minutes before I hear about politics in almost any conversation these days, but somehow money is still a taboo subject. Talk to your spouse about money. Ask others for help. Don't allow financial problems to linger and get worse.

15. **Material purchases won't make you happier in the long-run**. There is something of a short-term dopamine hit we get through retail therapy but it always wears off. Buying stuff won't make you happier or wealthier.

16. **Read a book or ten**. There are countless personal finance books out there. If it bores you to death then at least skim through a few and pick out the best pieces of advice from a few different sources to test out. This stuff should be taught in every high school and college, but we're often on our own. That means you have to take the initiative.

17. **Know where you stand**. Everyone should have a back-of-the-envelope idea about where their net worth (assets – liabilities) stands. Before knowing where you want to go you have to know where you are.

18. **Taxes matter**. I think everyone should try to do their own taxes at least once just to understand how it all works (maybe with an assist from TurboTax). It can be maddeningly complicated, but it can help you save money over time if you know where to look. Take advantage of as many tax breaks as you can and always understand your personal tax situation.

19. **Make more money**. Saving and/or cutting back is a great way to get ahead, but it's an incomplete strategy if you're not trying to earn more by enhancing your career. Too many people are stuck in the mindset that there's nothing they can do to get a better job, take on more responsibilities or earn a higher salary. That's nonsense.

20. **Don't think about retirement, but financial independence**. The goal shouldn't be about making it to a certain age so you can ride off into the sunset, but rather getting to the point where you don't have to worry about money anymore.

You may disagree with some of these but remember – personal finance is personal.

ABOUT BEN CARLSON

Ben Carlson is the Director of Institutional Asset Management at Ritholtz Wealth Management. He has spent his entire career managing institutional portfolios. He started out with an institutional investment consulting firm developing portfolio strategies and creating investment plans for various foundations, endowments, pensions, hospitals, insurance companies and high net worth individuals. More recently, he was part of the portfolio management team for an investment office that managed a large endowment fund for a charitable organization.

Ben is the author of the books *A Wealth of Common Sense: Why Simplicity Trumps Complexity in Any Investment Plan* and *Organizational Alpha: How to Add Value in Institutional Asset Management.*

Ben is the creator of the blog *A Wealth of Common Sense* and he is also a columnist for Bloomberg.

Life on the Edge

BY JOHN MAULDIN

"Where justice is denied, where poverty is enforced, where ignorance prevails, and where any one class is made to feel that society is an organized conspiracy to oppress, rob and degrade them, neither persons nor property will be safe."

– Frederick Douglass

"I am for doing good to the poor, but I differ in opinion about the means. I think the best way of doing good to the poor is not making them easy in poverty, but leading or driving them out of it."

– Benjamin Franklin

Like many of you, I'm trying to understand an economic landscape that's changing by the day – and rarely for the better, at least from the standpoint of the middle and lower classes. I am also trying to understand how in the world the two great US political parties have conspired to give us a choice, as Peggy Noonan has said, of "Crazy Man vs. Criminal."

I think these two questions are related, and not just in the United States. Populist angst is taking hold around the world. Like all anger, it isn't necessarily rational and may not bring the desired changes, but the anger and frustration are real. People have real problems, and increasingly they don't trust traditional leaders to solve them.

Last week I had the privilege of meeting first privately and then publicly with Peggy Noonan. For those who don't know, she was President Reagan's speech writer and is now a *Wall Street Journal* columnist and celebrated author. As a writer, she is one of my heroes, perhaps the greatest essayist of my generation – a true wordsmith.

Back in February, with the presidential campaign in full force, Peggy wrote a column that has been on my mind ever since. She titled it 'Trump and the Rise of the Unprotected'. Everyone should read it, preferably several times. It is that good.

Whatever you think of Donald Trump, he is a symptom of larger trends. So is Bernie Sanders. A major fraction of the population is living on the edge, vulnerable and unprotected. Most of you reading this letter aren't in that category; you have homes, steady incomes, and some investment capital. That puts you way ahead of average.

Today we're going to look at the real-world economic pain that so many people experience in daily life. Some of this will be hard reading, but it's important. Reading it, you will better understand what is going wrong and how badly we need solutions. You may also come away with a better idea of the direction this country is headed if we don't see real change in the near future.

Many establishment types in both the Republican and Democratic parties seem to think that Donald Trump and Bernie Sanders are anomalies. That goes double for the Republican Party establishment class that thinks their money can control things. Trump is not an anomaly; he is a harbinger of a growing frustration that is bigger than corporate donors and super PACs.

Protected vs. Unprotected

Peggy Noonan says the current unrest is the logical progression of trends that began long ago. The upper stratum of society is increasingly "protected" from sharing, and often even from seeing, the travails of daily life as most people experience them. Here is how she describes our situation (the boldface emphasis is mine):

> There are the protected and the unprotected. The protected make public policy. The unprotected live in it. The unprotected are starting to push back, powerfully.
>
> The protected are the accomplished, the secure, the successful – those who have power or access to it. They are protected from much of the

roughness of the world. More to the point, they are protected from the world they have created. Again, they make public policy and have for some time.

I want to call them the elite to load the rhetorical dice, but let's stick with the protected.

They are figures in government, politics and media. They live in nice neighborhoods, safe ones. Their families function, their kids go to good schools, they've got some money. **All of these things tend to isolate them, or provide buffers.** Some of them – in Washington it is important officials in the executive branch or on the Hill; in Brussels, significant figures in the European Union – literally have their own security details.

Because they are protected they feel they can do pretty much anything, impose any reality. They're insulated from many of the effects of their own decisions.

This insulation is now so common we don't even notice it – and not just in government. Business executives meet in a nice office, tweak a few numbers, and somewhere down the line people lose their jobs. Those folks are thousands of miles away, and the decision-makers never even see them. This is what it means to be "protected."

Peggy goes on to explain why immigration is such a watershed issue.

Many Americans suffered from illegal immigration – its impact on labor markets, financial costs, crime, the sense that the rule of law was collapsing. But the protected did fine – more workers at lower wages. No effect of illegal immigration was likely to hurt them personally.

It was good for the protected. But the unprotected watched and saw. They realized the protected were not looking out for them, and they inferred that they were not looking out for the country, either.

The unprotected came to think they owed the establishment – another word for the protected – nothing, no particular loyalty, no old allegiance.

Mr. Trump came from that.

Loyalty and allegiance flow in both directions. Yet somehow we've reached a point where the people who make decisions are so separated from the people who pay the cost of those decisions that neither group feels any loyalty to the other at all. This is not a recipe for a stable social order and a thriving economy.

I want to take Ms. Noonan's thoughts a little further. The protected are not just the politicians and bureaucrats who make and execute public policy; they are all the people who, because of their jobs and income, can generally protect themselves from the vagaries and vicissitudes of life. They have the money to hire the lawyers, doctors, mechanics, pay for the insurance, etc., to deal with whatever problems arise.

Are you in the protected class? If you're reading this newsletter, you probably are. At least for now. I do have some readers who are struggling. I read their comments online and sometimes get email from them. For the most part, though, people read me because they have money to invest and want to keep up with economic news. The unprotected have other priorities.

I think we have subcategories within the protected class, though. I know some of the top 0.1%, and their lives are not like mine. They have multiple mansions, bodyguards, private jets, chauffeurs, and people to take care of everything. Call them the Super-protected.

As for me, I'm just plain protected. I live in a nice apartment with a doorman downstairs. I have assistance to help me with a lot of the "busywork." I don't miss any meals unless I'm trying to lose weight. I drive my own well-used vehicle. I don't rate a private jet, but I can at least fly first class, usually, as my frequent flyer status with American Airlines allows me to be upgraded a large percentage of the time.

Another step down are what we might call the "semi-protected." These are people with secure jobs, college degrees, some money in the bank, and a modicum of leisure time. They have the luxury of wondering where Junior will go to college instead of *whether* they can even pay for it.

Middle Class Shame

Those three categories encompass maybe (being generous) 30% of the population. The rest are the unprotected. What is life like for them? It's a surprisingly hard question. You can't truly know unless you've lived it, but I found one very interesting account in *The Atlantic* magazine. The May 2016 cover story was 'The Secret Shame of the Middle Class'.

The writer, Neal Gabler, starts by noting a Federal Reserve survey that found 47% of Americans wouldn't be able to cover an unexpected $400 expense without borrowing or selling something. (That percentage is strikingly, even eerily, similar to the one in the 2012 Mitt Romney quote about the percentage of Americans who are dependent on government but pay no income tax.)

Read that again. Yes, nearly half the country can't come up with $400 cash in an emergency. That's stunning. The slightest mishap – a toothache, a minor car problem, a hot-summer electric bill – will send them into debt or force them to sell something.

Gabler says he knows how it feels because he is one of those people:

> I know what it is like to have to juggle creditors to make it through a week. I know what it is like to have to swallow my pride and constantly dun people to pay me so that I can pay others. I know what it is like to have liens slapped on me and to have my bank account levied by creditors. I know what it is like to be down to my last $5 – literally – while I wait for a paycheck to arrive, and I know what it is like to subsist for days on a diet of eggs.

> I know what it is like to dread going to the mailbox, because there will always be new bills to pay but seldom a check with which to pay them. I know what it is like to have to tell my daughter that I didn't know if I would be able to pay for her wedding; it all depended on whether something good happened. And I know what it is like to have to borrow money from my adult daughters because my wife and I ran out of heating oil.

That's life on the edge in USA 2016. The data tells us that millions of people live like this or even worse.

I should point out that many of the protected were once unprotected. I certainly spent the first 35 years of my life in the unprotected class. I know what it's like to wake up at 2 AM with your stomach in a knot as you try to figure out how you're going to make your little two-person payroll, pay the electric bill before they turn you off, get enough gas in the car to make it to your first sales call – and wonder how you're going to get one of your clients to pay you early so you can do all these things.

I lived in older mobile homes – not exactly considered even middle-class – (and in fact had my first two daughters while living in them) and was an enthusiastic supporter of the Reagan revolution because I wanted change. (Just for the record, I should note that I voted Democratic in the two presidential elections before that.)

When you have to borrow money at 18% and your taxes seem god-awful high compared to your income, your views on inflation and government participation change. For many years, as a young businessman, I kept a bank account in North Dakota to write checks on because it took between 7 and 10 days for them to clear. The polite term for that is cash management, but back in the day we called it kiting checks. Today, if I wanted to start a business, I could find a lot of people with a great deal of interest in investing. Back then I couldn't even get a loan on my own signature.

I understand having an old car that requires a lot of maintenance to get you where you need to go. I grew up knowing how to maintain and repair cars, swing a hammer, and do everything else needed to keep my life moving forward. I actually never thought of that approach to life as unusual; it was just normal. But I really didn't like where I saw our country and economy going.

So I can understand the frustration of people who don't feel that they are participating in the prosperity and growth of the country. I at least felt like I had a chance. As we're going to see as we go along in the letter, more and more people are feeling that circumstances – and the people who create those circumstance – are arrayed against them.

You might respond that even impoverished Americans live better than many others around the world. Maybe so. In some countries the poor and downtrodden simply accept their lot and remain happy. Here, we get angry. Why?

I suspect that much of the anger we see is felt by people who thought they would never suffer financially. They were doing well, but then something happened – a job loss, a medical crisis, drug addiction, bad investments, *something* pushed them down the ladder. Maybe it was their own mistakes, but they don't like life on the lower rungs and don't think they should be there.

Neal Gabler goes on to talk about the overriding shame that follows:

You wouldn't know any of that to look at me. I like to think I appear reasonably prosperous. Nor would you know it to look at my résumé. I have had a passably good career as a writer – five books, hundreds of articles published, a number of awards and fellowships, and a small (very small) but respectable reputation.

You wouldn't even know it to look at my tax return. I am nowhere near rich, but I have typically made a solid middle- or even, at times, upper-middle-class income, which is about all a writer can expect, even a writer who also teaches and lectures and writes television scripts, as I do. And you certainly wouldn't know it to talk to me, because the last thing I would ever do – until now – is admit to financial insecurity or, as I think of it, "financial impotence," because it has many of the characteristics of sexual impotence, not least of which is the desperate need to mask it and pretend everything is going swimmingly. In truth, it may be more embarrassing than sexual impotence.

"You are more likely to hear from your buddy that he is on Viagra than that he has credit-card problems," says Brad Klontz, a financial psychologist who teaches at Creighton University in Omaha, Nebraska, and ministers to individuals with financial issues. "Much more likely." America is a country, as Donald Trump has reminded us, of winners and losers, alphas and weaklings. To struggle financially is a source of shame, a daily humiliation – even a form of social suicide. Silence is the only protection.

I'm no psychologist, but I think psychologists would say that suppressing emotions like shame and anxiety, anger and frustration is terrible for your health. I would bet doing so is part of the reason for the rising middle-age death rate I wrote about last year (see 'Crime in the Jobs Report').

Yet I understand why people keep quiet about lifestyle setbacks. Our culture in the US preaches a survival-of-the-fittest "social Darwinism." We assume people get what they deserve; and if they don't succeed, it must be their own fault. So it's no surprise people hide or downplay their misfortune. Gabler is a brave exception on that point.

In fact, material success (or lack thereof) tells us almost nothing about a person's character, values, intelligence, or integrity. Sometimes good, hard-working people have bad luck. Lazy idiots can have good luck. I don't know why.

In either case, bad luck is not what enrages so many people. The unprotected are angry because they believe the game is rigged against them. Moreover, they think the protected class rigged has the game.

Permanent Damage

As bad as the situation is, official data says it's improving. Just look at the unemployment rate, down to 5% and job openings everywhere.

Those numbers look quite different from the perspective of the unprotected. The data doesn't account for underemployment, lowered wages, and job insecurity. If you spend a few hours cutting your neighbor's grass for 50 bucks and don't make another penny, you still count as "employed" that month.

Gallup has an enlightening statistic. Their Gallup Good Jobs Index measures the percentage of the adult population that works 30+ hours a week for a regular paycheck. It stood at 45.1% when I checked this week.

Last week's jobs report told us that 62.8% of the civilian noninstitutional population participates in the labor force, and 5% are unemployed, while Gallup tells us only 45.1% have what it considers a "good job." These aren't directly comparable datasets, but a rough estimate suggests that maybe a fifth of the labor force is either unemployed or have less-than-good jobs.

The picture gets even murkier. Last week my good friend (and onetime business partner) Gary Halbert reported a new survey from the Society for Human Resource Management. Their data says American workers actually feel pretty good. Some 88% of employees said they were either "very satisfied" or "somewhat satisfied" with their jobs.

Yet the same survey found that 45% were either "likely" or "very likely" to look for a new job in the next year. So it appears their satisfaction is limited. This survey doesn't include unemployed workers who also aren't satisfied with their status.

That 5% unemployment number masks a seriously low participation rate, falling productivity, and a serious surge in low-wage service jobs, coupled with a loss of middle-class jobs. It is skewed by the soaring number of temporary workers, involuntarily self-employed workers, and contractors and freelancers in the gig economy who are technically counted as employed. In other words, 5% unemployment today is not your father's 5% unemployment. There is a reason it feels substantially different.

So millions, dissatisfied with the eroding American Dream, struggle to make ends meet, despite a historically low unemployment rate. Merely finding a job, while necessary and welcome, didn't begin to solve their problems.

A May 9, 2016 *Wall Street Journal* story, 'The Recession's Economic Trauma Has Left Enduring Scars', reported some research on this point. People who lose jobs in a recession experience a variety of long-lasting effects. Their new jobs often pay them lower wages, and it takes years for them to reach their previous earnings peak. These people are less likely to own a home; they experience more psychological problems; and their children perform worse in school. The *WSJ* calls this phenomenon wage scarring.

We know from BLS data that about 40 million Americans lost their jobs in the 2007–2009 recession. Many still feel the financial pain, despite having landed new jobs. Says the *WSJ*:

> Only about one in four displaced workers gets back to pre-layoff earning levels after five years, according to University of California, Los Angeles economist Till von Wachter. A pay gap persists, even decades later, between workers who experienced a period of unemployment and similar workers who avoided a layoff. Estimates vary, but by one analysis, people who lost a job during recessions made 15% to 20% less than their nondisplaced peers after 10 to 20 years.

It gets worse. At some point these people will reach retirement age with little or no savings. They will either keep working – possibly in jobs that would otherwise go to younger workers – or they will live frugally and depress overall consumer spending. That's not good for anyone.

Think about it. These were probably people who had developed an acceptable lifestyle and were likely saving money and being responsible. Then they lost their jobs, and even now that they're working again, their pay is still 20% lower than it was. It's tough to maintain that former lifestyle and still save. And when your house is underwater, selling it and moving down is both difficult and gut-wrenching.

Young workers feel a different kind of pain. Too young to have lost jobs in the recession, they reached adulthood in a labor market that doesn't want them. That is especially true for those without college degrees.

The April jobs report showed a staggering 16.0% unemployment rate for teenagers ages 16–19. This sample includes only those who were actively looking for jobs, so these aren't full-time students. They have either dropped out, or they want to work while in school. They probably aren't happy with the situation, and their parents aren't, either.

Inflation Lives

While central bankers try to create inflation, for the unprotected inflation never disappeared. Last week in *Outside the Box*, I quoted Rob Arnott's study that found inflation for most Americans has been running around 3% annually since 1995. That figure includes the four categories that typical workers are most keenly affected by: rent, food, energy, and medical care. (See my article, 'Where's the Beef?')

I ran across another shocking data point after sharing Rob's story. It was in a May 8, 2016 *Wall Street Journal* story called 'Rising US Rents Squeeze the Middle Class'. It looks at data that shows middle-income renters have it worse than those above or below them. Buried in the middle of the article was this sentence:

> In Boston, median asking rents have increased at an annual rate of 13.2% since 2010, far outstripping the 2.4% average annual increase in income.

If Boston reflects other cities, we can see why people complain about rent and sleep on each other's couches. This kind of steep climb in the cost of living is very hard on people who have little income to spare.

The following chart comes from Sentier Research (via Doug Short). It shows the real median household income, which now stands at $59,361. That is, **half** of US households earn less than that. The picture is actually even worse since, as we saw above, the Consumer Price Index understates inflation for low-end households. Nominal wages may be growing – for those who have jobs – but in real terms the unprotected are falling farther behind every year.

Median Household Income in the 21st Century: Nominal and Real

Source: Advisor Perspectives. Data: Sentier Research.

When I look at that chart, I don't wonder that half the country is furious at the protected class; I wonder what took them so long.

Everything I've said about the US applies to most of the developed world. The UK will vote in June 2016 on whether to exit the European Union, in part because of the perception that EU policies leave UK workers at a disadvantage. Unemployment rates in Southern Europe are astronomically high, even as refugees pour in from the Middle East. Collapsing commodity and energy prices are hitting Canada and Australia very hard.

Yet in all these places, a portion of society is still doing very well. Why is that? One common thread is central bank policy. The Fed, the ECB, and others decided years ago to push rates down and keep them there. Maybe they honestly thought that would help restore growth. It hasn't, at least not growth that most people can appreciate.

Let's be generous and say the central banks made an honest mistake. Bernanke, Yellen, Draghi, and colleagues all wanted to help people. At some point, you would think they might have to say, "It hasn't worked."

Maybe they already say it among themselves but don't tell us because they want to preserve what is left of their credibility.

I'm sorry, but at this point there isn't much credibility left to preserve. The unprotected public has lost faith and is rising up, led by populists and demagogues.

The time for wondering where the anger came from is past. We know where it came from, and it's too strong to stop now. We will all be living on the edge before this is over. Even the protected don't have unlimited protection.

Conservative and Republican establishment types are trying to tell themselves that Trump is an anomaly. Things will go back to normal in time. But if there aren't major changes – and I'm really wondering how those changes can happen, especially in a Clinton presidency – what do you think the mood of the voters will be in 2020, after the near statistical certainty of a recession within the next four years? Unemployment will once again be high and climbing; pensions will be threatened left and right; and there will be even more people living on the edge.

I highlighted a recent study that shows the surprisingly higher death rate among middle-aged whites. That rate is the direct result of increased suicides and abuse of drugs and alcohol – all part of the psychological depression process. And then, while researching today's letter, I ran across a story in the *Washington Post* with the intriguing title 'Death predicts whether people vote for Donald Trump'. It turns out that there is a direct relationship between the middle-aged mortality rates and the percentage of voters who favor Donald Trump in counties where mortality rates are the highest.

> That fact becomes more alarming when you look at the context. Over the past decade, Hispanic people have been dying at a slower rate. Black people have been dying at a slower rate; white people in other countries have been dying at a slower rate.

Change in mortality rate, age 45–54

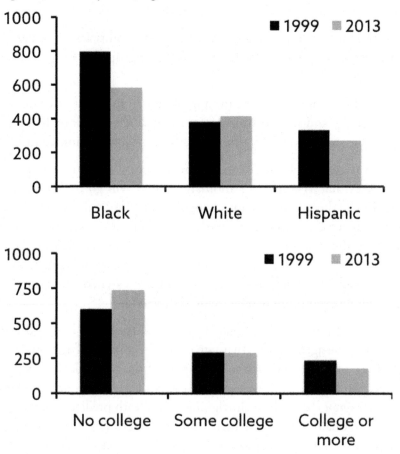

Change in number of deaths per 100,000 Americans. Most demographic groups saw a decline in their mortality rate over the past 15 years. Whites with little education saw an increase. Source: Case/Deaton (2015).

"There's something happening here; what it is ain't exactly clear."

I think we have crossed a political Rubicon. While money is important in the political process, the unprotected have discovered that their votes are even more important. And that there are more of them than there are of the protected. And that, if you're in the unprotected class, your vote is not for sale.

Anger and frustration are not limited to middle-class voters. They are roiling the ranks of the educated and people you would normally think of as the protected class. There is a growing recognition that the system no longer functions for many Americans. Donald Trump comes along and says he understands and sympathizes with average Americans; and he's the one who expresses that frustration in terms that a majority of the unprotected can understand. Other candidates may sympathize, too, but what comes out of their mouths sounds like conventional political yak-yak. Whatever you want to say about Donald Trump, when you hear him speak he doesn't sound like a normal politician.

I keep telling people to toss out their old investment models because the underlying economic tectonic plates are shifting under our feet, making our old models spit out unreliable predictions. So too, it's time to seriously think about throwing out our models for political predictions, because we're in the middle of what is likely to be an epic generational shift in voting patterns. Past performance is not indicative of future results. Now we have to apply that maxim to our political forecasts as well.

There is a fascinating quote attributed to Lord Salisbury, who was the Tory prime minister of England during Queen Victoria's reign. Supposedly, when she said that things must change, he rejoined, "Change? Change? Aren't things bad enough already?"

That response is generally read as an upper-class Victorian-era conservative reaction to a situation that might threaten his personal status and class. I read that quote now and wonder about the changes looming in our near future. I wonder whether we'll look back in ten years and wish we hadn't wanted things to change so much. – especially when we're so uncertain as to what the overall outcome of all that change will be. In addition to finding ourselves in the middle of a massive global monetary policy experiment with no clear understanding of what the consequences are, there is a real potential that we may be entering into a period of similar political experimentation. Fasten your seatbelt.

These are among the topics we are going to have to continue to explore in the coming months and years. I think they have all sorts of serious implications for our investments and financial planning.

Your more confused than ever analyst,

John Mauldin

Originally published May 14, 2016.

ABOUT JOHN MAULDIN

John Mauldin is President of Mauldin Solutions, LLC, an investment advisory firm registered with multiple states; and President and a registered principal of Mauldin Securities, LLC, member FINRA-SIPC.

He publishes *Thoughts from the Frontline* through Mauldin Economics, of which he is Chairman. Mauldin Economics publishes a growing number of investing resources, including both free and paid publications aimed at helping investors thrive in today's challenging economy.

John's books have appeared on the New York Times best-seller list four times. His current book count is six and includes *Bull's Eye Investing: Targeting Real Returns in a Smoke and Mirrors Market*, *Endgame: The End of the Debt Supercycle and How It Changes Everything*, *Code Red: How to Protect Your Savings from the Coming Crisis*, *A Great Leap Forward?: Making Sense of China's Cooling Credit Boom, Technological Transformation, High Stakes Rebalancing, Geopolitical Rise, & Reserve Currency Dream*, *Just One Thing: Twelve of the World's Best Investors Reveal the One Strategy You Can't Overlook* and *The Little Book of Bull's Eye Investing: Finding Value, Generating Absolute Returns and Controlling Risk in Turbulent Markets*.

John is a frequent speaker at conferences around the world and is a sought-after contributor to numerous financial publications, as well as a regular guest on TV and radio.

ABOUT HARRIMAN HOUSE

Established in 1995, and publishing actively since 2001, Harriman House previously operated as an online and mail order finance and business bookshop.

Harriman is now a leading independent business and finance publisher, dedicated to meeting the needs of finance professionals, private investors and traders, entrepreneurs and business leaders. We have over 300 titles currently available in print and eBook formats.

Our main areas of focus include:

- The fundamental skills of investing
- Techniques and systems for traders
- Great investors and their life stories
- Business and economics

Our highly regarded portfolio brings our readers top-quality content by leading practitioners.

At Harriman we are a dedicated team of creative publishing professionals who look to work closely with authors to help transform their ideas into any print or digital product.

www.harriman-house.com
@harrimanhouse

...AUGHNESSY MEB FABER **DAVID MERKEL** NORBERT KEIMLING **STAN ALTSHULLER** TOM MCCLE...

...D DILLIAN RAOUL PAL **BARRY RITHOLTZ** KEN FISHER **CHRIS MEREDITH** ASWATH DAMODARAN

...RLSON DAVE NADIG **JOSH BROWN** COREY HOFFSTEIN **JASON HSU** WES GRAY **JOHN REESE** LA...

...EDROE **CULLEN ROCHE** JONATHAN CLEMENTS **MICHAEL KITCES** CHARLIE BILELLO **JOHN MAUL...**

ADAM BUTLER JASON ZWEIG **GARY ANTONACCI** MORGAN HOUSEL **BEN HUNT** · TODD TRESIDDE...

...TRICK O'SHAUGHNESSY MEB FABER **DAVID MERKEL** NORBERT KEIMLING **STAN ALTSHULLER** T...

...CCLELLAN **JARED DILLIAN** RAOUL PAL **BARRY RITHOLTZ** KEN FISHER **CHRIS MEREDITH** ASWA...

...MODARAN **BEN CARLSON** DAVE NADIG **JOSH BROWN** COREY HOFFSTEIN **JASON HSU** WES GR...

...N REESE LARRY SWEDROE **CULLEN ROCHE** JONATHAN CLEMENTS **MICHAEL KITCES** CHARLIE BIL...

DILLIAN **RAOUL PAL** BARRY RITHOLTZ

EDROE CULLEN ROCHE **JONATHAN CLEMENTS**

LSON **DAVE NADIG** JOSH BROWN

DILLIAN **RAOUL PAL** BARRY RITHOLTZ **KEN FISHER** CHRIS MEREDITH **ASWATH DAMODARAN**

HAUGHNESSY **MEB FABER** DAVID MERKEL **NORBERT KEIMLING** STAN ALTSHULLER **TOM MCCLELL**

BUTLER **JASON ZWEIG** GARY ANTONACCI **MORGAN HOUSEL** BEN HUNT **TODD TRESIDDER** PA

EDROE CULLEN ROCHE **JONATHAN CLEMENTS** MICHAEL KITCES **CHARLIE BILELLO** JOHN MAUL

LSON **DAVE NADIG** JOSH BROWN **COREY HOFFSTEIN** JASON HSU **WES GRAY** JOHN REESE **LA**

DILLIAN **RAOUL PAL** BARRY RITHOLTZ **KEN FISHER** CHRIS MEREDITH **ASWATH DAMODARAN**

LSON **DAVE NADIG** JOSH BROWN **COREY HOFFSTEIN** JASON HSU **WES GRAY** JOHN REESE

EDROE CULLEN ROCHE **JONATHAN CLEMENTS** MICHAEL KITCES **CHARLIE BILELLO** JOHN MAUL

CPSIA information can be obtained
at www.ICGtesting.com
Printed in the USA
BVOW11*1931060817

491208BV00004B/6/P

9 780857 196194